Charles Wright
in Conversation

ALSO BY ROBERT D. DENHAM

Charles Wright: A Companion to the Late Poetry, 1988–2007 (McFarland, 2008)

Charles Wright in Conversation

Interviews, 1979–2006

Edited by ROBERT D. DENHAM

McFarland & Company, Inc., Publishers
Jefferson, North Carolina, and London

"An Interview by David St. John," originally published as "An Interview with Charles Wright" in *Wright: A Profile* (Iowa City: Grilled Flowers Press, 1979), 33–49, reprinted by permission of David St. John. "An Interview by David Remnick," originally published as "An Interview with Charles Wright" in *Partisan Review* 50, no. 4 (1983): 567–75, reprinted by permission of David Remnick. "Charles Wright on Eugenio Montale and Dino Campana: An Interview by Mary Zeppa," originally published as "Charles Wright on Eugenio Montale and Dino Campana" in *Poet News* October 1985: 1, 8–10, reprinted by permission of Mary Zeppa. "'Metaphysics of the Quotidian': A Conversation with Stan Sanvel Rubin and William Heyen," originally published as "'Metaphysics of the Quotidian': A Conversation with Charles Wright" in *The Post Confessionals: Conversations with American Poets of the Eighties*, ed. Earl Ingersoll, Judith Kitchen, and Stan Sanvel Rubin (Rutherford, NJ: Farleigh Dickinson University Press, 1989), 25–38, reprinted by permission of Stan Sanvel Rubin, William Heyen, and Earl G. Ingersoll. "A Conversation with Miriam Marty Clark and Michael McFee," originally published as "A Conversation with Charles Wright" in *Arts Journal* February 1989: 8–13, reprinted by permission of Miriam Clark and Michael McFee. "An Interview by Ernest Suarez and Amy Verner," originally published as "Charles Wright: An Interview by Ernest Suarez and Amy Verner" in *Five Points: A Journal of Literature & Art* 2 (Spring–Summer 1998): 7–32, reprinted by permission of Ernest Suarez and of David Bottoms, editor of *Five Points*. "An Interview by J.D. McClatchy" is transcribed from an audiotape produced by the Modern Poetry Association, portions of which appeared as "Charles Wright" in *Poets in Person*, ed. Joseph Parisi (Chicago: Modern Poetry Association, 1991; rev. ed. 1997). "An Interview by Andrew Zawacki," originally published as "Charles Wright" in *The Verse Book of Interviews*, ed. Brian Henry and Andrew Zawacki (Amherst, MA: Verse Press, 2005), 18–29, reprinted by permission of Andrew Zawacki and Verse Press/Wave Books. "An Interview by Troy Teegarden" was originally published as "1998 Interview with Charles Wright" in *The Metropolitan Review* 2, no. 1 (Spring–Summer 1999), reprinted by permission of Troy Teegarden. "Through Purgatory to Appalachia: An Interview by Martin Caseley," originally published as "Through Purgatory to Appalachia: An Interview with Charles Wright" in *PN Review* 27 (September–October 2000): 22–5, reprinted by permission of Martin Caseley. "An Interview by Willard Spiegelman," originally published as "Interview: Charles Wright with Willard Spiegelman" in *The Literary Imagination* 2, no. 1 (Winter 2000): 108–21, reprinted by permission of Willard Spiegelman and *The Literary Imagination*. "An Interview by Ted Genoways," originally published as "An Interview with Charles Wright" in *Southern Review* 36 (Spring 2000): 442–52, reprinted by permission of Ted Genoways. "An Interview by Morgan Schuldt," originally published as "An Interview with Charles Wright" in *Sonora Review*, No. 43 (2002): 74–80, reprinted by permission of Morgan Schuldt and *Sonora Review*. "Oblivion's Glow: The (Post)Southern Sides of Charles Wright: An Interview by Daniel Cross Turner," originally published as "Oblivion's Glow: The (Post)Southern Sides of Charles Wright: An Interview" in *storySouth*, Summer 2005, reprinted by permission of Daniel Cross Turner. "An Interview by Louis Bourgeois," originally published in *Carolina Quarterly* 56 (Spring–Summer, 2004); revised version appeared as "Interview with Charles Wright" in *VOX* 1, no. 2 (April 2006): 50–6, reprinted by permission of Louis Bourgeois. "Ars Poetica" appeared originally in *Antaeus* 40–41 (Spring 1981): 406. *The New Poem* and *Dog Creek Mainline* from *Country Music: Selected Early Poems* © 1991 by Charles Wright and reprinted by permission of Wesleyan University Press. *Night Rider, Ars Poetica*, and a passage from *Sprung Narratives* are reproduced by permission of Charles Wright.

LIBRARY OF CONGRESS CATALOGUING-IN-PUBLICATION DATA

Wright, Charles, 1935–
Charles Wright in conversation : interviews,
1979–2006 / edited by Robert D. Denham.
p.   cm.
Includes bibliographical references and index.

ISBN-13 978-0-7864-3965-2

softcover: 50# alkaline paper ∞

1. Wright, Charles, 1935– —Interviews.
2. Poets, American—20th century—Interviews.
I. Denham, Robert D.   II. Title.
PS3573.R52Z463   2008   811'.54—dc22   2008030634

British Library cataloguing data are available

©2008 Robert D. Denham. All rights reserved

*No part of this book may be reproduced or transmitted in any form
or by any means, electronic or mechanical, including photocopying
or recording, or by any information storage and retrieval system,
without permission in writing from the publisher.*

Cover photograph: Charles Wright, 1998 (photograph by Tom Cogill)

Manufactured in the United States of America

*McFarland & Company, Inc., Publishers
Box 611, Jefferson, North Carolina 28640
www.mcfarlandpub.com*

For Robin Reid and John Lang

Contents

Preface	1
Abbreviations and Shortened Forms	3
A Charles Wright Chronology	5
1. An Interview by David St. John	11
2. An Interview by David Remnick	21
3. Charles Wright on Eugenio Montale and Dino Campana: An Interview by Mary Zeppa	29
4. "Metaphysics of the Quotidian": A Conversation with Stan Sanvel Rubin and William Heyen	37
5. A Conversation with Miriam Marty Clark and Michael McFee	49
6. An Interview by J.D. McClatchy	59
7. An Interview by Ernest Suarez and Amy Verner	65
8. An Interview by Andrew Zawacki	83
9. An Interview by Troy Teegarden	93
10. Through Purgatory to Appalachia: An Interview by Martin Caseley	97
11. An Interview by Willard Spiegelman	105
12. An Interview by Ted Genoways	119
13. An Interview by Morgan Lucas Schuldt	127
14. Oblivion's Glow: The (Post)Southern Sides of Charles Wright— An Interview by Daniel Cross Turner	133
15. An Interview by Louis Bourgeois	143
Notes	149
A Selected Bibliography	155
Index	171

Preface

Because Charles Wright occupies a large space in the world of contemporary American poetry, it is natural that his readers over the years have wanted to engage him in conversation. Though private and self-effacing, he has always been generous in acceding to requests for interviews. He has granted dozens, and more than thirty have been published. Ten, including Wright's *Paris Review* interview with J.D. McClatchy, have been reprinted in the two collections of his prose, *Halflife* (1988) and *Quarter Notes* (1995). But all of these predate the books that were collected in Wright's second trilogy, *Negative Blue*, which represents the culmination of his trilogy-of-trilogies project. During the dozen or so years that have passed between the *Quarter Notes* and the present, a number of interviews have appeared that deserve wider circulation. I have selected nine of these for inclusion in the present volume. They are prefaced by six interviews which appeared between 1979 and 1991 but which were not included in *Halflife* or *Quarter Notes*. Together they form a composite portrait of the artist as a poet.

The fifteen interviews are rich with detail. One will find in them Wright's replies to queries about the beginning of his poetic career in Italy (Verona and Lake Garda); his experience at the University of Iowa; what he has learned from American poets (Dickinson, Pound, Crane, Stevens, Whitman, Justice); the Italian poets (Dante, Pavese, Montale, Campana); film directors (Fellini); his mother; and Augustine's *Confessions* ("the iconic book of my life"). He also comments on poets he has read in translation (Rimbaud, Baudelaire, Trakl, the late T'ang Chinese, Lorca, Attila József, Mandelstam, Rilke, Vallejo, Neruda [the *Residencias*], Celan, St. John of the Cross, among others), and he remarks, sometimes elliptically, on particular poems of his own, including *The New Poem, Tattoos, Skins, Bygones, 12 Lines at Midnight, Homage to Paul Cézanne, Portrait of the Poet in Abraham von Werdt's Dream*, his several poems entitled *Self-Portrait, Called Back, Virgo Descending, Delta Traveller, A Journal of True Confessions, Ars Poetica, Dog Creek Mainline, Meditation on Form and Measure, Black Zodiac, Reply to Wang Wei, A Bad Memory Makes You a Metaphysician, a Good One Makes You a Saint, Bar Giamaica, 1959–60, The Appalachian Book of the Dead, After Rereading Robert Graves, I Go Outside to Get My Head Together, Quotations, Night Rider*, and *Star Turn*.

Wright's interviewers ask about contemporary poets he admires and those he feels kinship with, the joys and struggles of translation, teaching creative writing, his view of the function of poetry, his writing habits, his quarrel with the Language poets, the importance of country music for him, his identity as a Southern poet, the function of memory, the difference between sentiment and sentimentality, and winning the Pulitzer Prize. They also ask Wright about numerous formal matters, including his lineation and rhythmic phrasing, the structure of his trilogies, his use of syllabics, and the development of his characteristic style. In addition, we learn about Wright's lover's quarrel with the Episcopal Church, landscape as revelation, the Christian subtext of his work, the negative sublime, and the thematic foundation of his poetic pilgrimage ("the contemplation of the divine"). The unexpected revelation crops up here and there. Knowing of Wright's interest in Gnosticism, we are not surprised to learn that he has read Elaine Pagels. But who would have guessed that his favorite American poet is Milosz and that "Xionia," the title of one of his books, comes from a variation on the name given to his home in Charlottesville by its former owners? The location of Wright's comments on such things as those just catalogued can be can be found in the index, which contains a full list of people, places, and things that appear in the fifteen conversations.

* * *

A note at the bottom of the first page of each interview gives the provenance. Editorial insertions are in square brackets. I have regularized the use of italics for poem titles, have silently corrected occasional misspellings, and have retained the ellipses in the originals.

I express my thanks to Charles Wright for agreeing to let me bring these interviews to a wider public and to the interviewers and editors for permission to recirculate these conversations.

Abbreviations and Shortened Forms

Andrews   Tom Andrews, ed. *The Point Where All Things Meet: Essays on Charles Wright*. Oberlin, Ohio: Oberlin College Press, 1995.

CM   Charles Wright. *Country Music*. 2nd ed. Hanover, N.H.: Wesleyan/New England Press, 1991.

Giannelli   Adam Giannelli, ed. *High Lonesome: On the Poetry of Charles Wright*. Oberlin, Ohio: Oberlin College Press, 2006. A revised and expanded version of Andrews, above.

GRH   Charles Wright. *The Grave of the Right Hand*. Middletown, CT: Wesleyan University Press, 1970.

Halflife   Charles Wright. *Halflife: Improvisations and Interviews, 1977–87*. Ann Arbor: University of Michigan Press, 1988.

NB   Charles Wright. *Negative Blue: Selected Later Poems*. New York: Farrar, Straus and Giroux, 2000.

Profile   *Wright: A Profile. New Poems by Charles Wright with an Interview and a Critical Essay by David St. John*. Iowa City: Grilled Flowers Press, 1979.

QN   Charles Wright. *Quarter Notes: Improvisations and Interviews*. Ann Arbor: University of Michigan Press, 1995.

SC   Charles Wright. *Southern Cross*. New York: Random House, 1981.

SHS   Charles Wright. *A Short History of the Shadow*. New York: Farrar Straus Giroux, 2002.

WTTT   Charles Wright. *The World of the Ten Thousand Things*. New York: Farrar Straus Giroux, 1990.

ZJ   Charles Wright. *Zone Journals*. New York: Farrar Straus Giroux, 1988. Exeter, Devon, England: Stride Publications, 1996.

A Charles Wright Chronology

1935	Born on his father's birthday, 25 August, in Pickwick Dam, Hardin County, Tennessee
1936	Moves to Knoxville, Tennessee
1937	Moves to Corinth, Mississippi
1941	Moves to Hiwassee Village, North Carolina
1943	Moves to Oak Ridge, Tennessee
1945	Moves to Kingsport, Tennessee
1948–50	Attends summer camp at Sky Valley School, Hendersonville, North Carolina
1950–51	Attends Sky Valley School
1951–53	Attends Christ School, Arden, North Carolina
1953	Takes a summer job as police reporter for the *Kingsport* [Tennessee] *Times-News*
1953–57	Attends Davidson College; graduates with a degree in history
1957	Commissioned as a 2nd Lt. in the U.S. Army Intelligence Corps; reports for active duty to Ft. Holabird, Maryland, November 2
1958	Studies Italian at the Presidio's Army Language School, Monterey, California
1959–61	Works for the 430th CIC Detachment, U.S. Army, in Verona, Italy, January 1959 to autumn 1961. Discharged with rank of captain
1959	In March visits Catullus' villa on the peninsula of Sirmione, Lake Garda. Reads Pound's *Selected Poems*
1961	Turns down acceptance for study at the Columbia School of Journalism in order to study creative writing

A CHARLES WRIGHT CHRONOLOGY

1961	Begins study in the creative writing program at the University of Iowa
1961	Begins translating Montale's *Motets*
1963	Receives M.F.A. from the University of Iowa
1963	Publishes *The Voyage* (Iowa City: Patrician Press)
1963–65	Studies at the University of Rome as a Fulbright student; reads Dante with Maria Sampoli; completes translation of Montale
1964	Publishes *Six Poems* (London: Royal College of Art)
1964	Death of mother, Mary Winter Wright, at age 54
1965–66	Returns to the University of Iowa for further study
1966	Begins teaching in the Creative Writing Center at the University of California, Irvine
1968	Publishes *The Dream Animal* (Toronto: House of Anansi)
1968–69	Serves as Fulbright lecturer at the University of Padua, Italy
1969	Publishes *Private Madrigals* (Madison, WI: Abraxas Press)
1969	Marries Holly McIntire, April 6
1969	Receives the Eunice Tietjens Award from *Poetry* magazine
1970	Publishes *The Grave of the Right Hand* (Middletown, CT: Wesleyan University Press)
1970	Birth of son, Luke Savin Herrick Wright
1971	Publishes *The Venice Notebook* (Boston: Barn Dream Press)
1972	Death of father, Charles Penzel Wright, at age 67
1973	Publishes *Backwater* (Santa Ana, CA: Golem Press)
1973	Publishes *Hard Freight* (Middletown, CT: Wesleyan University Press)
1974	Receives National Endowment for the Arts Award
1975	Publishes *Bloodlines* (Middletown, CT: Wesleyan University Press)
1975	Receives a Guggenheim Fellowship
1976	Receives the Melville Cane Award from the Poetry Society of America and the Edgar Allan Poe Award from the Academy of American Poets—both for *Bloodlines*
1977	Publishes *Colophons* (Iowa City: Windhover Press)
1977	Publishes *China Trace* (Middletown, CT: Wesleyan University Press)
1977	Writer in residence at Oberlin College
1977	Receives the Academy-Institute Award, American Academy and Institute of the Arts

1978	Oberlin College publishes Wright's translation of Eugenio Montale, *The Storm and Other Poems* (Field Translation Series 1)
1978	Begins systematic reading of Dante's *Commedia*
1979	Publication of *Wright: A Profile. New Poems by Charles Wright with an Interview and a Critical Essay by David St. John* (Iowa City: Grilled Flowers Press)
1979	Receives the PEN translation award for *The Storm and Other Poems*
1980	Publishes *Dead Color* (San Francisco: Meadow Press)
1980	Receives the Ingram Merrill Fellowship in Poetry
1981	Publishes *The Southern Cross* (New York: Random House)
1982	Publishes *Country Music: Selected Early Poems* (Middletown, CT: Wesleyan University Press)
1983	Publishes *Four Poems of Departure* (Portland, OR: Trace Editions)
1983	Receives the National Book Award for *Country Music*
1983	Visits London, September–December
1983	Begins teaching at the University of Virginia and settles permanently in Charlottesville
1983	Receives National Endowment for the Arts Award
1984	Publishes *The Other Side of the River* (New York: Vintage/Random House)
1984	Oberlin College publishes Wright's translation of Dino Campana, *Orphic Songs* (Field Translation Series 9)
1984	Nominated for the National Book Critics Circle Award for *The Other Side of the River*
1985	Publishes *Five Journals* (New York: Red Ozier Press)
1985	Spends part of the summer with Mark Strand at an Italian villa, Cà Paruta
1987	Receives the Brandeis Creative Arts Citation for poetry
1988	Publishes *A Journal of the Year of the Ox* (1988)
1988	Publishes *Zone Journals* (New York: Farrar Straus Giroux)
1988	Publishes *Halflife: Improvisations and Interviews, 1977–87* (Ann Arbor: University of Michigan Press)
1988	Is appointed Souter Family Professor of English at the University of Virginia
1988	Travels to China to attend meeting of American and Chinese writers at the 4th Sino-American Writer's Conference, 12 April

1990	Publishes *The World of the Ten Thousand Things: Poems 1980–1990* (New York: Farrar Straus Giroux)
1990	Publishes *Xionia* (Iowa City: Windhover Press)
1991	Becomes a member of the Fellowship of Southern Writers
1991	Is the subject of the annual Literary Festival at Emory & Henry College, Emory, VA
1992	Receives and Award of Merit Medal from the American Academy of Arts and Letters
1992	Serves as distinguished visiting professor, Universita Degli Studi, Florence, Italy
1993	Receives the Ruth Lilly Poetry Prize
1993	Receives Distinguished Contribution to Letters Award from the Ingram Merrill Foundation
1993	Reads at the Library of Congress, December 16
1995	Publishes *Chickamauga* (New York: Farrar, Straus and Giroux)
1995	Publishes *Quarter Notes: Improvisations and Interviews* (Ann Arbor: University of Michigan Press)
1995	Oberlin College publishes *The Point Where All Things Meet: Essays on Charles Wright*, ed. Tom Andrews
1995	Is elected to membership in the American Academy of Arts and Letters
1996	Receives the Lenore Marshall Poetry Prize from the Academy of American Poets
1997	Publishes *Black Zodiac* (New York: Farrar, Straus and Giroux)
1997	Receives the Book Prize, *Los Angeles Times*, and National Book Critics Circle Award for Poetry—both for *Black Zodiac*
1997	Receives an honorary Doctor of Letters degree from Davidson College
1998	Receives the Pulitzer Prize for Poetry and the Premio Antico Fattore Alla Poesia—both for *Black Zodiac*
1998	Receives the Ambassador Book Award from the English-Speaking Union for *Black Zodiac*
1998	Publishes *Appalachia* (New York: Farrar Straus Giroux)
1999	Publishes *North American Bear* (La Crosse, WI: Sutton Hoo Press)
1999	Begins two-year stint as poetry editor of the *New Republic*
2000	Publishes *Negative Blue: Selected Later Poems* (New York: Farrar, Straus and Giroux)
2001	Publishes *Night Music* (Exeter, Devon, England: Stride Publications)

2001	Italian translation of poems (*L'altra riva del fiume* [ExCogita Editore] and *Crepuscolo americano e altre poesie 1980–2000* [Jaca Book]) presented by Gaetano Pramapolini and Barbara Lanati at Salone del Libro, Turin (19 May)
2001	Attends a discussion of his work on May 25 at Fondazione Il Fiore, Florence
2002	Publishes *A Short History of the Shadow* (New York: Farrar Straus Giroux)
2002	Is elected as a fellow of the American Academy of Arts and Sciences
2004	Publishes *Buffalo Yoga* (New York: Farrar Straus Giroux)
2005	Publishes *The Wrong End of the Rainbow* (Louisville, KY: Sarabande Books)
2005	"Charles Wright at 70: A Celebration and Retrospective," Vancouver, BC, 31 March. Annual Meeting of the Associated Writing Programs
2006	Publishes *Scar Tissue* (New York: Farrar Straus Giroux)
2006	Oberlin College Press publishes *High Lonesome: On the Poetry of Charles Wright*, a revised and expanded edition of *The Point Where All Things Meet* (1995)
2007	Publishes *Littlefoot: A Poem* (New York: Farrar Straus Giroux)
2007	Receives the Griffin Prize for *Scar Tissue*
2007	Receives the Leoncino d'Oro award at the Palazzo Comunale of Pistoia
2008	McFarland & Company publishes *Charles Wright: A Companion to the Late Poetry, 1998–2007*
2008	Receives the Rebekah Johnson Bobbitt National Prize for Poetry
2008	Receives the Premio Internazionale Mario Luzi Award for lifetime achievement
2009	Publishes *Sestets* (New York: Farrar Straus Giroux)

CHAPTER 1

An Interview by David St. John

DSt.J.: *How has translating—particularly Montale—affected your own work? What writers outside of the English language, both contemporary and otherwise, are you fond of and/or have influenced your work?*

CW: The translations I did of Pavese, Pasolini, and Elio Pagliarani had no effect on my own work at all, all three of them writing a more discursive poetry than I was interested in at the time, or am now. Pavese has a lot to teach anyone, however, at least through William Arrowsmith's brilliant versions,[1] which are, I think, more interesting in English than they were in Italian, sounding so Hemingwayesque in Italian (a writer Pavese translated into Italian). Montale, of course, is a different story. There was always some thread in Montale's work that was tied to my sensibility, and every poem tugged on it to one degree or another. What was fortunate for me was that I began to translate him at the same time I began to write poems seriously. Mark Strand was the first person to encourage me to try my hand at translating, back in 1961, saying it was a good thing to do when you were "between poems."[2] I thought it was true then and I still do. After I had been in graduate school for two years, I got a Fulbright grant to go back to Italy (I had been there for three years in the Army) to work on Montale, Pavese, and Pasolini. It came at a very good time for me, as I had spent two very intense years trying to get surfaces to work or beginning to understand what the surface of a poem was about, and now I had the chance to see what the insides were about, as I spent the next two years, 1963–65, translating *The Storm & Other Poems* while living in Rome.[3] Translating Montale at such a formative time in my own development was

Originally published in Wright: A Profile *(Iowa City: Grilled Flowers Press, 1979), 33–49. Reprinted in David St. John,* Where the Angels Come Toward Us: Selected Essays, Reviews & Interviews *(Fredonia, NY: White Pine Press, 1995). This interview was conducted by David St. John as a follow-up to an earlier interview, conducted by David Young and Stuart Friebert in November 1976 at Oberlin College and published as "Charles Wright at Oberlin,"* Field *17 (Fall 1977): 46–85, and reprinted in* A Field Guide to Contemporary Poetry and Poetics, *ed. Stuart Friebert and David Young (New York: Longman, 1980), 241–71. The earlier interview was later reprinted as "At Oberlin College" in* Halflife, *59–88. Wright responded to the questions in the present interview by mail.*

a real gift—I was able to see the grooves and dovetailings, the suspensions and stresses and, in general, most of the physical ways he put poems together; I was also able to see how the poems often worked conceptually, spatially, and dramatically. Some of this I have been able to take over and assimilate in my own work. A great deal of it I can merely admire at second hand and hope someday to be good enough to be able to do in my own and different way. There was also a certain spiritual quality in the work I admired, and a way of using hard-edged imagery with genuine sentiment, something lacking in Italian poetry since Dante. I also liked the generally large themes he took on, and the way he took them on—clear-eyed and down-to-earth and unapologetically.

I haven't done any serious translating since then, so I have no *pronunciamentos* on the art in general, except to say that what everyone says is true—it's an impossible task. The one who gets the most from a translation is the translator, not the reader. Which is unfortunate for me, as some of my favorite poets, poets whose work I have loved and been changed by, I have read only in translations—Rimbaud, Baudelaire, Trakl, the late T'ang Chinese, Lorca, Attila József, Mandelstam, Rilke, Vallejo, Neruda (the *Residencias*)—the list could go on, but it makes one realize why Pound wanted to know all those languages—Celan, Campana, St. John of the Cross...

Do you feel as though you are influenced by your American contemporaries? If so, who? If not, can you pinpoint why—do you believe it unhealthy for a poet to read his contemporaries?

No—regarding your first question—if you mean poets of my own generation. I suppose there is some affinity with the ones I feel closest to—Mark Strand, Charles Simic, and James Tate—but someone else would have to say what it is, or what it is not. I don't really feel any mutual influence going on, though. As for the generation before me, as I've said elsewhere, Donald Justice was an early influence on me, as he was my teacher and I was an empty blackboard just waiting to be written on. I still feel fortunate that he had the chalk. Later, I find that W.S. Merwin and I share a certain spiritual affinity, one I also share with Peter Matthiessen, I think, though he is primarily a prose writer. I suppose there are many poets I have picked up a phrase from here, a turn there or an image here and there. This seems inevitable to me if one reads at all and is open to good things. One thinks of the poets one admires and realizes that some burrs have stuck as one passes through their fields on the way to one's own plot of ground. But none of this is very serious down deep, and would not come under the seminal heading of influence, which is a way of hearing things, a way of seeing, and seeing through, things. For that, I think, one has to—in my case—jump two or three generations back to get at what was really happening to me in my malleable years. I think of Pound and Crane (Hart) as primary sources and, earlier, Emily Dickinson (and, from England, Father Hopkins). Perhaps even more basic was early country music, and the lifey/deathy/after-deathy themes inherent in the songs, say, of The Carter Family, Roy Acuff, Merle Travis, and early Lester Flatt and Earl Scruggs. This is a roundabout way of saying that I think one should try to avoid being influenced by one's American contemporaries in any deep sense. One reads them, of course, just as you

1. An Interview by David St. John

hope they read you, with appreciation and sometimes great admiration, but there are greater lessons to be learned from the dead than from the living, ultimately, as they have all the secrets.

In the Field *interview [November 1976; see note, p. 11] you remarked: "I'm not interested in a flat line, or the flat language that has been fairly popular in the last, say, ten to twelve years" [Halflife, 66]. Could you elaborate on this? It seems to me that this popularity germinates from the erroneous equating of honesty /directness/and clean diction with flatness. How does that strike you? You also mentioned, in the* Field *piece, "I suspect that* Skins *[CM, 82–102], and* Tattoos *[CM, 56–76] as well, is over-written to a certain extent." Could you speak toward pinpointing a middle way between flat language and overwriting?*

I'm not sure how much elaboration is either called for or is possible. As I try to look back on my motives for saying such a thing from the vantage point of today [January 1979], it seems likely that they were at least two: one, surely, was because it [the flat line] was so popular and had been used so much and, so often, badly. And, two, since I had worked hard in the opposite field, I felt, I'm sure, some real stake in supporting my own position. And, three, since I hadn't really "chosen" a more "musical" line, it coming more or less naturally to me (as I tried to explain in the interview), it seems probable that I felt more evangelical in its defense than I might have otherwise. And, fourth, I guess, I just prefer music to drone, in whatever form it comes. I still feel these ways and, if anything, have an even greater interest in the sound and weight and rub and glint of words.

As for the popularity of the flat line, I think you're probably correct in your reasons for its popularity. It also, I might add, seems so easy to write. In this it's like free verse, which seems so easy to do, and is, but is so difficult to do well.

And as for *Skins* [CM, 82–102] and *Tattoos* [CM, 56–76] being over-written, if I really felt that at the time (which I doubt; it sounds like a very defensive statement to me), I no longer believe it. They both got, I hope, the closest I could come at the time to the rhythms and rhetoric I thought they needed. And I look at them now—even though I probably wouldn't write them again in exactly the same way—as a middle way, given their subject matter and my leanings, between a flat style and one that is over-written and excessive.

Speaking of China Trace *in the* Field *interview, you remarked: "I'm trying to talk about things that I don't know anything about, because I haven't been there, in terms of something I do know something about, because I'm standing in the middle of them" [Halflife, 77]. I'm wondering if the antithesis of this statement could not as well apply to the book, if someone couldn't make a case for the opposite: that you found a form of projecting, for objectification, certain subject matter onto this China trace, and came to understand the things you were "standing in the middle of" via this new perspective. It's a weird epistemological problem—the particular is cast out on the general, the abstract, for form (as Plato would have it), and then retrieved and dealt with in a certain context. What do you think?*

I think we should break for lunch. But before we do, I'd say you could certainly do it that way, as the main thing is to understand the things one is "standing in the middle of"—one's life and how one lives it. Writing poems should have to do with helping you live and understand your life. Your poems should help you to understand yourself and the world around you, no? Your poems should, if you work hard enough at them, help you to come to terms with whatever there is, wherever it is. They perhaps won't solve anything (although often they might), but they should at least ease your passage from one place to the next. Poems are both reliquary and transubstantiational, as our lives should be.

Are you interested in speaking further regarding the use of the line, the use of the page's white space (the doughnut hole, as Mandelstam called it)[4] and/or your counting of stresses and syllables?

The white space is really white sound (the technical term is "white noise"), sound the ear doesn't always pick up but which is always there, humming, backgrounding, like silences. It's what pulls the lines through the poem, gauging their weights and durations, even their distances. It is the larger sound out of which the more measured and interruptible sounds of the line are cut. And it is always there, the faint hissing that tells us where to go and where to avoid.

 The line, of course, is what separates us from the beasts. I think a line has specific weight and heft, that it is melodic and tactile. It is as though the lines were each sections of the poem attached by invisible strings to the title, the way the various parts of a marionette are attached by strings to the control board. Each line exists in itself as each separate part of the marionette exists independently and interdependently. It is only when the strings are all being used in unison from the board that the marionette operates properly. The same with lines/poem/title. Lines have movements, turns, and meanings independent of the poem as a whole, etc., etc....

 I don't count stresses and syllables quite as assiduously as I did a couple of years ago. I still count them, but more after the fact, to confirm my ear rather than to guide and control it. I still like to know exactly what's there, and if a rhythmic repetition is done on purpose or has happened by unfortunate accident. It's just something I do, and has no theoretical value other than contributing to the weight and duration of the line itself. And the line, as we all know, and as I've just repeated, is the linchpin of the poem. Without it, the wheels come off. With badly made ones, the entire vehicle moves awkwardly. Weak ones snap.

Could you speak about the poems printed in the Profile *[see note, p. 11; the poems in* Profile *are* Homage to Paul Cézanne, *the five* Self Portrait *poems,* Mt. Caribou at Night, Holy Thursday, Virginia Reel, *and* Called Back*] in their relation to the trilogy? When the trilogy, after many years work, was completed, you were no doubt confronted with aesthetic decisions—can you address yourself to these decisions and their manifestations as presented in the* Profile*?*

1. An Interview by David St. John

Rather than a "trilogy," I prefer to think of the books as a triptych, three different and separate instances in the same life instead of the linkage that the literary term "trilogy" seems to carry. It may be nit-picking, but I don't see the books as interrelated as a "trilogy" signifies. The linkage is my life, not any superimposition that the books posit. Mantegna's triptych of Christ in Perugia is of three separate ages in his life, and uses three discrete panels. In my case the panels are yesterday, today, and tomorrow. Somehow, looking at the books in this way makes a difference: they stand as individual books, but are on the same background, in the same frame. One doesn't need the others, but all are informed by each other.

As for the *Profile* poems, their relationship to *Hard Freight*, *Bloodlines* and *China Trace* is minimal, if even extant. *Homage to Paul Cézanne* has an energy runover from *China Trace*, but that's all. There may be some autobiographical tie-in in the odd poem, but that's unintentional and inevitable. I am trying to make what I'm working on now as little like what I did before as my style and subject matter will allow. Since I write out of obsessions, I don't know how far away this will be, but I hope it's far enough. There are, of course, technical follow-throughs and extensions in the ten poems here, especially from *China Trace*. I was trying for a perhaps unreachable compression in the *China Trace* line and stanza. One of the technical considerations I'm interested in in these new poems is an attempt to put the heavily freighted and compressed, synaptically-linked line into a more expanded context, i.e., longer lines and longer poems. I'm also still very involved with making the stanza a unit of measure (Hopkins and Williams both did this, in differing ways; and others, too, I suppose) the way certain color constructions become focal points in paintings.

In the Field *interview you mentioned the hope of writing, after completion of* China Trace, *a long poem which would attempt to translate a painter's technique to the page. Is* Homage to Paul Cezanne *[WTTT, 3–10] that poem? If so, could you elaborate on this technique? Could you offer anything else about the poem that might be of help or interest?*

It is, indeed, the poem, although "painter's technique" is surely too inclusive a term. How it comes closest is in its non-linear approach to plot. Which is to say that I doubt you could "plot" the poem if you were of a mind to do so. The structure of the poem is presentational, and it works accumulatively. Which, again, is to say that it works in layers or overlays, much as a painting would do, until it has reached completion. The sections aren't haphazard or substitutable, however, any more than certain layers or brushstrokes or colors are. They go in the order they have, which is, I hope, an accumulative order, but they are not numbered, hence they are not sections as we usually understand them in poems. As far as other painterly techniques are concerned, I was conscious of working in blocks of lines, stanzas, and pages, much as Cézanne might have used his dabs and columns and blotches of color (in many of the Mt. St. Victoire landscapes you can't find a line at all—everything is dab and spread and knife-stroke and, in the finished painting, extremely representational). The poem as painting, etc., visualization of abstracts, filling in the corners...

I deliberately chose an abstract subject matter (the Dead) that was as close to a tactile and animate one as I could come up with. It made the theoretical possibilities (i.e., language for paint) more plastic and malleable. The poem has nothing to do with him as a man, and everything to do with him as a painter, the way he painted in the last twenty to thirty years of his life. The poem began as a technical experiment and rapidly (after the first page) became something much more. As is the case in most anything you do that you eventually value, what you say becomes so much more important than how you say it. And that aspect of the poem will have to speak for itself. As for the so-called "painter's technique," I had used it in parts of *Bloodlines* and to a real extent in *China Trace*. I am now doing it even more extensively in this "book" [*SC*]. As I say, "painter's technique" is, I believe, inaccurate for the most part. And whatever it is I'm doing will have to wait for its term, if it deserves one.

In the poem 12 Lines at Midnight *there is a line "The breath inside my breath is the breath of the dream" [CM, 132]. I sense, from this line and the* Field *interview, a sense of both "you are what you are going to be" and that you're not, that, as many writers are, you are motivated by imperfection, a strive toward something greater, toward saying It in perfection once and for all, toward over-stepping—as Nietzsche would put it—yourself. On the one hand, as soon as you say It you're doomed, because there's nothing beyond It but silence; on the other hand, there seems to be the horrible truth that language can never accomplish It, cannot communicate—cannot function—in these quintessential spheres. To bring this to a less theoretical issue, Faulkner commented, "Always dream and shoot higher than you know you can do. Don't bother just to be better than your contemporaries or predecessors. Try to be better than yourself."[5] Can you respond, somehow, to this?*

Well, you've just given the answers. What, as Gertrude Stein said, is the question?[6] I do think you're correct in the first two sentences, but one out of two in the third one. Certainly I am guilty of sentence #2 (and #1), although it is a guilt I wear with a certain amount of vanity. The first half of the third sentence I think is wrong because of the word "doomed." If you ever said It, you'd be saved, not doomed. And what a glorious silence! I am becoming more and more aware of the truth of the second half of the third sentence, and I mention that awareness twice in poems in this *Profile*. And, of course, Faulkner is right. Still, as Homer knew, and others after him, what's important is the journey itself. My true Penelope is Penelope.

Could you speak about your use of the self-portrait (which seems to be almost a sharper focus on your use of autobiographical material in general)?

In general, I think it's true that these five self-portraits [*WTTT*, 11, 13, 16, 19, 21] are more autobiographical than descriptive. They stand as a model in miniature of a process I am trying to bring across in the entire body of the projected "book" I'm working on, and which the ten poems in the *Profile* form, or will form, the first two sections of.

Francis Bacon has done series of self-portraits (3–4 in a series) in which the image is broken down and distorted a little more in each succeeding picture, all the while retaining the central focus and outline of the picture as a whole and as a composite. If brushstrokes and brushwork can be equated, in this case, with language, and form can still be considered form, then I'm after something like this. And not merely for oddity's sake, but as a further step in trying to understand the elasticity, availability, and ultimate desirability of language as a means.

The first two self-portraits I did (one in *The Grave of the Right Hand* [57] and one in *Hard Freight—Portrait of the Poet in Abraham von Werdt's Dream* [*CM*, 18]) were purely technical exercises. The third (in *China Trace* [*CM*, 113]) was more serious, and these five, even though originally technically oriented, have come to be the most serious of all, in that I hope they say something about my life, and how I look at it. The second and third ones in the *Profile* group are made up, for the most part, from postcards and photographs that are above my desk. Four has to do with my years in Italy, and five uses rearranged material, in part, from John Donne and Emily Dickinson. All five are separated and punctuated by four longer poems about rebirth, and all nine poems are supposed to work together in the movement of the Bacon paintings. *Called Back* [*WTTT*, 20], for instance, is supposed to be the least narratively inclined of all the nine poems, each section being more or less independent. The same goes for the last self-portrait. Finally, of course, the poems have no referents but the language, as they have nothing to do contextually with anyone's paintings. They have to do, as I say, with my life, and where and how I live it.

Do you, as many poets do, keep a journal?

No, but I do keep, off and on, or have kept off and on over the past year or so, a sort of "commonplace notebook" where I jot down quotes or thoughts of my own that I happen to cotton to at the moment. What follows is most of the notebook, so you can see that it hasn't been extensive or obsessive.[7]

A Pound (and Whitman) Sampler
— The unseen is proved by the seen, which in its turn becomes the unseen and is proved.[8]
— The image is the poet's pigment.[9]
— The vortex is the point of maximum energy.[10]
— Every emotion has its rhythm.[11]
— Symbols have a fixed value, as 1, 2, 7 in arithmetic. Images have a variable significance, as a, b, or x in algebra.[12]
— A symbol is a permanent metaphor.[13]
— An image is an intellectual and emotional complex in a given instant.[14]
— The image records the instant when an outward and objective thing is transformed to a thing inward and subjective.[15]

"The outward and visible sign of an inward and spiritual grace."[16]

"A place belongs forever to whoever claims it hardest, remembers it most obsessively, wrenches it from itself, shapes it, renders it, loves it so radically that he remakes it in his image..."
—Joan Didion on James Jones[17]

Two new lines for *Holy Thursday*. The 'fly jump' in the second stanza is a warning shot, a tracer...[18]

People keep saying, Life is like war. Life is not like war, life is like summer camp.

Never break into lines and try to pass off as a poem something you would be embarrassed to write down in prose.

"Cézanne: 'I have my motif.' (He joins his hands.)
Gasquet: 'What?'
Cézanne: 'Yes...' (He repeats his gesture, spreads his hands, the ten fingers open, brings them together slowly, slowly, then joins them, squeezes them, clenches them, inserts them together.) 'There's what must be attained... There must not be a single link too loose, a hole through which the emotion, the light or the truth may escape. I advance my entire picture at one time, you understand ... I bring together in the same spirit, the same faith, all that is scattered ... I take from right, from left, from here, there, everywhere, tones, colors, shades; I fix them; I bring them together... My canvas joins hands. It does not vacillate.'"
—(J. Gasquet, *Cézanne*, Paris, 1921, p. 80, based on a translation by Lawrence Cowing)

"A little glimpse of death, and the looseness and tolerance that brings."
—Allen Ginsberg on what he 'needs' to write[19]

Rimbaud, Trakl and Hart Crane: 3 favorites. It's their passion I love. They are great 'I' poets, whatever persona they use.

"The great ones always speak from the other side."
—Leonard Michaels[20]

"...the symbolic imagination ... a dramatic imagination in the sense that its fullest image is an action in the shapes of this world: it does not reject, it includes: it sees not only with, but through, the natural world to what may lie beyond it."
—Allen Tate[21]

A painting is occupying (inhabiting) a given space in front of you. A poem is the same thing.

"...he defined himself as a supporter of 'Western liberal democracy, favoring an intellectual elite and a progressive middle class and based on a moral order derived from Christian absolutes.'"
—Tom Stoppard[22]

"There is a kind of cleanness and virginity in it, in this looking away from oneself; it is as though one were drawing, one's gaze bound to the object, inwoven with Nature, while one's hand goes its own way somewhere below, goes on and on, gets timid, wavers, is glad again, goes on and on far below the face that stands like a star above it, not looking, only shining. I feel as though I had always worked that way; face gazing at far things, hands alone. And so it surely ought to be. I shall be like that again in time."

—Rilke[23]

"My business is circumference."

—Emily Dickinson[24]

"The move toward a disintegration of the object in some of the most memorable works of a painter so passionately attached to objects is the attraction and the riddle of Cézanne's last phase. The element that usurped its place, the patch of color in itself..."
—Gowing on Cézanne[25]

The object is the poem, the patch of color is the stanza (the line?).

A Japanese student in America quoted in Pound's *ABC of Reading* on the difference between prose and poetry: "Poetry consists of gists and piths."[26]

"Night be good, do not let me die."
—Apache invocation

The primary level of the poem is bread mold. The secondary meaning, the resonance, is the mystery that heals, the penicillin.

Imagistic tone of voice
Imagistic structure
———
Narrative tone of voice
Narrative structure
———

Hard Freight: imagistic tone, narrative structure
Bloodlines: all 4
China Trace: imagistic structure narrative tone

"The recourse to talent shows a defect in the imagination."
—Georges Braque[27]

The rhetorical silences in the long, image-freighted line—the rhetoric of silence ...
    (from "Cézanne..." on)
Pure technique is the spider web without the spider—it glitters and catches but it
    doesn't kill.

Poems should come out of the body, like webbing from the spider.
"Momentous depths of speculation."
—Keats[28]

For M., who wants 'eyesight, not vision'—There's more to poetry than meets the eye (see Crane's comment on 'retinal registration.')[29]

Art tends toward the certainty of making connections. The artist's job is to keep things apart, allowing the synapses to speak.

When the finger of God appears, it's usually the wrong finger.

Language is always the big winner in pot limit poetry. And pot limit is the only real game in town.

The best narrative is that which is least in evidence to the eye.

"The ultimate fate and duty of the poet is visionary..."
—Denis Donoghue

"Transform? Yes; for our task is so deeply and so passionately to impress upon ourselves this provisional and perishable earth, that its essential being will rise again 'invisibly' in us. We are the bees of the invisible. We frantically plunder the visible of its honey, to accumulate it in the great golden hive of the invisible."
—Rilke[30]

CHAPTER 2

An Interview by David Remnick

DR: *I think most readers will be surprised to learn you didn't start writing until you were twenty-five years old.*

CW: That's true. I was in the army in Italy in 1959 and I was given a copy of Ezra Pound's *Selected Poems*. The poems had many references to places in Northern Italy where I was stationed, so I started reading them and going to places that he mentions. One place, Lake Garda, was one of Pound's sacred places. He met Joyce there for the first time; and Catullus supposedly had a villa there. I was stationed only fifteen miles away, in Verona, and I would go out to the ruins—very romantic with all the beautiful leaves and trees—and I would read Pound's poems. And naturally, once you start liking something, whatever it is, you try to do it. I started trying to imitate him and that's how I got into writing poems. I would also go to the army base library which had Eliot, e. e. cummings, Robert Frost, and the usual five or ten books of poetry, and that's what I read for two years until I got out of the army. Then I went to a graduate writing program at the University of Iowa. I kept my mouth shut there, listened for a couple of years, and I've been writing ever since, or trying to.

Don't you remember having read poetry before then?

Only to a certain extent. One has to read poetry if one goes to school and takes English courses. I never studied poetry at all in college other than in the regular freshman English course. My mother had gone to the University of Mississippi, was interested in writing and, at the time, used to date William Faulkner's brother, which made for a literary aura around my house. It was never poetry, though; it was always fiction. There was always good fiction around the house. My mother was a great admirer of Jane Austen, Eudora Welty, and people like that, and so, even in high school, I was reading Thomas Wolfe and had read all of Faulkner before I graduated. In college, I

Originally published in Partisan Review *50, no. 4 (1983): 567–75.*

read all of Dylan Thomas's prose, like *Adventures in the Skin Trade* and *Portrait of the Artist as a Young Dog*. So there was some background early on: it was a good thing to read books in my house. Puns and language play were also encouraged. Love of language is the primary thing for a poet even before he has anything to say. W.H. Auden said that[1] and he was right.

Did you do any writing before the army?

I used to try to write stories in college but I wasn't very good at it. I've always said that I am the one Southerner I know who can't tell a story. My mind doesn't seem to work that way, but in short flashes and bursts, which is more akin to writing poems. Also, the kind of language I like is much more conducive to poetry than to fiction in that it's more condensed than fiction is able to carry for the most part.

You've said elsewhere that a poet is "stuck" with the first poet he reads and enjoys.

To a certain extent I think that's so. For instance, I know my teacher at Iowa, Donald Justice, first read Kenneth Patchen, who is so far away from Don Justice's esthetic and his whole road to and from poetry that you could hardly imagine one being more different; however, he still says he retains to this day a great affection for Kenneth Patchen because he was the first poet he read. The first poet I read who was important to me was Pound, and one tends to stick with that. He was a beautifully gifted poet, but one who had problems that I didn't really know about when I first started reading him.

Political problems?

Yes, politically he made many missteps, shall we say, and had at least several very wrongheaded, incorrect opinions that he pushed as vigorously as he pushed anything. And perhaps he was also more professorial in his poetry than I would have liked him to be. As my experience widens and I see more things that are possible and not possible in poetry, I still think that Pound was a great poet and, so far, probably the leading figure in American poetry in this century.

Did Williams's poetry help you at all?

I am a great admirer of Williams. I love him. You can't write poetry in this century without having read Williams, and how can you read Williams and not love him? Imagine getting that kind of simplicity, specificity, emotion, and power out of little things. He was able to do it simply—for the rest of us it seems too contorted. But I would still be more in the line of Pound, Crane, and Stevens than Williams and Creeley.

The New Poem [CM, 17], which is the first poem in your trilogy of books, is, at least in part, a very political poem.

2. An Interview by David Remnick

To a certain extent it mirrors or echoes W.H. Auden's statement that "poetry makes nothing happen,"[2] which I think is both true and untrue. It makes nothing happen in the world but it can make a lot happen to you and your inner life. That poem was written in 1970 toward the end of the Vietnam War. It's a political poem, and while poems against the Vietnam War were a big thing at the time, I thought that no matter how many poems you write against the war, it's not going to help us. It's not going to stop anything because political poetry only encourages people who think the way the poem thinks. It does not affect anyone who does not think the way the poem thinks.

Do you ever feel any kind of burden as a poet?

I've only felt the burden once in my life. One wants one's poems to be important to other people. One is writing for oneself—I am talking to myself—but I want to be overheard.[3] One time I got a letter from a young man after I had given a reading in California. I had read from *China Trace*, which is a book that is about spiritual anxieties and spiritual hopings for the future. He said he had decided to change his religion, to give up Christianity, because he felt I had thought so much about my own exposure to Christianity for so long and had come to such a reasoned renunciation of it and expressed it to him in such a reasonable way that he had been thinking about it for two months and had decided to do the same. That was a terrible burden. You want poems to change your life and perhaps to change other people's lives but that's a huge change. It was, at the same time, the most frightening and uplifting letter I've ever received. But that doesn't happen very often.

You've written a trilogy of books, Hard Freight, Bloodlines, *and* China Trace, *and you've written long poems within those collections, most notably* Skins *[CM, 82–102] and* Tattoos *[CM, 56–76]. I think it's fair to say that the trilogy is not one poem in the way that Dante's* Commedia *is, but it is still very unusual in our times to attempt anything so comprehensive. Why do you think so few long poems are written now?*

It's too hard and it takes too long; the novel; the movies; desire for instant recognition; the instant lives our lives have become through television; the current popularity of the "lyric" poem; it's too hard and it takes too long. One might also add that nothing is a poem the way the *Commedia* is a poem or one poem. It is the great triptych of literary history. My three little mice huddle in the vast shadow of its wings.

The fifth section of Tattoos *is one of your most skeptical poems on religion.*

Not only this poem, but almost all of *Bloodlines* and *Hard Freight* are about my ten-year struggle with the Episcopal Church, from age six to sixteen. In this poem I faint at the altar as an acolyte because they wouldn't let you eat before you took communion. I must have been eleven or twelve and I just sort of keeled over. I was all right but that all seemed a little foolish to me. A ten-year-old can't eat before he takes the wafer and the wine? There's not much point in getting into that, but it has given me much subject matter and has directed my life to a great extent; which is to say, had I not been forced by my mother (my father couldn't have cared less) to go to Sunday school and to church, I would not have the nature I have now. It's a little more of spiritual nature than it might have been otherwise and I'm glad of that. Also, going to Sunday school was good because you learned the Old Testament, which you wouldn't have done otherwise. You come to know all the wonderful stories and you get to read the Bible. The greatest translation that I know of is the King James Version of the Bible. So my work is full of Christianity and ex–Christianity. It's funny. I woke up this morning, remembering my last dream. A man came up to me in a Volvo agency and said, "You look like the kind of person who would contribute to this cause." And I turned around and he handed me these papers and said, "Here. Take this. I know you're a person who loves his mother. You'll contribute to this, won't you?" I said, "What's this? Oh yes. Maybe so. How would I make out the check?" And he said, "Just make it out to Jesus." I said, "I'm sorry. I can't do that. Please excuse me." I felt a very terrible coldness in the pit of my stomach knowing that I was doing what I shouldn't have done according to what my mother would have thought. So one grows up and one moves away, but the thing still remains. I haven't been in church for twenty years except for funerals! "Just make it out to Jesus." I thought that was a great line.

A Willie Nelson country music line.

Exactly.

Could you provide some background on #14 of the Tattoos?

It's interesting. That was a dream poem, dreamed after having seen Diane Arbus's photographs of mentally retarded people.[4] If you go back and look at the pictures of them dressed in sheets (it might have been Halloween), you can see where the image comes from; but it was a dream.

Much of the beauty achieved in the Tattoos *series is a result of the connections made from section to section. Generally, what is your attitude toward that technique of making connections using numbered sections?*

Making connections is the impulse of all art, I think. The artist's job is to try and keep the connections from being made completely, so that the synapses can snap and spark. That is where the real connections are, in the electricity and energy that goes back and forth between the parts. When Emily Dickinson said, in a note to her sister-in-law Sue, regarding the unexpected and devastating death of little Gilbert, Emily's nephew and Sue's son, "Our little Ajax spans the whole,"[5] she is pointing out a great synapse in her life and a connection to all art. One wonders if she might not have subconsciously died of grief a few years later. Connections are everything, but never perfect connections. Always the gap for the electricity to arc.

2. AN INTERVIEW BY DAVID REMNICK

I'd like to know a little about the composition of Virgo Descending *[CM, 51–2]. You appear to be a very meticulous worker. Does improvisation enter your composition in the sense that Ginsberg talks about it?*

No, there really isn't any improvisation. Doesn't he say "first thought, best thought"? I don't agree with that. How are you going to know what thought is best until you have worked at it? It's funny you picked *Virgo Descending* because it didn't take that long. It came right out of a dream. My dreams are usually very flashy and disjointed, as most people's are, like the #14 from *Tattoos*, or my dream from this morning when the man approached me for the check to Jesus. *Virgo Descending* came out, though, as a very narrative dream. Obviously, I fleshed it out, but the image of seeing my grandmother, of walking through these cavernous halls, emerged very narratively. I don't know exactly, but that took only two or three days to write. Some poems, some of the little poems in *China Trace*, for instance, took a month to six weeks. So spontaneity exists in the beginning of the poem, and each time you come back to it you make little spontaneous insights into how it might be done, but there is not one long continuous writing as if it were a dictation. That never happens to me. My mind works in flashes and starts and not in continuous movements as Ginsberg's; he must have a mind like that in order to have written *Howl* in the length of time he describes[6] or *Kaddish*, which he wrote overnight at long sittings. I can't sit still for that long and still concentrate.

When do you work?

Catch as catch can. I can't sit for that long a period. I work for an hour or two, get something down, get up, read, walk around, come back to it, try to get something else down, and work on what I have. No long stretches. I envy people who can do that. A friend of mine, the poet Jon Anderson, writes out every one of his poems completely over a night and then goes back the next night and begins to rework. The first versions are done in one sitting. Never for me. No matter how long or short the poem. The one-line poem in *China Trace—Bygones* [*CM*, 128]—was the result of days of work.

How did it start?

As a one-line poem, and then it got longer and then shrank. I thought that I could get one line with a title that made sense. I was trying to write a one-line poem—try it. It's hard as hell!

You've tried many technical experiments. Bygones *is only one example. Are technical experiments a real impulse to write for you?*

Technical experiments are a major source of interest to me. Every poem should have something new to me in it; otherwise, it holds little interest to me as a writer. What I have to say, I say. How I say it is a continual discovery.

Could you talk a bit about the Southernness of your voice?

I would always like to be thought of as a Southern poet, even though I haven't lived there in twenty-two years. Most of what I have written about comes out of the South, or Italy. The emotions drawn on are out of the South. I'd just like to have the texture and richness of language that we've come to think of as Southern.

Do you aim for a particular and consistent voice?

You know, it's funny and it sounds so naive to say this, but I really don't. I write it down the way I hear it, as it pops into my head. I think in a metaphysical way; that's why my poems are structured that way. That's why I can believe Emily Dickinson thought the way that she wrote because I tend to also. I don't think it's weird. I could write differently if I wanted to, but that wouldn't be me. I think in metaphor. I explain things in class in metaphor. So it's not a street poetry and it's not East Tennessee hill language, which I also know. I think it was Goethe who said "genius is only naturalness"; and it is natural for me to write and think this way and unnatural any other way. Now that might be because of my background, and the level of conversation in my house, or my immersion in the Bible and the Book of Common Prayer. It's not street speech and it's not salon speech either. It's some kind of speech on the outside of the stained-glass window looking in.

What does distance mean to you and your poetry?

Do you remember an old Colgate commercial in which the baseball pitcher Don Drysdale would throw a baseball at the announcer? He would throw the ball and it would go right up to the announcer's face and then ... Wham! It would hit an invisible pane of lucite and fall to the ground. Well, that's the distance I want. You see it all but there is that invisible pane of glass. If it were to smash into your face, the artifice would be lost to a certain extent. That's what rescued Sylvia Plath. It's that one step back and making a character out of her suffering rather than saying, "I, I, I, Me, Me, Me" all the time. That becomes boring and merely therapy, whereas if you create your own myth, which was what Plath did or what John Ashbery does, you will convey yourself or your emotional sense more believably. Of course, that distance is a matter of taste; I feel that for art's sake distance should be there. But not too much. I don't want personas with emotion in the basement either.

Isn't sentimentality a dominant problem in people's first efforts?

Yes, I think you have to know the difference between sentiment and sentimentality. It's a little like jazz—if you don't know what it is, I can't explain it to you. Again, it comes with practice, and reading, and someone pointing out to you what is sentimental. It's good practice because it becomes an emotional value. I keep going back to him, but Pound said "Poetry is the verbal expression of an emotional value."[7] The key word, of course, is value. Some things are more valuable emotionally than others.

What will distinguish the possible poet from the non-possible poet is this love of language, because that is something that goes above and beyond a need to say something like, "My boyfriend went out with someone else and smoked a reefer and now I feel so bad I'm going to write this poem." Language is beyond that. Of course I keep talking about language. Poetry is not all language. What is important is what is being said—I know that—but without language it's a long dark road.

Also, to get back to sentimentality, you can't ask for an emotional response. You must elicit the emotion from the reader of the poem. The poem has to elicit the response. It becomes an object that you create, and out of that has to come the response. You are not being morally fair with the poem when you are imposing on the poem; the poem takes on a life of its own once it gets started. It does the work, you can't do the work for it.

Do you recall the composition of Delta Traveller *[CM, 79–81]?*

I was in Laguna Beach, California, in a little shack in the backyard of our house in which I used to write. I had written *Tattoos* and *Skins* and I knew I wanted to write a poem about my mother and one about my father. As most of my poems do, *Delta Traveller* probably started with a rhythm rather than a structure. This was at a time when my son was two or three years old, and I had very few stretches of writing time. I would have maybe an hour or so that I could sneak in before I had to help out. That's why the poem came out in those little sections. Each one of them was written at a different time. I know it took somewhere between three weeks and a month. I would work on a section at a time, but what holds the poem together is that it is an elegy. It doesn't go logically from one section to another, nor would I want it to. The skull part was from a dream; the armed lawn chair was actually a chair of my mother's; she had bone cancer, therefore "bones like paint." The first part arises from the fact that I was the first child born in this particular hospital and Dr. Hurt was my doctor; the fertility business comes from a *National Geographic* I was reading. The last stanza is about nothing ever being really lost because it stays in the memory and is part of the natural process.

But you can't pin down what started it off?

I did have in mind a poem about my mother, but that was not what started it. Something other than the desire to write the poem actually got it going. Perhaps even the word "quarternight." It's the sort of word that might get me to hearing a rhythm. I remember I read Andy Adams' *The Story of a Cowboy,* and there was a cowhand in it named Fox Quarternight. I thought that was a marvelous name and I may have been saying it to myself and the first line happened, as I was born in the early morning hours in that hospital. (Hence, "brash / Tongue on the tongueless ward.") That may have started it all and it flowed from there. I don't really remember, but it's a good story, and it could be true.

CHAPTER 3

Charles Wright on Eugenio Montale and Dino Campana: An Interview by Mary Zeppa

MZ: *Let me make sure I have the sequence right: you first studied Italian at the Army Language School in Monterey.*

CW: Right. I went to Monterey in the summer of 1958. It was the first time I had had any Italian at all. I had a six-month course there, and then in January of 1959, I went over to Italy and was there two, almost three, years. Until the fall of 1961. That's when my Italian was best. It's sort of been falling off steadily since. I did the Montale translations two years later, 1963–65, when I was back in Rome on a Fulbright fellowship, not to translate Italian, but to study Montale and Pasolini and Pavase. But basically what I did was translate *La Bufera*.[1] And my Italian was all right then too, although I had some help on the first part of the book from my teacher, Maria Sampoli. I did the basic work and then asked other people to look at it. I later had them looked over twice again by Italianists, one an Italian and one an American Italian. And that's how the poems arrived at their final conclusions.

And you wrote your own first poems in Italy? You hadn't written poems before?

No. I tried to write a little fiction in college, but I wasn't any good at it.

From the beginning then your own poems were involved with the Italian language?

Certainly with the landscape of Italy. And even the English poems I was reading—the poems of Pound—were very much involved with Italian landscape. So Italy kept com-

This interview, conducted by telephone during the summer of 1984, was published in Poet News *(October 1985): 1, 8–10.*

ing in, even in my attempts to write English poems. Which were really Pound translations until I got to Iowa and was disabused of that notion. Fortunately. But I did train my ear on Pound, and that's what stayed with me.

Do you think the fact that you started writing poems and were very conscious of both the landscape and the language has had an effect on your work?

I *suppose* it has. I used to have a more facile answer to that, which was "Yes." [Laughs]. I don't know to what extent it's true any more. Early on, I was so obsessed with Italy and with the landscape and it's being the place where I started writing, that I kind of *imprinted* it and kept returning to it and returning to it. The same way I return to my childhood in eastern Tennessee and western North Carolina. Because *that* was the place I started finding out about the world around me. In Italy I started finding out about the world around me *and* inside me. It took me a long time obviously. A late bloomer. But that's where it happened. So of course those two places will continue to come back. Italy has always been a profoundly important place for me. Both physically and, if one can use such a word, spiritually. Italian itself was important, not in the *beginning* of my own writing, but in an early stage. Which was after I'd been to Iowa and learned some of the things I shouldn't be doing. Then I started translating Montale and learned a *lot* about how to put a poem together. Of course I was fortunate in picking a brilliant poet. And there was a real, sort of psychic, transference between the two of us. There are certain things about Montale I just believe to be true. For *my* life as well.

Can you set Montale and Campana, chronologically and culturally, in the Italian tradition for us?

Campana was born in 1885—the same year Pound was, which I find interesting—he was born in 1885 and died in 1932 in an insane asylum in Tuscany. He spent the last eighteen years of his life in the asylum, and he said that was where he belonged. He was quite lucid about that part. He said, "I'm crazy. This is where I belong. I used to write. I don't write any more." He ended up writing one book, *Canti Orfici* (*Orphic Songs*), which is a combination of prose and poetry. He was a wanderer. He had a wandering heart. A gypsy from an early age, he just couldn't sit still. He started wandering off from home when he was about fifteen. And he wandered all over Europe and South America and so forth. He is the *poète maudit* of Italian literature. The Italian Rimbaud, the Gérard de Nerval. He's kind of the wild man of the Italian literary scene. That's his niche. And even though he has only one book and a handful of good poems, he's kept this niche and kept his reputation because he was unique in Italian letters. Montale was around just a little bit after Dino—Dino's book came out in 1914, and Montale started writing right around the time of World War I. And he's much more from the tradition, the Dantescan tradition. A hard-edged, very imagistically concise and incisive kind of poetry, as opposed to the fuzzy and what we would now think of as sentimental poetry of, say, people like Pascoli or D'Annunzio. He is in, I think, an almost direct line from Dante that doesn't go through too many other people. He pretty much resurrected that tradition in Italian poetry. What attracted me to Dino early on was his legend, not his poems. That's why it took me so long to translate his stuff. I thought I owed two debts to Italian poets. Certainly, Montale was one because I learned so much from him when I translated him. But the other one was Dino because ... just the *idea* of him, the idea of the "poet" was very interesting to me and important to me when I first started writing. And I translated him to pay that debt.[2] And I'm glad I did, although I probably did it twenty years too late, and I did Montale twenty years too soon. But I probably wouldn't have done either one had I switched the twenty years around.

You once called Montale the greatest poet of the century. You said, "If I'd known more Italian, I'd never have attempted anything so insane [as to translate him]." Were you being a little bit hyperbolic?

A little bit, but not really. He's truly untranslatable. I probably would have been much more leery of trying to do it had I known how much of the Dantescan tradition was involved. I didn't *know* anything about that tradition. I don't know *much* about it now. But then I see other people who know a lot about the Italian tradition and the Italian language and I read their translations and I don't like them any better than mine. Less, actually. Translators are inordinately proud of their translations, even if they're not about their own poems. You figure you've got the answer. And then someone else says, "Oh, no, it should be this," you take great umbrage. "How can it *possibly* be that? I've figured it out and it's this!" And you *never* think that about your own work.

What about *trying to translate from another tradition? Poets always stand in the tradition of literature whether then intend to, whether they fight against it, or not. There's really no choice. They are* in *the culture. And a translator outside that culture doesn't have easy access to all the things that involves.*

So what you usually do is bring it over to your own culture. That's why Poe is apparently such a great poet in French. And to be honest, in English he isn't very good, I think. Even though he *has* a room right over here on the lawn at U. Va. [Laughs]. And I revere his spirit. The poems aren't that interesting, but the French worked him into their tradition in the late 1800s, and he's marvelous, apparently. You can't help but bend a little into your own tradition. Kenneth Rexroth said something very funny in an article I read about how the perfect example of this is the American Indian and the Great Spirit, who apparently didn't exist until the French Jesuits came over and started talking about the Holy Father. Then suddenly the North American Indians had a Great Spirit. They just translated that into their own tradition and manufactured a Great Spirit that would correspond with what the Jesuit missionaries were telling them. Rexroth said the Great Spirit migrated bodily from the age of reason in France over the ocean into the North American Indian culture.[3] [Laughs].

Are you aware that when you speak of Eugenio Montale you always say "Montale," and when you speak of Dino Campana you always say "Dino"? At first—I didn't know anything about where he was set in the culture—I actually thought that you knew *Campana, because of your* tone.

There's just something about Dino. Dino is unique. As Steve Martin would say, he's a kind of wild and crazy guy. Montale is much more of a statuesque figure, someone one looks up to. Campana...

You feel a different kind *of closeness to him?*

Yes, I would never call Montale "Eugenio," but I'd want to go up and say, "Hey, Dino! What's happening?" [Laughs]. And he'd answer back. It's something about how he wrote, what he wrote, how he conducted himself. Montale was known as a reserved, very patrician sort of fellow.

Since you responded more to Campana's spirit than to his work, did you ever have the impulse to improve his work?

Yes, I did. At least to punctuate it. And then Jon Galassi talked me out of it.[4] And absolutely rightly so, because a great part of Dino's presence in his poems comes from his sort on onrushing, overrushing syntactical excesses. And the non-punctuation, the rush of language that keeps coming out—that sort of hyperactivity drives the poems. I was just trying to make it easier to read in English. And then I realized that Jon was right. If you want to get as close to Dino as you can then you better at least have the syntax and the grammatical construction the same, and then you can let the people worry about it in English just the way I worried about it in Italian.

I could sense some of that torrential quality.

It did seem to sort of spill out of him all his life. That's how he lived. That's how he wrote. And that's apparently how he talked and how he acted. It was absolutely wrong to try to change it. And I wouldn't change any of his words. Oh, I tried to add a word here and there, but, again, I eventually took them all out. I over-translated and then cut back as close as possible to the original.

What do you mean by "over-translate"?

You add things. You try to improve. You do this and you do that that's not in the text. And when you cut back the English to the almost literalness of the original text, what you have is an English that wasn't literal to start with, so you have different kinds of words and different kinds of rhythms. It seems to work for me. I did that on both the Montale and the Campana. It's a *way* of working. You can't fool yourself that you're kind of vamping on your own out there, but, in fact, when you get it cut back, you've remained as true as you can to the text. But you also have the illusion, and sometimes the actuality, of having a looser kind of translation than you might have if you had done it word for word. And you also avoid the academic notation that you get in a lot of translations.

Somewhere in between that and Robert Bly's approach, for instance?

Yes. Now that's too loose. I don't know the languages he translates from, but I've seen examples, and it seems to me he goes much too far out of the line that *I* would want a translation to take.

So you think he does an injustice to the poets?

I don't know the languages, so it isn't fair for me to say. But if he were doing it in Italian, I would say, "Absolutely." Obviously, you don't do word for word. But you also don't do imitations, unless, like Lowell, you *call* them "Imitations."

So the reader knows where he is right away.

Exactly. As Dryden said, "There are three kinds [of translations]: paraphrase, metaphrase, and imitation."[5] Metaphrase is word for word, paraphrase you do as best you can in your own time and in your own language. And it seems to me from what I can gather and what I have seen that some of Bly's translations fall somewhere between paraphrase and imitation, instead of between metaphrase and paraphrase. Well, as Frost said, "What worked for them might work for you."[6] [Laughs]. But that's not workable if you're going to call it a translation.

What about translation generally? You've said that the translator is the one who gets the most out of the translation no matter how good the translation turns out to be.

I think that's true. But of course a great deal of our fund of intellectual knowledge comes from translation. So translation is absolutely necessary. We couldn't get along without it. Even a poor translation is better than no translation at all, isn't it? Of course, the more you know about the language, the more you know about translation and then the more you get incensed. But if you don't know anything about it, you're happy to have what you've got there. You might think it's terrific. You might think that Louise Varese's translations of *Illuminations* by Rimbaud are great, as I always did, because it was all I knew for a while. And I still don't know French, and I still like them. But somebody who translates French and knows Rimbaud would probably say, "Are you kidding?"

Bob Hass once said that translation is like making love with gloves on.

Well, he shouldn't use his hand so often. [Laughs]. No. That sounds about right. It's getting the feel of it. And it's truly a thankless occupation, but an endlessly fascinating one for someone who's trying to learn about another language or about how another writer thinks, lives, all those commonplaces that everybody knows. And it has served me, certainly, very well. But I never think of myself as a translator or even as someone who translates. I once translated two books. That's about all. It goes back to your original question. I got into translation mostly through love of Italy, rather than through love of particular poets. I was lucky in the two that I chose. It was an extension of my Italian obsession as opposed to an extension of my obsession with Italian literature. And I suppose it was more an extension of my interest in American poems than it was in Italian poems, which may be a very unusual case. I don't know how other people get involved in translation.

One of the first books I read about the process of translation was George Steiner's After Babel. *One of his most intriguing ideas is that there is a pure speech, an* Ur-Sprache *that "precedes and underlies all languages, and in which all languages are fused." He says that such a language* must *exist because "human beings mean the same things, that the human voice springs from the same hopes and fears, though different words are said ... a poor translation ... misses the bond of meaning."*[7] *Does that make any sense to you?*

Sure. A poor anything misses that bond of meaning, doesn't it? It sounds very neo-Platonic to me, and I rather fancy it. It's like something I've always said: all poems are translations. Even original poems. I truly do *believe* that there is some perfection out there that we keep trying to cut off little bits and pieces of, to shape in our own way, to *make* translations from some great language, from some great river of words. And we all scoop out our little handfuls from time to time.

It is *an appealing idea. Galway Kinnell once said, "I think we do really want to know, insofar as it's possible, what ... others in the past thought and felt. The translator should ... try to completely suppress himself, or to put it the other way around, try to flow into that person he's translating and do it faithfully."*[8]

That's the opposite of what you asked earlier about bringing someone over into your own cultural milieu. What Galway's saying sounds like a perfect definition of Negative Capability. [Laughs]. Which I think it is. And that's always a good thing. It's hard to argue with Keats. But then there's also the Egotistical Sublime, which, if it works for Wordsworth, maybe it'll work for certain translators![9] It's probably a good thing if you can flow into another person's thinking and juices, as it were. It's probably the *optimum* thing. I find it very difficult. If you can do it at certain key points or in certain key grooves, maybe then the poem will start to click together, like little Lego pieces. I find it hard to completely become, well, I don't *want* to become Rilke, even to translate his poems. I don't want to *be* anybody else. I would like to get a *feeling* and a *sense* of, but I don't want to *become*. I think the only person I would like to become would be Emily Dickinson. [Laughs].

A good choice! You felt a metaphysical closeness with Montale. Did you ever feel anything approaching that kind of unity when you were working on his poems?

No. Only with his beliefs—with his sort of stance toward things. Certainly not to such an extent that I would become something behind his eyes and try to take it in with his point of view. No, I never did that. I just felt that we believed some of the same things. And that seemed to me important. That's why I think my Montale translations are better than my Campana translations. I *wanted* to do the Campana and did it with great good will. But I felt after starting the Montale I *had* to finish those. I had to keep finding out what they were because I was learning stuff about myself. I felt I was learning things about Campana when I translated him. It's always interesting to find out things about yourself, and I really felt that with Montale. If I could find somebody else who would give me the same things, maybe I would try translating again.

Do you know any other language well enough to...

No. I don't even know Italian well enough anymore. See, that's again the problem. I've been away from it for so long. Doing Dino was quite difficult, because even though I could read the progress of the syntax, I still had to use the dictionary so much more than I used to.

What about the idea that we'd all be better off sitting down with a dictionary and a grammar and the original poem?

Well, that's a great idea, but it's really hard to do, isn't it? I think you ought to have a prose trot and a dictionary and the poem in front of you. Then you can see how the grammar goes and how the language goes in the original. When you sort of know what it's saying, then you can *hear* it. And you can't hear it, I think, if you have to keep turning to the dictionary. If you know *what* it's saying, you can listen to the *way* it's said.

A friend of mine who's translating contemporary German poets says that method would be fine if dictionaries were ever good enough. And then there are all those phrases that you can't possibly...

Yes. Which is one of the good things about having a prose trot. Someone who knows the language has already gone to some trouble to give you those possibilities. It's important that we hear the original. It just is.

What about *sound? Is there any way even to* approach *getting the music in the translation?*

You have to try. You have to deal with the original form the poem was written in. But there's no point in slavishly trying to imitate, for instance, the hendecasyllabic Italian line. The closest thing in English to the Italian hendecasyllabic line would be iambic pentameter, since that's our basic traditional line. But they're not writing in iambic pentameter. So you try to find something that's kind of an accentual line in English that close—that sounds something like the line but that's flexible as well. You don't try to imitate but you try to get it in a decent number of stresses and syllable crossovers so that it sounds close enough to the original. Italian is basically a syllabic language and obviously that's very important when you're translating it. Not just the *counting* of syllables, but the *length* of them and the way they sound. The feel in the mouth is what's important—very much more so than trying to put their traditional line into our traditional line. I tried to make Montale's lines sound in English they way I thought at the time they sounded in Italian—of course, I *hear* differently now than I did twenty years ago. And I certainly did that with Dino. I tried to make an English equivalent of that, to use your word, "torrential" flow of language. Yes, one tries. You arm yourself with all the good will and intelligence that you can, and you do what you can with what you've got.

Sound, music, "the feel in the mouth" is obviously very important to you. Do you think a writer who loves music but is not a musician *pushes all that musicality into language?*

I think there's something to that, yes. Montale was a singer, you know, before he became a poet. He studied *bel canto* as a young man. Then he stopped doing that and started writing poems, and surely that comes into the poems. Now my teacher, Donald Justice, plays the piano very well and once wanted to be a composer, and there's certainly music in his poems. But I don't imagine he's as *obsessed* about it as I am. Because I can't get it out any other way. As Pound said about Yeats, he couldn't carry a tune, except on the page.

What are you working on now?

I'm working on some verse journals. I've been working on these the last couple of years. I have one called *Night Journal* and one called *A Journal of English Days*. *English Days* was the first one. I started it when I was in London two years ago. After Port Townsend last summer, I did one called *A Journal of True Confessions*. [Laughs]. It started out with the assignment I gave everybody—I figured I'd better do it—the eight lines about the weather. So I did that, and then it expanded *somehow* into a nine-page prose poem called *A Journal of True Confessions*. [Laughs]. It starts out at Port Townsend and works its way across the country over four months. And right now, well, I probably shouldn't talk about it ... I'm trying to do a year-long one which is very.... Well, there's not a lot of immediate gratification in doing a year-long poem. But I'm slogging away at it. And I'm *slugging* away at it too. What I'm mostly interested in is structure. The various structures possible in English: the possibilities of the tight, long line, the infinite possibilities of certain forms. I'm trying to *explore* that and see how far I can go before it all collapses—either under the weight of its own boredom or the weight of its own excesses. And I hope that I'll stop it before it does either one.[10] [Laughs].

CHAPTER 4

"Metaphysics of the Quotidian": A Conversation with Stan Sanvel Rubin and William Heyen

The New Poem

It will not resemble the sea.
It will not have dirt on its thick hands.
It will not be part of the weather.

It will not reveal its name.
It will not have dreams you can count on.
It will not be photogenic.

It will not attend our sorrow.
It will not console our children.
It will not be able to help us.

Ars Poetica

I like it back here

Under the green swatch of the pepper tree and the aloe vera.
I like it because the wind strips down the leaves without a word.
I like it because the wind repeats itself,
                               and the leaves do.

This conversation took place on 3 April 1986 as part of the Writers Forum program at the State University of New York College at Brockport. Interviewers were Stan Sanvel Rubin and William Heyen. Wright began the interview by reading two poems, The New Poem *[CM, 17] and* Ars Poetica *[later published in WTTT, 38]. The interview was published in* The Post-Confessionals: Conversations with American Poets of the Eighties, *ed. Earl Ingersoll, Judith Kitchen, and Stan Sanvel Rubin (Rutherford, NJ: Farleigh Dickinson University Press, 1989), 25–38.*

> I like it because I'm better here than I am there,
>
> Surrounded by fetishes and figures of speech:
> Dog's tooth and whale's tooth, my father's shoe, the dead weight
> Of winter, the inarticulation of joy...
>
> The spirits are everywhere.
>
> And once I have them called down from the sky, and spinning around
>   and dancing in the palm of my hand,
> What will it satisfy?
>   I'll still have
> The voices rising out of the ground,
> The fallen star my blood feeds,
>   this business I waste my heart on.
> And nothing stops that.

SR: *You read two poems about poetics and poetry. I'd like to go back to the first of the two,* The New Poem *[CM, 17], which says that it will not offer us consolation and it will not be able to help us. What can we expect from* The New Poem?

CW: That poem was written in the time of the Vietnam War, in the late sixties, when political poetry was, if not *de rigueur*, certainly all the vogue. There were read-ins against the War, as you remember, and political poetry was experiencing a kind of rebirth, as it were, in this country. My point in that poem is only about political poetry—not poetry itself—which is not going to help our children over there. It's not going to be any consolation. It won't do the job; something else has to stop the War. As Auden said, "Poetry makes nothing happen."[1] He meant it in that kind of political sense. That's what I mean in that poem; I don't mean it as encompassing all of poetry, because I think poetry can change your life; but it can't change a war, or it couldn't change that one.

SR: You won't even grant Shelley's "unacknowledged-legislators" claim that poetry is somehow changing the world?[2]

Again, I have to tip my nonexistent hat to Wystan Auden and say that the "unacknowledged legislators of the world" are now the secret police and not the poets.[3]

WH: The poem says, "It will not attend our sorrow." That line makes me sad. I want the poem to accompany my emotions through the world.

Certainly the political poem can't. Accompanying us through the world could be the poem's finest moment, and ours as well. But I don't think it'll help us on the battlefield. That really is beside the point, because what the read-ins were about was changing the government, and it wasn't the poetry that changed the government's mind, but all the people finally getting together. Maybe poetry had a little to do with it, but it was the inevitability of the asininity of the enterprise that finally changed things.

4. A Conversation with Stan Sanvel Rubin and William Heyen

WH: When I first read that poem, I wasn't connecting it with you and Vietnam and the time you wrote it; I was reading it as a kind of prophetic statement—that's how readers will come to it.

I hope that if they will not read just that poem but something else I've written they will see that *The New Poem* is not a total *ars poetica*, or poetic statement on my part.

SR: Now the other one you just read is an Ars Poetica *[WTTT, 38]. You say in that poem, "I like it because I'm better here than there."*

"Here," because if I had been reading that poem before an audience live, instead of an audience out there behind the glass, I would've said that here is where I write, my little room, and there is the rest of the house or the world. I am more myself when I'm writing than when I'm out doing daily things. Somehow my job is to bring what's here, there. My business is the metaphysics of the quotidian.

SR: Then the act or process of writing does offer you something of value.

Oh, it changed my life totally, when I started writing! I was just someone looking for something to do, and then I found it.

SR: The line, "This business I waste my heart on," implies a certain degree of irony or pain, or both.

It's a self-inflicted pain, of course. It's what we all do as writers. You waste your heart on it, because it's never quite right and it never quite is satisfying; but it's the closest thing to being satisfying that I've been able to come up with in my life.

WH: This is maybe a bad question because it has to do with "idea" and I think you'd agree that we find out what we know and feel by writing; but you did just now use the phrase "the metaphysics of the quotidian," and yet when I read your poems they're always edging toward something beyond that. You say, "The spirits are everywhere," for example; and you say that you want to get to that "still, small pinpoint of light at the center of the universe," where all things come together and intersect—this is a romantic view of the integrity and the harmony of the universe out there. So the focus is on the here and now, but there does seem to be something inside you of a greater connection or a greater feeling.

Certainly a greater aspiration; and one can only get there through the tangible, tactile things of the everyday, I think. There's a passage I came across in the letters of Paul Cézanne in which he says that colors were to him numinous essences beyond which he knew nothing—"the diamond zones of God remaining white."[4] For me if you replace the word *colors* with words and *white* with *blank*, you would get how I try to find out what those "zones" are. I admit that I think they exist; I'm just not very sure of them.

WH: Roethke says, "The flesh can make the spirit visible."[5] Richard Wilbur says that Poe's aesthetic, for example, is insane.[6] He uses the word insane; *that is, Poe tries to knock people out into some aesthetic realm out there, forsaking the earth.*

I think that's very foolish. I won't try to top Mr. Wilbur's word, but it seems fairly accurate from my point of view because I don't think it works that way. If Lowell was right that "I myself am hell,"[7] then you can fill in the blank in "I myself am————."

WH: There is so much "thingness" in your poetry—the heavy, drenched thingness of the world. That's one of the most beautiful things about your poems, I think.

You only get to the invisible through the visible—an old idea, but it seems workable to me. As Frost said, "What worked for them might work for you."[8] That's why I say that almost all of my poems seem to be part of this ongoing argument I have with myself over my rather foolish enterprise of ... what? Perhaps the possibility of salvation—again I go back to what Cézanne was saying because that's as close as I can get to it in any rational way.

SR: Has that always been your motivating impulse? Is that what got you started writing in the first place?

It's been my motivating impulse ever since I realized what I thought I was about. What got me interested first in writing was the fact that my mother used to date William Faulkner's brother at the University of Mississippi and used to talk about it at the house, and I thought writing a great thing to do. Like everyone else I tried to write stories in school, but I can't tell a story—I'm the only Southerner I know who cannot tell a story. When I got to Italy in the Army, I went to a place called Sirmione, where the Latin poet Catullus supposedly had had a villa. Someone handed me *The Selected Poems of Ezra Pound* and said, "You should read *Blandula, Tenulla, Vagula*; Pound wrote it right here in Sirmione." It was like a lightning bolt out of the sky. I read it, it was beautiful; it was a poem about a place I was sitting in, and it wasn't narrative. It wasn't Mr. Frost. Much as I love his poems, I can't write those long narratives. This was associational, imagistic, fabulous! It worked the way my mind worked, in jumps and starts, synaptically, and my life was changed. So I tried to rewrite the *Cantos*, a very foolish enterprise, which I gave up after a few years. I showed up at the University of Iowa, thinking I wanted to go to graduate school; but I had neglected to get myself accepted into the program. It was so unstructured at that time that no one knew I hadn't been let in, so I just signed up for classes and started going. The very first class, I walked in and sat down—I think it was Mark Strand who was in my class that said, "I don't think the iambic pentameter line is working very well here in this poem." I'm dead, I thought. I was a history major in college, and I didn't even know what an iambic pentameter line was! So I shut up for two years and listened very intently. To answer your question, it was the desire to be a writer that made me get started, and once I got started, somehow all my life's obsessions, my ten-year lover's quarrel with the Episcopal Church and all the accoutrements of growing up in East Tennessee with the country music and all of that life-and-death, lyric theme in country music started to well up in me, and I knew what I was interested in—this constant struggle with, well, Will we be, or won't we be? I'm one of those few people who think there is a difference between content, subject matter, and form. The content remains like a Greek chorus behind everything I write—the contemplation of the divine, if you will. The subject matter is how you tell the story to get to that content. The form is however you put it together.

SR: Pound was important to you, as you said, because of the movement of mind, I suppose.

The whole associational modernist way of putting together a poem was important to me. Pound was the first poet I ever read. I think anybody's first poet whom he really reads is very important. If you're lucky, you get a great poet; if not, you still like the one you started out with.

SR: Were there other poets who were important to you in a shaping way in terms of this content, the contemplation of the divine?

Wallace Stevens. He said that "the proper study of all poetry is the contemplation of the divine."[9] There are obviously other things that are important in poetry: restitution of the past, rescue from oblivion—a lot of things are important as content. This happens to be the one that obsesses me, and if you don't go with your obsessions, then you're kind of faking it, you know. I intend to continue with my obsessions, although I hope the story lines and the examples change from time to time; but the main idea of what I am worming my way toward would be there. Pound was important for me, as I said, because he was the first poet. He also allowed me to try things that you weren't supposed to try when I was learning to write poems, particularly at the Iowa Workshop, which was much more structured and formal. I was, to a certain extent just because I didn't know anything, a slightly odd thorn in that context. Iowa was very good for me, because I spent three or four years trying to learn forms. If you don't know them, then you can't do the other. You've got to know what you're *not* doing.

WH: You've said that in the beginning your music was the music of the stanza, and you worked awfully hard on stanzaic integrity and stanzaic balance. In general you've moved toward a more free-flowing or synaptic or associational poem. I guess this is a question of form, content, and subject matter all at once. How do you think you came to that other way of writing?

I'm a fairly—that's not true—I'm an excessively orderly person. Stanzas seemed to me the proper study of poetkind. Which is to say if the poem isn't in stanzas, it's all kind of unorganized. Wrenching order out of chaos is one of the things we know poetry does. During those three or four years I was trying to write formal verse, I fell into stanzas, because if you're trying to do sonnets or quatrains.... I had a fortunate occurrence. I mentioned to you yesterday that I used to have a little shack at the back of my house in California. When my son was born, the first several years were very hectic and there wasn't a lot of free time to do things. I would start a poem and I'd get the idea, and maybe a stanza, and then I'd have to rush off to do something else. The next day I'd come back to it and write another stanza. After a period of time, I started to realize that the stanzas were all cohering to the title, but they weren't necessarily narratively following each other. This was a great discovery for me, because it went back to my original idea of how things worked in my mind, which was synaptically, and I'd been trying to force myself into a logic of narrative, just because I thought I should learn how to do it. Unbeknownst to myself, I was breaking back out into where I should've been in the first place. But with the great exception that I had learned that the organization was very important as well, so I was leading from organization instead of leading from chaos. As the stanzas got larger and looser, there still remained the idea of a stanzaic or a patterned organization. And no matter how long the poems get—my last one is forty-two pages—they are still built up of stanzas, but you really wouldn't know it to look at them.

WH: I looked up that word synapse *this morning, and it has to do with impulse from nerve to nerve. But it also has to do with the way that when a cell divides the chromosomes are realigned again somehow.*

One of my pet little theories is that most art—and certainly poems—tends toward the condition of circularity: we try to make things complete. The artist's job, or at least my job when I'm writing a poem, is to try to keep it from meeting completely, because once it meets completely the energy stops. So what you should be doing is keeping it apart and working in that synapse—that's where the sparks are—in that synapse from nerve to nerve. Again, that goes back to the stanzaic pattern, but not a complete stanzaic patterning. That's one of the things I don't like about—even though I love many of them—accepted forms. The accepted, given, traditional form, if it's executed perfectly, is a completion, a circle. Since I truly believe that considerations of form are at the heart of all poetry, all considerations of poetry are considerations of form—I don't mean forms, but form—then one should try as hard as possible to generate forms that are one's own, but out of the given, out of the tradition. I don't mean standing in a field and lighting your hair on fire and jumping up and down saying, "Look, I'm doing something new and different." Form means everything to me. Larkin said, "Content means everything to me, form is nothing."[10] Form means everything to me, content is nothing. I don't believe that, of course, but it's a provocative thing to say, because people say, "What do you mean?" My point is that once you know your content, the way Larkin knew his forms, then it's not something you have to think about any more.

WH: The older I get, the more I understand what Williams meant when he said, "The only way to stay alive is through technique." 'He uses the word technique, *but he means the exploration of the form.*

4. A Conversation with Stan Sanvel Rubin and William Heyen

And he talks about the "measure"—that's the word nowadays. It's not the metrics; it's the measure. I have to admit I'm dedicated to free verse the way Frank Stella says he's dedicated to abstract art. You know, he knows a lot, if not everything, about the history and traditions of art. That is where he's staked his territory; this is where I stake mine. When I talk about formal organization, I'm always talking about working in free verse. It's the one meter where the rock hits the water as far as I'm concerned.

SR: I suppose once you found prosody at Iowa, it never let you go.

It's true. I love formal poems, and I teach a course in prosody. It's endlessly fascinating to me—the variations in iambic pentameter and tetrameter, and syllabics, accentuals, and all of this; but at this point I'm not particularly interested in working in those meters. I'm interested in what those meters can give to the free verse I try to work in, which is not really all that "free." It's quite ordered and structured, and its idea of line comes from having studied the formal line. The trouble now with most of the kids is that they don't know what the formal meters were so they don't know that lineation really exists as lineation. They're thinking in sentences and ideas, so they write them down and sort of just chop the line wherever it looks good. Lineation in free verse originally came from traditional meters. All of the great modern masters of free verse—including Whitman—always wrote in accepted, traditional meters before they broke away. They had a sense of the line; they knew what a line was, or had been. If you don't know what a line has been, how the hell can you make it different?

SR: I'd like to push this a little further into how you actually work. How conscious, for example, are you of syllabics and stress while you're writing?

Totally. I count the syllables of every line I write, and I tend to work in lines from, say, three to nineteen syllables. Mostly they're an odd number for some reason.

WH: You count them consciously? That's very surprising to me, because I sensed a more intuitive engagement with your music as you wrote—which I guess is a good effect when I read your poems.

I love you for saying that, because that's what, of course, I would like it to be. I'm conscious of stress only to try not to make it regular. If you're working with a thirteen-syllable line, you're going to have somewhere between four and seven stresses. Stresses, in a way, tend to be like little staples for me to keep the line down, as the line gets longer and longer. I'm listening to syllables; I'm listening to the sound and to what used to be known as quantitative meters, which we cannot write in, because the English language will not accept them; but the idea of them—the weight, the duration, the length, the syllable, is very important in my line. That's what Pound was talking about in the "sequence of the musical phrase": he was trying to get the idea of quantitative meters into English and not to work with the metronome or syllable stress. So, yes, I count them all. I find that after ten or fifteen years of doing this I hear what they are before I've counted them and I know basically where I want a long one or a short one. Music—to use the word you brought up—is extremely important to me. Sound is extremely important to me in my poems, I hope not to the detriment of what I'm trying to say, because as we all know there is the "how" and the "what." Someone said, "Great poets write the 'what,' minor poets write the 'how.'" But you can't get to the "what" except through the "how." You can't just start with the "what," as many examples of beginning poets will show. They have something they want to tell you, but they don't know how to say it. To make "how" you say it an end in itself seems foolish because then you end up with this gorgeous structure out here in the middle of the desert. It's not very fashionable, but I'm extremely interested in style as well. Style is a dirty word in poetry now, because it seems to imply surface, and surface only. I don't think it has to. Painters know that style is important. You can get fifteen painters to go out and paint the exact same motif, and the great painter will make a great painting out of it and the others will just make a painting out of it. Ultimately I would like to be able—if you put ten poems on the wall as they do paintings in a museum—you'd be able to say, "Oh, that's the one by Charles Wright."

WH: The trouble with words like style *and* content *and* subject matter *is that you can only talk about one of them at a time. This is something that is very much on my mind right now. Robert Penn Warren once said that he went through a school as an English major and didn't realize until he was done that he'd never really had a course in literature. All the courses were courses in history, philosophy, biography—whatever. Everything except poetry. What is the "poetry" of poetry? What is the essential experience of poetry, beyond the other talk we find ourselves doing?*

All I know is that essence is not ironic. Emily Dickinson says, "When the hair stands up on my head, I know it's true poetry."[11]

WH: I think it has something to do with not being able to separate the "dancer" from the "dance," when you're in the presence of the poem at least.

You read my mind! I was going to say that I wrote down in this little journal or commonplace notebook I keep, "If you can tell the dancer from the dance, one of you is not doing his job."[12] There is no division between form, subject matter, and content. It seems to me there are three stages you go through. When you're a young writer, it's the singer, not the song—you're learning how to do it. When you hit your prime, it's the song, not the singer. Then, in old age, you go back to "It's the singer, not the song." Of course, the great poet knows it's always both at the same time. *The Divine Comedy* is the singer and the *song*.

SR: Does the concept of voice, which is such a catchword in workshops, mean anything to you?

I never really—I know sort of what I think of as voice, and someone has his own voice and so forth—no, it doesn't mean a lot to me. So many people mean different things by it: the authority of the way the poem is presented, the style, the manner that is being brought to it, either from tradition or some newfangled way. I never know quite what voice is. Tenor and voice—tenor and vehicle—voice and subject matter. I have no answer for that.

SR: The persona poem, the poem as if spoken by someone else?

That's an obvious voice; but it's a different kind of "voice" from what a lot of people mean.

SR: That seems really beside the point for you. It's a kind of poetry that people write in abundance these days. It would seem almost an evasion of the real work as you are describing it.

I've written one book that I think is in a persona, and all the rest of the I's are thinly disguised me.

SR: Are you thinking of China Trace?

That's the only real persona poem. It's interesting that, when you think about Keats and the "negative capability" of submerging your own personality or voice for the voice of the character, he says that there's only one person who can't do this, and that's Wordsworth because of the "egotistical sublime." When he walks through a field of daffodils, he can pull it off; everyone else had better work with "negative capability." Surely there's been some fusion now after almost two hundred years of the Romantic movement. Maybe it's an egotistical necessity or a negative sublime—maybe I write out of a negative sublime. I don't know.[13]

SR: Does all this attention to form that you've been describing and all this care for the "music" imply a lot of hard work and revision in your writing process?

Yes, it does. I've been sitting here talking a lot of theoretics, but when it gets down to the work you have to just write, and in my case erase. Most writers don't erase; they just cross out, because they want to save earlier versions for posterity. I revise constantly. I used to revise whole poems; now I revise as I go along, from line to line. Sometimes I erase so much I tear a hole in the paper. I don't believe in "first-thought, best-thought." I know that when Allen Ginsberg talks about that, it's a Zen concept;[14] but you can't get into that until you've put yourself into a Zen condition where you're completely empty and ready to receive. Then first thought may be best thought, but don't tell that to young poets unless they're practicing Zen Buddhists. First thought is usually worst thought—you have to work at it!

WH: He has reworked every one of his poems, including Wales Visitation.

I think that was "first-thought, best-thought" with *Wales Visitation*, which used to be called *Wales Visitation Sutra*. It's one of my favorite poems of his. The way he uses the line is so strong and so hooked together—the way he says he's learned from Cézanne about one word hooking into another. I thought that was a fabulous poem. I wish he hadn't even changed the title.[15]

WH: Charles, we need to hear you read one of your poems.

All right, I'll read *Dog Creek Mainline* [*CM*, 36]. It's about a little town in Western North Carolina I lived in at the age of six. It's a poem about memory and how we change memory, how memory changes and memory becomes imagination. And imagination becomes language. Last night when we were talking about this, Bill [Heyen] added a coda: language goes back into memory again. I liked that so much I thought I'd repeat it here. There are some place names here I should explain. Ducktown and Copper Hill are two little towns in East Tennessee. The poem ends up commenting on itself, on the process of memory and how it becomes imagination—how it becomes true in its untruth.

Dog Creek Mainline

Dog Creek: cat track and bird splay,
Spindrift and windfall; woodrot;
Odor of muscadine, the blue creep
Of kingsnake and copperhead;
Nightweed; frog spit and floating heart,
Backwash and snag pool; Dog Creek.

Starts in the leaf reach and shoal run of the blood;
Starts in the falling light just back
Of the fingertips; starts
Forever in the black throat
You ask redemption of, in wants
You waken to, the odd door:

Its sky, old empty valise,
Stands open, departure in mind; its three streets,
Y-shaped and brown,
Go up the hills like a fever;
Its houses link and deploy
—This ointment, false flesh in another color.

*

Five cutouts, five silhouettes
Against the American twilight; the year
Is 1941; remembered names
—Rosendale, Perry and Smith—

4. A Conversation with Stan Sanvel Rubin and William Heyen

Rise like dust in the deaf air;
The tops spin, the poison swells in the arm:

The trees in their jade death-suits,
The birds with their opal feet,
Shimmer and weave on the shoreline;
The moths, like forget-me-nots, blow
Up from the earth, their wet teeth
Breaking the dark, the raw grain;

The lake in its cradle hums
The old songs; out of its ooze, their heads
Like tomahawks, the turtles ascend
And settle back, leaving their chill breath
In blisters along the bank;
Locked in their wide drawer, the pike lie still as knives.

*

Hard freight. It's hard freight
From Ducktown to Copper Hill, from Six
To Piled High: Dog Creek is on this line,
Indigent spur; cross-tie by cross-tie it takes
You back, the red wind
Caught at your neck like a prize:

(The heart is a hieroglyph;
The fingers, like praying mantises, poise
Over what they have once loved;
The ear, cold cave, is an absence,
Tapping its own thin wires;
The eye turns in on itself.

The tongue is a white water.
In its slick ceremonies the light
Gathers, and is refracted, and moves
Outward, over the lips,
Over the dry skin of the world.
The tongue is a white water.)

SR: Earlier you mentioned the poem Dog Creek Mainline *[CM, 36] as the first poem you wrote that was yours. What did you mean by that? What makes it "yours"?*

Well, it's about my own life. I spent ten years learning to write, and I'm still learning; but those ten years were extremely important to me, because as I've been saying I was learning more traditional forms and learning what might work and what might not. As I look back at them, there's not a bad poem in the bunch that I saved; there's not a good one either. They're just all O.K. Anybody could've written them. There they are—well put together, nice little Lego assemblages. Then I discovered that I had a childhood, a past, something I wanted to say; and that's the start of finding my own burden and my own job of work, as they say down in East Tennessee, and my own language, since I had chosen writing as my job. This is the first poem that came out of my own life directly, the first poem that nobody else could've written, because no one else had been there and had had the same experiences.

SR: I wonder if you could say something about what you're trying for now in your work.

What I'm working on now is something I call "verse journals." They are quotidian situations I write about in a journalistic fashion, but in verse. It started out as an exercise in lengthening the line and how far up against prose it can go before it stops being a poetic line. This seems to be the right kind of format, since journals are supposed to be prose, so let's see what one can do with them. What I'm after is what I've always been after—to make the "diamond zones" unblank.[16] I just say to myself, "Good luck," because I need it! I don't know that I can be any more expansive in form after this; I may try to go back and write short poems. But the intent will still be the same—to punch a hole through the invisible.

SR: Hearing you read aloud is for me, and I think for others, a revelation in telling us how to read you. Do you speak your lines aloud in the privacy of writing?

No, I write for the inner ear; but I'm very conscious of my inner ear. I say them over and over to myself, but not out loud. But they are oral; they are *all* oral.

CHAPTER 5

A Conversation with Miriam Marty Clark and Michael McFee

MC: *You spent some time in Arden, at Christ School, as a boy. Would you care to reminisce a little?*

CW: That's an interesting way of putting it. Yes, I did do time here, about two years' worth. Actually, I loved it. I had a wonderful time but I don't remember much about it. I was sixteen and seventeen at the time.

MM: It turns up in your poems, though.

There's one poem about Christ School in the sequence in *Bloodlines* called *Tattoos*. I think it's number nine. The note says "A temporary evangelical certitude; Christ School, 1952," or something like that. Actually, I haven't used it much. I've used a lot of the stuff from Sky Valley and Hendersonville. But from Christ School through Davidson College I somehow haven't used any of that. And then it picks up again once I get into the army.

MM: What is the Hendersonville stuff? That wasn't while you were at Christ School?

That was a summer camp that I went to for about four years, and then I went to school there for a year. In tenth grade, the year before I came to Christ school, I went to a place called Sky Valley School that had eight students, seven boys and one girl. She was a senior and we were all younger. She was a music student who studied with Mrs. Perry who ran the place, that's why she was there. It was a very odd, odd school, so when I saw Christ School I thought I'd gone to New York. I mean there were more

This interview was conducted at Christ School in Arden, North Carolina, on 29 October 1988. Wright had gone to Arden to speak to the benefactors of the school. The interview was published in The Arts Journal *[Asheville, North Carolina], February 1989: 8–13.*

than eight students there. There was more than one building. I was sort of in shock. I was fifteen when I was at Sky Valley and it was a very formative time. I had been there during the summers from ages twelve through fourteen, too, so all of that period was settling inside me in those days. Somehow that's what I go back to when I go back to that time in my life. Christ School was sort of fun. I didn't do any kind of intellectual fossiling away there like I'd done previously.

MC: *How would you describe what it is that "settled inside" you?*

Sky Valley was, like Christ School, very Episcopalian, very church oriented. Mrs. Perry who ran Sky Valley was the daughter of Bishop Guerry, Episcopal bishop of South Carolina, and very much an evangelical. I started to say "do-gooder," and I guess she was a do-gooder but a do-gooder in a very good sense. She didn't believe in sitting still and letting the Lord come to you. She went out and proselytized as hard as she could, and she was always bringing displaced persons after the Second World War over from Russia and places like that and putting them in Sky Valley. They have 2000 acres up at the top of this mountain above Zirconia. And she'd put them out there to work, and then they'd always go to Detroit where all the rest of the Ukranians were, or to Chicago. But she would do that sort of thing. She ran a very tight evangelical ship there at Sky Valley, which settled into me, obviously. It mostly settled into me as something to fight against for the rest of my life, but it's in there. I fight against it, but I wouldn't change it for anything. Obviously it spoke to some part of my nature that I—even at the time—secretly felt was all right and that went begging during the years of my late teens and twenties. But I've come back to it over the last twenty years, and I write about it constantly. All my poems seem to be about the impossibility of salvation. What she inserted into us is that there is a possibility of salvation, and I'm still arguing with her. At Christ School, too, we had chapel and vespers every night, but it seemed kind of dissipated once I got there, because it wasn't just her and me. There were a hundred and forty other guys around, and they had a regular preacher and all.

MC: *Certainly the liturgical language has stayed with you.*

If not the solemnity, yes. It seeped out of my soul and seeped into my lines. I like it or I wouldn't put it in there. I guess it goes back even further to when I used to go to Sunday School with my mother. I was brought up on it all the way from the age of six up through sixteen until I made a break here at Christ School, and I said, "No more of this stuff." Basically it's been "no more of this stuff" on the surface ever since for thirty-five or thirty-six years but it won't ever go away. I don't really want it to go away. I keep sticking my bucket down there and pulling up a little bit each time I need to.

MC: *Reading your poems, I can see the autobiographical bucket going down and coming back. On the other hand, in many of your poems there isn't—at least on the surface—the sort of strong narrative line that often goes with the use of the past.*

That's because of my ... I don't know why that is. I started to make up a story but I won't. I can't tell stories. The main reason I don't use narrative is because I can't tell the story. I do think part of it is the scatteredness of my background growing up. I was always moving around and I went to three different high schools. I lived ten different places from birth until the age of ten. I have no narrative in me. I have a *sub-narrative* in me, which I try to exploit as much as possible. And I think that is underneath the lyric impulse, which is my main impulse in writing—toward song instead of storytelling. Obviously both are quite workable. Right now it's fashionable to tell the story, so fortunately I'm unfashionable. It's a nice position to be in, actually. The great Southern tradition is narrative, we all know that. I'm starting an alternative tradition, which is to be the non-narrative Southern poem.

MC: You grew up in the South, you were away for a long time living in Italy and California, and now you're back, at the University of Virginia. Do you think of yourself as a Southern poet?

Oh yeah. I always have. Other Southerners don't seem to think of me as one, except for Michael McFee and Dave Smith maybe, but most of the others don't. But that's not my problem. I'm not in the tradition. I don't have long narrative poems. I have long lyric poems, and that's a very odd thing indeed and maybe not even a genre yet.

MC: I'm interested in what you call a "sub-narrative impulse"—in other places you call it a "buried narrative." Could you tell me what you mean by that?

In Italian it would be *sottonarrativa*, an under-narrative. That's what I mean, a narrative that's always underneath the lyric and every once in a while it will spurt up and you'll get a little anecdote, just enough of an azimuth reading so you can see which way the poem is going. This all sounds very theoretical, and I couldn't really play it out to you, but I know it's there, and I know it works that way. If I were capable, and I feel fortunate not being capable, it would be right up on top, and I'd be telling a story. If I were doing that I'd be writing fiction.

MC: Still, that sub-narrative always seems to be there and seems to set you apart from contemporary poets who write without narrative at all—say, from the Language poets or those who whose work can be talked about as "chance generated" or "machine generated."

I believe in narrative. It's just a narrative that's not in view. I think it's Beckett who says the best narrative is that which is least in evidence, or something like that. I like that and it seems to fit what happens in my poems, which is to say it is there. You just can't see it most of the time, but it is what controls the poem.

MC: It's been about twenty years since the first poems of your first volume were published. Would you talk some about how your work has evolved over those two decades?

It's gotten more garrulous, that's for sure. I'm not sure that's a good thing. It's found a subject matter, for one thing, which I wouldn't say my first book, *The Grave of the Right Hand*, had. In *Hard Freight* it started to get a subject matter which runs, as far as I'm concerned, all the way through *Zone Journals* and past it to this next book called *Xionia*, the last of the journals. I think it's a fairly evident quest, if you want to use such a word.

MM: You mean the impossibility of salvation?

Yeah. The first book was just about writing poems, trying to figure out how to put a poem together. All of them are ultimately that, too. All our books are training books. You can't say "that's my apprentice volume." All my volumes are my apprentice volumes. I keep on doing it, but they get more and more involved, and the apprenticeship takes on more and more weight, and it tries for more and more things, has larger and larger aspirations. My poetry has moved toward larger gestures—less Dickinsonian and more Whitmanian, to throw our old dichotomy up in the air again, although I think my impulse still remains Dickinsonian, which is toward concentration as opposed to a larger, more rambling Whitmanian aspect, which is probably the true genius of American poetry—which of course is one of the reasons I wanted to try longer things. I'm not sure that the true genius of American literature is the true genius of all poetry, which may be great concentration, but you want to try whatever you haven't done and whatever you think you're not as good at is what you want to try. And so I try to write longer poems, which now I look back to see ... well obviously they're a succession of small things, but that's all right. It's changed in that I've become more aware of what I want to try to do, and I'm more willing to try to do it and more willing to fail at doing it and more willing to take larger chances. Because once you start doing what you know how to do, you're a dead person.

MC: That leads me to something else I want to ask. By now, and for some time already, your work has been the subject not only of reviews but of larger discussions of contemporary poetry. Robert Pinsky writes about you in his book.[1] Charles Altieri and Helen Vendler[2] both write about your poetry. Does such discussion affect your writing at all?

No, it doesn't affect me at all. One of the nicest things ever said to me was said two nights ago in Knoxville. A student came up and said to me, "You know, I'm drawn to your work, it's so out of the mainstream." And I said, "Great!" So to circle back to your question, I like to be out of the mainstream. That's a current that I'm comfortable in. As Cézanne says, I have my motif.[3] I have my motif, there's my mountain, that's what I paint. I have my quest, that's what I write about. I have two-thirds of it done.[4]

MC: I agree, it is out of the mainstream. On the other hand, you teach at a university—a university known for its writing program. Your publications have all been through major commercial and academic houses.

It's very strange. The weirder the poem was that I sent to Howard Moss, the quicker he would put it in the *New Yorker*. The damnedest thing. And then I'd read those other things and I'd say, "Howard, how could you print mine and then print "Flower in the sunlight, tra la, tra la"? The first poem he ever printed was back in 1965, and it was a syllabic poem, a seven-syllable line, almost-narrative poem. And then my work kept changing, as I said, getting larger and stranger, and he would invariably pick the one poem I would think he would not touch with a ten-foot pole. And I also have to say, since he's now dead, to his memory and for his good sense, that later I would come to think of the one he chose as the poem of the batch. At the time I wouldn't have thought so but when I look back, I think his taste—at least for my work—was very good. But it was always for the odd, odd poem. He excerpted from this long poem *The Journal of the Year of the Ox*, which is not your mainstream kind of poem. He took hunks of it and he said, "This is the longest poem the *New Yorker* has ever accepted." And he had to run it in two separate issues[5] and then two other issues for two little pieces, so it ended up in four different issues of the magazine, just the one thing he took. I would never in my wildest dreams have thought he would take that much of that strange a poem.

So I have published in these magazines—*Paris Review*, *Field*, and so on—all these mainstream magazines.

MC: So a person can be out of the mainstream and still in the mainstream?

Yeah, I think so.

MC: I ask because there are some critics who say the reason American poetry isn't very interesting right now is that it's all coming through the same channels—the workshops and the publishing houses. They suggest that interesting things are happening, but outside the channels.

Perhaps they are. There are things happening outside the channels and perhaps they are innovative. I think of the Language poets...

MC: I was thinking of them.

I don't know whether that's a positive thing, overall. I think experimentation is positive. I think the Language poets are akin to Dada. I think it's a dead end. I don't think they're akin to surrealism, which was absorbed into the main body of poetry. I can't imagine Language Poetry doing that because it is deconstructive to the point where I think it's a dead end, and it eschews meaning or purpose. Maybe since poetry is a dying art, maybe its swan song is a poetry merely of words that has no meaning. Maybe that's true. I don't want to believe it. So yes, that's going on on this side, Scylla. And Charybdis over here. We have the New Formalism. I think some interesting things are happening in between those two.

MC: What are those things, for your money?

What I'm doing. [Laughter all around]. No, I do think that experimenting with language that *has* meaning, that has an emotional quotient is helpful. I like the idea of the language poets being interested in language, just the sound. I like half of their purpose. It's the other half I disagree with.

Also, have you ever tried to read them? I've read a lot of them. I mean I don't want to miss the train if it's the only train going through. I've read this stuff and concentrated on it. It's junk. Michael Palmer's terrific, I mean he's really got something going on that you can hear. I don't know yet what it is but I can hear it. But did you ever read Leslie Scalapino, seriously? Bad. I guess they would say, "Well yes, but everybody else's language is no different from the ads in the *New Yorker* or the *Saturday Evening Post*." Maybe so. I think John Ashbery is interesting. I think that's a use of language that has meaning and also has a beauty of language itself. There's a reason for both sides of the equation to exist. I don't have any real interest in the new formalism. It's just like the old formalism to me. If you're good at it, fine, you're a good poet. But as a movement I find very little interest in it because I don't think that's where the future of language and experimental poetry is.

MM: But you seem very concerned with form.

Form is everything to me. Content is nothing. But there's Form with a capital F and there are forms. And I think the new formalism might be better called the new formsalism, which is going back to writing in forms, which is fine if people need that. That's good for them. But over the years I like to fool myself into thinking that I've been able to find the kind of formal guidelines and formal interests that will channel my poems in the way that I want them to go without having to use an old form. I like to think I've made my own forms. It's not that way for everybody. Look at James Merrill. He doesn't do that and he's terrific. But it seems to have worked for me. But I'm always happy to talk about sonnets and sestinas, villanelles. I tried to write a couple of them once.

MM: You said you're done with the journals now?

Yeah.

MM: That was an interesting kind of stretching out, teasing out of form.

Yeah. That was as far toward conversation, toward colloquial turn of phrase as I've gone and still had a poetic line.

MM: What do you see now that you've finished those?

Great darkness. Endless speculation. Well, I wasn't kidding when I say I've done about two-thirds of it. In 1990, Farrar, Straus is going to put the last four books together: *Southern Cross*, *The Other Side of the River*, *Zone Journals* and this next one, which is called *Xionia*. Then I've got the last third and I don't know what the last third is and that's why I've got a humming in my ears and headaches and stiff necks because I don't know what I'm going to do now. For four months—I finished the last book in May—I've been this way. Now I just have to go on. I have my motif and I know what I have to do. Like Cézanne I just continue to paint the mountain. But I buy no brushes; there's no paint. I hope and I feel that I will come back to find another way of trying to go after it. I don't want to keep writing journals. I don't want to go back to writing *Bloodlines*. I want to try to figure out something, some other way of going after the same mountain again, which is what the other two books have done—*Country Music* and this one, which is to be called *The World of the Ten Thousand Things*.

MC: Tell me about Xionia, *the title and what it refers to.*

It has so many layers, my dear, I can hardly tell you. We bought a house in Charlottesville, a very pretentious house, that was fixed up by an art historian and an artist. It's an old Victorian house—1913—with pillars on the front, columns. They called it Ionia. Well, it was odd to live in a house called Ionia in 1983, odd having a house with a name. So we thought we'll put an X in front of it and call it X-ionia. Xion is also an alternative spelling for Zion. So it becomes Zionia, which is not only the house where I wrote the poems but it also is the end of the movement that the journals make. That's known only to us. It's a wonderful house.

MC: So where does one go from Zion—or Xionia.

Indeed, one goes back down the hill and starts back up. Lately I've written some little poems but they don't add anything to my motif, with what's coming. They're just occasional things,

MC: We talked before about what is mainstream. Of the poets being published right now, who do you like best to read?

My favorite American poet is Milosz. I don't know if he's a true American poet but he publishes his books in this country. I know they're translations but I like him a lot. I think Joseph Brodsky is off and on a brilliant poet. Those eclogues that he did are very good. And I read. I read my friends. Mark Strand, Charles Simic—I think they're both marvelous. I've read an awful lot of Robert Morgan lately. I finished his *Selected Poems* and his new book which is called *Sigodlin*. After *Xionia* that's the second greatest title I've ever heard.

MM: I asked one of my relatives if she'd ever heard this word "sigodlin" and she said, "Why sure, it's just a little wee wad."

I remember it from around here. So anyway, I read all this material of Bob's. But I've been reading mostly prose all summer, something I never do. I've been reading novels. I've read a couple of things by a woman named Elaine Pagels, *The Gnostic Gospels* and *Adam, Eve, and the Serpent*. I've been reading the new Eliot biographies. I've read some Italian novels. And I'm usually so busy reading student manuscripts that I can hardly get a book of poems read. But there are a lot of poets I enjoy. Phil Levine is somebody I always read with pleasure.

MC: As a poet, do you find that teaching is something you benefit from or is it just a necessity of life?

Right now it's a necessity of life. It used to be that I benefited a lot because I would work out all of my so-called ideas at the time. I was just thinking about this in the last week or so. There are two kinds of teachers. One who does it because it's a necessity and one because he has a drive to explain things to people. There's a period in most writers lives when they are bettered by teaching. And it's usually that period when they are discovering what they are trying to do, and as they work it out with themselves, they talk about it all the time because they want to explain it to themselves. It helps if you have somebody in class to explain it to. When I was in my 30s and 40s I was trying to work out my ideas about what a line should be, how a poem should be put together, what the structural imperative really is, what the lineation of a poem should be. All these things it took me twenty years to think about and I would talk about that. Then I finally figured it out—how I could put poems together that were different from the way other people put poems together and a line that I think has—through accumulation of other people—become my own line. Now I find that I'm one of these teachers over here. I don't want to explain it to anybody. I figured it out. Let them figure it out for themselves now. I don't have that necessity to explain things to people anymore. For twenty years teaching was very wonderful. How, I don't know. I've got a handle on it, and of course I crank it up and I try to be interesting, but it's not as exciting to me and it's not as nourishing as it once was. It's probably a product of age, but I think it's primarily a product of having figured out what you're trying to figure out. Or at least you think you have. Of course you never really have. Teaching is good because it keeps you close to literature and it keeps you away from the shovel or the advertising firm or whatever.

MC: You've done a lot of translating. How have you benefited from that?

You really learn how people write poems. Don't pick somebody who's easy to translate. Pick somebody who's difficult and someone who's a great poet and translate. Even if you translate poorly you can figure out how he put those little things together. You can learn more from translating a poet than you can from sitting in a million workshops. You have to take it apart in one language and put it together in another language. That lets you see how it's put together because you can't take it apart without learning. That's what I learned from Montale, how he put that poem together, how he did that with language, how he could take could take a basically soft-edged language and make it into hard-edged poems—first person to do that since Dante. I could have read him in translation or in Italian but I would never have figured that out to a point of real interest and almost a point of knowledge if I hadn't translated it myself. I think translation is a necessity, and finding a great poet to translate.

MM: Has your work been translated?

There's somebody over in Italy working on it now.[6] We'll see. He's a friend of mine and tends to procrastinate.

MC: Do you ever write criticism? You've never published a prose collection.

MM: You have this book coming out from Michigan.

MC: That's my next question. Tell me about Halflife.

It's mostly interviews. Six interviews including one on translation by an Italian woman. Then there are fifty or sixty pages of little prose improvisations that I've done over a period of ten years—one on Montale, one on Pound, and others. The part of it called "Halflife" is a commonplace notebook that I kept for about two years, quotes from other people. I like the form because you can comment on the quotes if you feel like it, although you tend to comment more on your own stuff.

MC: That makes me think of Theodore Roethke's book, Straw for the Fire *or Auden's* A Certain World.

Actually, the Auden book is where I got the idea for a commonplace book. And that will probably be my only prose book. Who knows, if I can't write poems anymore, maybe I'll start writing prose. I admire people who can write prose but I'm just not good at it. Well, I said you should try to do what you're not good at so maybe that's what I should do.[7]

MM: But it may not be in your nature. You said you're not a storyteller.

MC: Who have your important teachers been over the years?

Well Montale was, surely. And Pound was a teacher, the first poet I ever read. Donald Justice was my actual teacher and he was wonderful. I've learned from Giorgio Morandi a lot about writing by looking at his paintings. I've learned from Paul Cézanne by looking at how he puts his paintings together.

MC: You talk a lot about learning how things are put together. Have there been critics over the years who have helped you see either how your own poems or other poems are put together?

Not really. The only time I tried to do something that a critic suggested was after Helen Vendler's first long piece on my work. She said it would be nice to have some people in the poems so I tried, particularly in *The Other Side of the River*. But then I also saw that that wasn't my major interest. I did listen and I did do it, and I must say it's probably on account of that my most approachable book. I realize that. It's not that I'm trying to be perverse by not continuing that. It's just not my motif. I didn't listen to Robert Pinsky in *The Situation of Poetry* at all.[8] I'm trying to think of others who've written on me, Calvin Bedient had a piece in *Parnassus*.[9] Helen Vendler had those two.[10] She doesn't either praise or damn. If she finds you interesting enough to her taste to talk about, that's the praise. Therefore she examines your work, which I think is a good way to do criticism. That's why I took her seriously.

MC: Tell me about the dedication of Zone Journals. *It's "To Merle Travis and Glenn Gould."*

They're two musicians I've liked a lot. Merle Travis was a very, very early love of mine, first discovered in 1951. "Dark as a Dungeon Way Down in the Mines"—I used to play it over and over. I had it by him and I had it by Grandpa Jones. He has several really great songs: "Dark as a Dungeon," "Sixteen Tons" ... Classic country songs. And then, as I've grown older I loved Glenn Gould. Not long ago I was trying to do a Glenn Gould fugue-like little poem and I had somebody humming in it, just like Glenn Gould does in all his recordings. What a weird guy. But a great, great musician. But about the dedication, I'd used up my family and my friends so I thought, why not?

MM: No, I thought it was terrific and it really did point out the musicality of your poems.

I'm not musical at all. My brother played the trombone but I couldn't even play the bass drum without missing a beat. My wife is extremely musical, plays the piano and the harp, all kinds of things, but I'm totally unmusical and my son is just like me, totally tone-deaf.

MC: I'm sorry to say we're out of time. It would be nice to go on a while longer.

CHAPTER 6

An Interview by J.D. McClatchy

JM: *When you came back to Virginia, did you notice that the South had changed?*

CW: Well, there are more moths, for one thing, and the people talked a lot funnier when I came back than they did when I was here, which is to say that my ear had grown unaccustomed to the kind of language with which I was familiar as I was growing up. But the South is much more energetic now. I grew up in a very rural, deprived, poor—dirt poor—area of the country. Now there are obviously still pockets, but that is not so pervasive now. It's much more of an upscale place.

But when you write about the South, you write about the South of thirty years ago?

I do write about the South of thirty years ago. All of my South is locked into 1945 to 1955 probably—say 1940 to 1955—from the age of five to fifteen. That's the South that I will always remember as an engendering force for my life.

But what you're then writing about is memory itself?

Yes, I'm writing about memory and my coming to age and to grips with the world around me. I think the instinct comes out of that experience.

You've mentioned your experience of working on a construction crew and holding other jobs as a teenager in East Tennessee. Could you elaborate on the atmosphere of that?

This interview is part of a longer interview conducted for the "Poems in Person" audio project sponsored by the Modern Poetry Association and the American Library Association and funded by the National Endowment for the Humanities. The audiotapes that resulted were accompanied by a listener's guide, Poets in Person, *written by Joseph Parisi (Chicago: Modern Poetry Association, 1991; rev. ed. 1997). Some of Wright's responses are reproduced in the chapter on him in that book. Part of one paragraph in the present transcription comes from the listener's guide: it does not appear on the audiotape. The tape was transcribed by Robert Denham.*

All of the people I would work with in construction or in what not were more "characters" from Southern novels than, say, I consider myself to have been. But all of that informed me in the same way that religion informs my work. It was just always *there*. You couldn't turn on the radio, you couldn't do anything—religion just suffused the whole air and the mentality of the South during the time that I was growing up. But there are certain things about the South that come in by osmosis, even if you didn't have a grandfather who held you on his knee and told you stories about this, that, and the other. No one in my family ever told a story—ever—in my life. I never remember my father telling one story—ever—or my mother, or my grandmother, on either aide. No one told stories, which is why I can't tell one, I suppose. I'm not used to hearing stories told. And I was always fascinated by these things that were not exactly me but surrounded me, constantly. When one starts writing about one's background and one's childhood, one writes about what one did, but basically what one *didn't* do, and what one might have liked to have done. Most all the stories that come out in my poems are things that not necessarily happened to me but I would like to have happened to me.

In Skins *you write, "There comes that moment when what you are is what you will be." What do you mean by that?*

It just suddenly occurred to me that there is a moment when what you are is what you're going to be. You will not be able to alter yourself. You have already made yourself into what you are. That time comes at different ages for everyone. Mine came in the fifth grade, when I realized that I was the onlooker. I was always with what I considered the right crowd, but I was never in the center of the right crowd. I was always on the edges. I was always the observer. Even though I was included, I was the person who was always doing the observing. That has continued in my life to this day. This came out of my writing *Tattoos*. I had spent six to eight months trying to dredge up things in my life that I wanted to write about. Then after I'd written them, I suddenly realized that I became what I am in the fifth grade. Obviously, the psychologists say that it happens by the time you're five, you're unable to change your ... but that's not quite what I mean, because there are ways that we can add or subtract, but the main stem stays the same, I think. That was it for me, and that has controlled the way I have gone through my life. My personality was the same. How I reacted to people was the same. What I was interested in was the same, because the fifth grade was when I got interested in words and language. I was stuck with the kind spiritual awareness that I think I still have, but I was already beginning to be uncomfortable with the organization of the religion in which I had first discovered this spiritual awareness. And, again, that's gone on to manifest itself throughout my life.

You say that it was in the fifth grade that you discovered language. Do you think of yourself as being made out of words?

I think of the self that I write about as being made out of words, as being reconstructed constantly over and over and over again out of words. I think I am a product of language much more than other people I know.

Dr. Johnson said of Milton that he looked at the world through the spectacles of language.

Well, I do, and I have. One of the things that helped that along was my mother, who always thought that being a writer would be a wonderful thing. How many mothers think it would be a wonderful thing for their sons to be writer! She was, I think, a failed writer herself. I discovered after her death some years ago that there were some short stories that she had written when she was at the University of Mississippi. Her steady boyfriend for a year or two was William Faulkner's middle brother, Dean, the one who was killed in the airplane crash—that Faulkner never really got over. They were a real item, apparently, and she was very interested in Faulkner, as well as a writer, and had me read all of Faulkner by the time I was out of high school. Which was why I thought the only thing you could do would be write stories if you wanted to be a writer. And I thought I'm a failure already, because I'll never be able to do this. But the idea of language, reading, and what-not was always in my family, even though no one had ever told any stories, they read books, constantly, constantly. That was the way they did it—instead of telling you a story they'd say, "Read a book." So, yes, I do look at the world through language. Absolutely.

When did you start writing?

I was twenty-three when I started writing poems—when I started writing poems of all places in the United States Army, in Italy. I was stationed in Verona, Italy, as a second lieutenant in the Counter-Intelligence Corps. Outside of Verona, Italy, is a place called Lake Garda, and on Lake Garda is a peninsula called Sermione, where the Latin poet Catullus reportedly had a villa, the ruins of which are still there. When I was going out there one day, this friend of mine gave me a book called *The Selected Poems of Ezra Pound*, and said, "Read this poem. It's about the place where you're going to go." And so I went and sat under an olive tree in the March sunshine and read this poem, and, as Emily Dickinson said, the hairs on the back of my neck stood up. Now, I don't know what it was about the poem that I particularly liked. I suspect nowadays it was the iambic pentameter, the blank verse that it was written in. But I didn't know what blank verse was or iambic pentameter was at the time. It just sounded good to me, and it was also about the view that I was looking down the lake at. And I thought that this was fabulous. Then I got very interested in poems—at that particular moment. I had always wanted to write, as they say, but I thought to write meant to write stories and fiction, and I couldn't write stories, as I just said. I cannot tell a story. And now I found something that I thought I could do, which was the lyric poem. I didn't know it was called "the lyric poem" at the time, but it was an associational kind of progression, and not a straight Frostian, Dickensian narrative. And I thought, well, I could do that, because that's the way my mind seems to work—in fits and starts. It jumps from one thing to another, and if you can jump from the right thing to the next right thing, then you can have an organization, an associational organization to a poem. And I liked the sound. And all of my, I suppose, repressed musical ambitions were able to finally find a way of coming out. And it was through language, because I was certainly never able to play anything, any instrument.

In Halflife *you refer to your poems as hymns, and you mention the influence of Emily Dickinson, another poet who wrote in a kind of hymn form. Could you elaborate on that?*

When I mentioned her writing in a hymn form, I was speaking of the meters, really, and I was speaking of hymnals, and I was speaking of hymns as regards my poems, as poems of praise. I've always thought that the true purpose of poetry, at least in my case, was the contemplation of the divine, however or wherever one finds that, and everyone finds it differently for himself. Emily Dickinson affected me at my heart's core—and *does*—because what she writes about is what concerns me—the inability to get to heaven. I don't think she ever believed truly in the accepted religious dogma or attitudes of her day, although she was a religious person. I feel the same things affect me. Whitman's *Song of Myself* is a religious poem, obviously, but it's of a different kind. Emily Dickinson's poems are much more concentrated, condensed, non-stories, as it were, exclamations of desire. I like to listen to Walt talk, but she speaks to me.

In an interview you once said that no matter how well a poem was written, it always comes down to the same thing: is it a telegram, or is it a recipe. What did you mean by that?

That sounds pretty clever, but [laughter] I don't know what I meant by it. I think what I meant by that is that a telegram is an urgent message to someone; a recipe is a way that you could continue to do the same thing over and over and over again. Emily Dickinson's poems are always telegrams from the other side, as it were, telling you how it is, telling you what to expect. I would be much more interested in my poems being like that than merely fulfilling a recipe. Each poem is a different urgent message, a different urgent telegram.

You've been very concerned with form, as opposed to forms. And when I read your comment about the difference between the telegram and the recipe I thought, well, telegram is news or maybe a vision, something you didn't know before, that spark of inspiration, whereas a recipe gives you instructions of how to put things together or maybe to rearrange them.

What you just said about the telegram and the recipe is what I should have said about it. I'm a little suspicious of forms *per se*. I don't quite know why, because some of the poems that I love best in the world are written in standard forms. I feel my poems are dedicated to free verse, to proving that free verse can be just as structured, as tight, and as formally organized as any kind of received, traditional form is. And I find that much more of a challenge. I find it's an impetus to me that is freeing without being lawless. I understand when people say that free verse is lawless, because most free verse *is* lawless. But most forms are boring. Most poetry is not good: we all know that. Most drivers are bad, but there are good things in everything, and there is good free verse. It is where the rubber meets the road.

How did the example of the painter Cézanne help with your own poetic technique?

Cézanne was the one who got me interested in the idea of trying to slide over into free verse, in some of the processes that the painter often uses in abstract painting. Now Cézanne is not an abstract painter, but the way he would put together his landscapes in particular toward the end of his life—to make them representational—was not done by the usual line and outline. It was done by patches of color, daubs here, little hooks, and so on and so forth. When you look up close at a Cézanne landscape, it looks like layerings of mismatched coloration. And as you step farther and farther back, you see that all of these are starting to coalesce into a picture, and the farther back you get, the more representational it becomes with Cézanne, and of course it made him a great painter. But it seemed to me an interesting way of trying to put poems together, which is to say, that to make a representational, i.e., narrative poem, you did not have to do the straight narrative. You could do it in various other ways. Those are the various other ways that I have been interested in since 1975 of trying to juxtapose an overlay—description, incidents, and so on—that makes a poem look perhaps abstract in its individual parts, but by the time you've finished reading the whole poem, there's an understood story that's been going on.

And interviewer once asked you what was the major emotion that prompted your poetry, and your response was, "I write from fear." What did you mean by that?

Well, I was being a little quippy, but fear that you will not write something that is acceptable to the great dead or the people you want to show that you're doing all right, that you're doing with your little gift the best that you can. With the little gift you've been given—the only thing apparently that I've been given, there's always the fear that you're not doing the job, that you're not pushing yourself enough, that you're not being serious enough about the one thing that is important to you. So fear plays a great part in that—not drooling, sweating fear but the inner fear that's worse, that you didn't live up to what you could have done.

But you've talked too in that past about the way in which when you look at the landscape you see the dead. And many of your poems seem haunted by ghosts. I wonder if there is any sense in which you feel haunted by the dead?

Particularly haunted? Probably not more so than other people, although maybe all artists are particularly haunted by the dead, by the preceding dead greats or the preceding dead makers who have done things that are important to you. Poetry seems even more so, because we tend more than other arts perhaps to write out of past performances, which is to say, we learn from what went on before—even more so than painting, I think. The previous ways that poets have talked about landscape, the way Dante's fabulous similes talk about landscape, the way Dante takes landscape and makes it into human emotions, the way the Chinese—the great T'ang poets—had that reciprocal imagination, where they put into the landscape what they want back out into the human experience. All that becomes part of you. When I say I write for the dead, I write for the landscape, I write for the dead in the landscape. I don't mean them buried in the landscape. I mean that they have become part of my not only literary landscape but mental landscape, my imaginative landscape, indeed my obsessive landscape, because most of my poems tend to be about landscape, again, which may have something to do with the painterly aspect of my influences, as opposed to the literary aspect of the influences.

You say somewhere, "All poems are about dying."[1] Do you think that's true?

No, actually, I think that all poems are about not dying. I must have been much younger when I said that. Most poems seem to be about death in that, as Stevens said, "death is the mother of beauty."[2] There is a certain slipping, sliding away, a disintegration into nothingness that a certain cast of imagination finds beautiful. I happen to have that cast of imagination. Therefore, in my younger days I would have said all poems are about dying. Death means no more poems. So all poems are about dying or all poems are about not dying. I think it's the same coin. It's just either side.

You quote Montale's famous statement that the ancients said that poetry is a stairway to God,[3] and at that time when you talked about it, you said you agreed. Do you still feel that way?

I still feel that way. It was meant differently back then, of course, in that a great many of the poems were religious poems. Of course, I still think poems are religious, but in a different way. They are stairways to whatever god is for me. Poems are the only things that are going to put the coin between my teeth and to get me my ride across the river, as it were. They do tend to be constantly my argument with myself against the improbability of salvation. They tend to be my contemplation of things beyond us, yet ourselves.

But the divine and the beyond is everywhere around you.

Of course. And you get there by ... it's right under your fingertips. Theodore Roethke said, "All finite things reveal infinitude."[4] I agree with that. The tactile is the highway to the sky.

CHAPTER 7

An Interview by Ernest Suarez and Amy Verner

ES: *Your poems often focus on the interplay between the narrator's subjective perception and the exterior world, particularly landscapes. To what extent are you trying to create an aesthetics of perception, perhaps something like what we see in Wallace Stevens's poems?*

CW: I'm not consciously trying to do that. If such a thing comes about as a by-product, that's another thing. But I suppose, more than anything else, I'm trying to convince myself that the way I perceive the world is the way that I should perceive the world, and that I can recreate the exterior landscape into an interior landscape in which I feel comfortable. The exterior landscape is not always comfortable to be in, but it contains all the elements of comfort. If you can take it inside, if you can transfer it into your own perception, or being, then I suppose one could live more at ease in one's life. I'm not consciously trying, as I say, to establish a mode of perception, or a way that everyone should look at the world. I am only trying to establish for myself a way that not only acknowledges an exterior world and an interior world, but an *It* which is a combination of the two.

ES: Is Stevens a poet whom you've read?

Stevens is a poet whom everyone has read. I have not read him in the sense that I'm often accused of having read him. I'm not a Stevensian in ways that probably I should be, which is to say, maybe I should have been more influenced by Wallace Stevens

Originally published in Five Points: A Journal of Literature & Art *2 (Spring-Summer 1998): 7–32; reprinted as "Interview with Charles Wright" in* Southbound: Interviews with Southern Poets, *by Ernest Suarez with T.W. Stanford III and Amy Verner (Columbia: University of Missouri Press, 1999), 39–61. The interview was conducted on 30–31 January 1998, at Wright's home in Charlottesville, Virginia.*

than by Eugenic Montale and Ezra Pound and Hart Crane and Emily Dickinson and Gerard Manley Hopkins, who I think were influences for me. I have read Stevens; I admire Stevens. I find as I get older that there is more and more of old Wally in me than I thought when I was younger. I don't know if it's a good thing or a bad thing, but I tend to see the world more through language, through the experience of language, through the transformation of language, as I think he did, the older I get. And I seem to see the world more as a transformation of sentences that were handed down to me through the generations of writers. I tend to find myself trying to alter that language in terms of my personal perception. Yes, I read Wallace Stevens; yes, I admire the pants off Wallace Stevens, but I was not, early on, influenced by Wallace Stevens, although maybe the best influence is the last influence.

ES: Do you see yourself as a poet in the Romantic tradition?

First of all, I don't see myself as a poet. I hope others might see me as that. But I think Frost was right when he said a poet is something that other people call you. You don't call yourself one. I try, through writing poems, to come to terms with myself. One, of course, wants to be thought of as a poet, or one wouldn't write any poems, obviously. But I still feel that it is a kind of sacred trade, and I'm not sure that I have passed all the barriers yet for my working papers. I do think of myself in a Romantic tradition, yes, when I write my poems. I do think of myself as a Romantic as opposed to, say, a Classicist.

ES: Your poems often reflect a subject-object split.

This is getting into a very spongy area. If I say I'm aware of subject matter more than I am of the way I present the subject matter, that's not true. If I say I'm more aware of the way I present the subject matter than the subject matter, that's not true either. So I am aware of myself trying to come to terms with subject and object. Trying to come to terms with the what and the how. You're always out there screaming, tearing your clothes off. But, yes, I like to see things in a diffused light. I like to think that there's something alterable about what I see. Again to go back to the first question we talked about: if I didn't think I could alter the world in terms of personal existence, and whatever it is that might be beyond any existence, then I don't think I would be doing this in the first place. I would be working for Colgate-Palmolive-Peet and writing zippy advertising phrases. Or something like that.

ES: To what extent is your poetry an attempt to understand the past emotionally? How do the objects that you focus on, the landscapes, for instance, serve as conduits, sources of mediation between memory and emotion?

I don't know. I suppose that, in a way, what you saw is what you'll get. And if your childhood was basically happy—certainly mine was—then you want it to mean a lot. I'm a visual person. I'm much more attuned to what I see than what I read, actually. I'm much more attuned to looking at paintings, for the most part, than just reading, *per se*, to be reading. That doesn't mean the important books, but some people just read because that's what they do. They just read. I don't read a lot. My wife reads constantly. That's the way Richard Howard is, too. That's the way a lot of people I admire are. They just read. I don't. I, on the other hand, walk around; I look at things, look at paintings, look at reproductions. I'm much more interested in the visual. So I've tried, over the years, to retranslate that visual sense into a more written result. And so, naturally, childhood comes into play because we are so much more aware of things when we are children because it's all new. It's all just discovered. That's what made Rimbaud such a great poet. He was a child three or four years into the time of his mature writing period, so he had that incredible visionary newness from the age of fourteen through eighteen that most everybody else doesn't have because by the time they get mature enough to write well, it's gone, and they have to remember it. Nothing remembered is as good as the actual moment because you change it so much. Or it's better, but it's not the same thing; it's not the same electricity, and that's why Rimbaud is so fabulous, among other reasons. So earlier on I depended a lot on memory, and of course, as Rilke says, everybody has a subject matter, his childhood.[1] You can't say you don't have subject matter; everyone has it. Now to what extent you use it, and how you use it, is up to you. He used it very well. I've tried to use it myself. As I get older, again, I find that I don't write about memory so much. Or I write about memory in a different way, which is to say that memory is not as count-on-able as I once thought it to be. It is not as all-giving and sustaining and nourishing as I once thought it to be. There was a time when memory meant everything to me. And what you remembered, if you remembered it well, was the basis to all you were able to transfer or to translate into your waking current life. But it tends to loom alone on the horizon more often now than it tends to engulf me.

ES: What's the relationship here between reason, rationality, and emotion?

I don't know. I'm an emotional person, more often than I am a reasoning person. In other words, I'm not a debater. I am someone who gets excited and carried away by the currents of what is being talked about. That's why I always pray for a reasoned and articulate student in every class, so I'll have somebody to argue with, and he can do that part. Emotion is, of course, at the core of our romanticism. My mind doesn't work in a logical, reasoning, narrative manner, for the most part. Therefore, I'm much more, as I said before, impressionistic. Things seem to work their way out, I hope, in a reasoned form, but not through clear steps of reasoning. They work their way through the poem by some kind of logical impressionism. In other words, there will be an imagistic logic to a poem as opposed to a kind of narrative reasoned discourse that leads from point A through point B to point C. I may go right from A to C to B to A right back to C. That sort of thing. But still, I'll get there. My mind works synaptically; it just sort of jumps from one thing to the next, one synapse to the next, as opposed to some methodical step pattern. So I suppose one would have to say that emotion rules me, and I try to rule my emotions in the best ways I can, as far as language is concerned.

ES: Your poems move from object to object, but the associations tend to be emotional, rather than intellectual.

But I think that they are rational, or emotionally rational, if not intellectually rational. And that's the distinction that I would want to make. Reason in itself, in my poetry, has no interest, holds no interest for me. Emotion is everything.

ES: You've been called a spiritual poet. Do you see yourself as such?

No. I don't see myself as any kind of spiritual creature at all. I suppose that what I'm trying to do is write a kind of quasi-spiritual autobiography. That's what all my poems tend to accumulate toward, I think, and certainly what I have been working on for the last twenty-seven years now, this project that I've had underway since 1971. It's three trilogies. One group was collected in the book called *Country Music*. Another group was collected in a book called *The World of the Ten Thousand Things*. And the last group will be collected in a book as yet untitled. As I look back on it, the whole thing does seem to be a kind of searching. A kind of movement, if not a narrative, an emotionally organized movement, in an ascending path.

ES: What do you mean by "an ascending path"?

Ascending path. Going upward.

ES: Upward toward...?

Upward towards. Being a secular person, I don't know what it's going upward toward. But the imagery seems to keep moving upward. The iconic book of my life is the *Confessions* of Saint Augustine. The idea of that book, spiritual confessions, has had a pretty controlling hand over my imagination for many, many years. In my own way, I try to reproduce that sort of movement, or that sort of confession, and what such confession has led my life to be. It's not going to be the same thing as Saint Augustine, of course, because we don't believe in the same things. I did have quite a religious upbringing, however, and so some of that has, obviously, had to wear off on me. And that's okay, I don't mind. But to say that my poetry is a spiritual poetry is, I think, problematic. Of course, in the long run, I would like to think that others might think that.

ES: Can you relate any of this to Gerard Manley Hopkins's notion of inscape?

I like his idea of inscape, though he wasn't the first one to talk about it. All of the notions of the immediate perception of the essence of things, since the first religious man came down from the mountain, have been more or less the same thing. When Joyce talks about his epiphanies, when Hopkins talks about his inscape, when other people talk about their revelation of intellect at a given moment, when they first saw what a certain object meant to them, what a certain passage meant to them, when they saw a certain memory exfoliate into its full meaning, they're all talking about the same sensation. And that's what he means by inscape. It's the essence of being of the object, the word, the whatever. And yes, I believe in that sort of thing. I believe in that sort of thing, and I believe in trying to get there through language. That impossibility. All revelation is intuition and just immediate knowing.... Therefore, you give yourself a job of work to try and tell those feelings. But then, of course, the only job that's worth doing is the one which can never be finished. Yes, I was a great admirer of Hopkins, at first intoxicated by his language, as I think most writers are because you can't believe that anyone could get away with all that and have it be so fabulous at the same time. And so non-imitatable. The more I read him, the more I saw what he was trying to get at, and the more it seemed to me that his language got in the way. I have read some of the T'ang poets. They were, in their way, trying to get to the same essence of things by a different, much more simple, much more uncluttered way, and you think, well, that's the way to do it. Then you find out that maybe there isn't enough language to do it that way. And then you realize that there is no language that can do it, and so you just do the best you can with the language you've got. I think that inscape is good. I think it's a valid enterprise. Actually, I wish I'd thought of the word myself, because I think that it is more exact than epiphany, particularly if one works in landscape and what things look like. The idea of the inscape of a thing as opposed to the landscape or the outerscape of the thing, or its seascape or skyscape or the particular....

ES: At what point did you make a conscious move in the direction of the particular journey you've been on?

I wrote a poem called *Dog Creek Mainline* [*CM*, 36], about a place I grew up in at the age of six and seven in the North Carolina mountains, and that's when I realized that Rilke was right, that I did have a subject matter. For the ten years before that I had been just writing poems—some of them were interesting, most of them not, none of them bad, none of them good. They were technical exercises. Well, everything I've written has been a technical exercise to some degree, I suppose. But then I realized that I wanted to tell my story. Everybody wants to tell his story. Some people have stories to tell; some don't. If you don't have a particularly fascinating one, then the work really begins, and you have to sort of make one up. And that's what I had to do. I had to go make one up. And since I couldn't tell it narratively, I was going to have to do it by accretion and by conjunctions of things with building blocks that made a kind of edifice. In any case, I can't say that at that moment, in the fall of 1971, when I wrote *Dog Creek Mainline*, I knew I was going to write a series of trilogies, nine books plus a couple of codas and an introduction that the first one had. But I did know that I was starting on something that was not going to be finished for a while. I knew that it was not going to be a narrative journey; therefore, it can't be like *Piers Plowman* or *The Divine Comedy* or something like that. It was going to have to be separate books where I hoped eventually I would see what form I was working toward, and then once I saw that, it would start to coalesce. And that is more or less what happened after I finished the first group of books, *Hard Freight*, *Bloodlines*, and *China Trace*, which became *Country Music*. And I said, "Oh, this is a trilogy. It moves from here to here. Now, I wonder if I can write another one and then a third one, so that I get a series of pyramids that basically have the same structure but would be, instead of next to each other, superimposed, one on top of the other." And so, that's what I set out to do. But each book was separate, each book was individual. The ones that have the most linear connection to them are, I think, the last three: *Chickamauga*, *Black Zodiac*, and the one I just finished, called *Appalachia*.

During the time that I was doing this, there were also technical matters—which I've talked about in other places—I was interested in doing. I was interested in making the poem as short and as tight and as complex as possible—which I think I finally did in *China Trace*, actually a book-length poem made up of forty-six tiny parts—and then trying to take the line of the poem and stretch it out as far as possible, which I finally did in a couple of books, collected and called *The World of the Ten Thousand Things*. I take the line as far as I could toward prose, still keeping it a line of poetry. So I squeezed it down and then stretched it out in those two groups of books. Then in this third group, I am taking the condensed form of the first trilogy and the long line of the second trilogy and combining them into the poems that I've been writing since 1988. Well, I didn't know exactly what I was going to do, but I did know I was going to try to do something that was, if not singular, at least not plural.

ES: I want to get at the relationship between technique and subject in your work. Your use of the line has changed at various points in your career, though your themes have remained fairly constant. Do different technical approaches, such as the varying use of lines, allow you to explore the material in a different manner?

To a certain extent, yes. They obviously have to. The longer line lets you linger a bit, lets you look at the material from different vantage points, lets you savor it a little bit more. It lets you think about things a little more. It lets you include more. One of the reasons I always said I couldn't do narrative was that story didn't really interest me. What's interesting about a story is the telling of the story, not the point. I always want to get to the point. And in the poems—for instance, in *China Trace*, in short poems— you get to the point much more quickly than you do with longer lines in longer poems. Same point, different path to get there. With longer lines, say, you don't go on the interstate, you take the blue highway. You see more, you dawdle, but you're going to the same place. They both have their pleasures. They both have their seductions. One of the reasons the last three books have shorter poems with the longer line is that my main interest is getting there, not *how* I got there. So, somehow, I've gone back to a tighter version of things, even though the line is longer. So the idea of the long line has changed somewhat for me, even though the central idea remains the same. Now, I'm not sure that experiencing more of the subject matter gives you a truer understanding of the nature, or the inscape, of that subject matter, but it's a different way of looking at it. If you try to squeeze it down for ten or fifteen years, the natural thing is to want to open it up. That's how it came about with me. After that it became more of an aesthetic than it was at the beginning, where it was an experiment. And now I think that the longer line with the shorter, compacted poem is something that I find unavoidably seductive.

ES: But does the longer line alter the final point?

No, the final point is the final point. Compostela is always Compostela. You can get there by the main pilgrimage road, or you can go the long way through the Pyrenees and come back, but the final point remains the final point. Sometimes you like to take a hike in the mountains, and sometimes you like to go down the highway. The big thing about the spiritual journey is that you never get to where you want to get. You may get to Compostela, but once you get to Compostela you realize, "Oh, this is the starting point."

ES: In terms of the longer line, is there anyone that you feel an affinity with?

Again, soggy terrain. I suppose I would have to say Whitman. I first got interested in *Song of Myself*, and its long, self-contained line, one long unit and then another long unit. I was not able to keep the line buoyant for that long myself, so I started to break it. I broke it rather than having it break under its own weight. Breaking the line is nothing new. A lot of people have done it. Pound did it; Jeffers did it. A lot of people have broken the line. However, I maintain that my broken line is still one line, while most other broken lines become two lines. It may be merely a difference in perception on my part. C.K. Williams's long line is a rhetorical one. Mine is an imagistic one. Rhetoric is easier, I think, to keep afloat than a series of packed images, because images tend to separate themselves. The challenge of trying to keep a long, image-freighted line independent is still of some interest to me. I think that Ginsberg's line, when he was really doing it well, in the fifties, is really quite strong. Part of his strength lay in his idea of the connections between words that would lock them together and keep the line up, not letting it sink under its own weight. When Ginsberg was good, he was pretty good and showed how the long line could be used. Whitman was the best at it. I was never a great Whitman fan, but it's sort of like your question about Stevens. I read Whitman late, and I read him very limitedly. I read *Song of Myself*. I've read the other stuff too, but *Song of Myself* is the one I like. So I'm not Whitmanian; I'm not a Stevensian. I'm much more an Emily Dickinson kind of person. At one point I got the idea of putting Emily Dickinson into the long line, and that's where the image-freighted long line came about, at least for me. So that's what I've worked on ever since. Jeffers. The only interest to me in Jeffers is his double-pentameter line, you know, the twenty-syllable double pentameters. Actually none of the long-line people we've mentioned, except for dear, sweet Gerard, Father Hopkins, are great interests of mine as writers.

ES: What about Warren?

Warren was someone whom I liked toward the end of his writing career, in *Can I See*

Arcturus from Where I Stand? The old-age poems were fabulous; I just love them. I like the early stuff less; I'm not a great Warrenite. I'm not a great Dickeyite either after *The May Day Sermon*—which shoves me pretty much out of the Southern pathway because, as we know, Southern poetry is pretty much based on Warren and Dickey, all the narrative, long, and expounded people.

AV: Do you think of yourself as a Southern poet?

I do. Much more so than anyone else does, I think. I'm not thought of as one mostly because I'm not in the narrative, storytelling tradition. And that's okay. But I certainly think of myself as one. I mean, I'm a Southerner; have been for generations.

AV: How do you differ from other recent poets from the South?

There is an accepted line, and I think it's a decent accepted line, from Sidney Lanier, down through Warren, Dickey, Dave Smith, David Bottoms, and a few people like that. Almost everyone who's thought of as a Southern poet is a narrative poet, as I've been saying. There's a real flowering, I think, of Southern poetry now, a really strong Southern poetry assembling at the edges of everything. Particularly with the generation right under me, you know, the half generation—Dave Smith, that group on down. I'm sort of in the middle, between Dickey/Warren and Smith/Bottoms, and that's a good place to be if you're not part of the narrative tradition. No one ever told a story in my family. My father spoke very little, and my mother didn't talk much either. I didn't have any old-hat uncles who told stories, so there you are. I was narrative-deprived from the cradle, and so I had to make up my own stories. At least, I think of them as stories. They all have story lines. There is an undernarrative that runs through all of my work, but my stories are put together differently in my poems from those that are considered Southern.

ES: What do you mean by "undernarrative"?

That's the story line that's underneath the imagistic line on the top. I discussed it once in terms of going through a series of tunnels on a train, then back out to the landscape again.[2] You come out to the landscape and you see where you are and then you go back in the tunnel, then back out to the landscape again. And so on. The story line is what the poem is about, the journey you are reminded of each time you come back out to the landscape. And that's always running underneath the imagistic examples, rhetorical examples, or the narrative tidbits. What goes on in the tunnels is something else and often more exciting and mysterious.

ES: It's not in the foreground?

It's not in the foreground. It's very much, oh I don't know if you'd want to say that it's backgrounded, but it's often undergrounded. Like some electric wire.

7. An Interview by Ernest Suarez and Amy Verner

ES: I've read your poetry here and there for a few years, but reading it in a concentrated manner over the last few weeks, I detected more of a narrative than people have supposed.

One of the reasons I think you can say that, perhaps, is because you did read several things over a shorter period of time, so you see how the concerns are continuing ones. The concerns, what the poems are about, go on as you go from book to book. I would like to think that if one spent the time and took on more than just a poem or two, he could see there's a movement.

ES: And there's a definite consciousness working through different situations in poem after poem. There's a narrative going on within that consciousness and the things exterior to it. I think what throws some readers off is that your poems aren't filled with people, particularly in cause-and-effect relationships. There are cause-and-effect relationships in your poetry, but the cause and effect is the interaction between a consciousness making its way through these concerns and doing it primarily with this interplay between the internal self and the landscape. But there's a narrative.

I like to think that's true. And it's also true that there are not any people in my poems. There's a wonderful photographer named Josef Sudek, who just died recently. He had only one arm, his left arm, and he had a big stand-up camera. And someone once said to him, your photographs are always churches, or landscapes, or still lifes. Why aren't there ever any people? And he said, well when I start out there are always people there, but by the time I get everything ready and I take the picture, they're all gone. And that's sort of the way I feel. The people are sort of there, but by the time I get through going through everything, the people are out and the concerns are left.

ES: There's a case to be made that Faulkner relies on narrative disruptions rather than narrative.

Well, that's true, but when he comes back after the disruption, it is still narrative. When I come back from my disruptions, it's still an image. And a little understory that's going on. I do think some of the other younger people, like Yusef Komunyakaa, for instance, are much more imagistically oriented than narratively oriented. Yusef writes this imagistic narrative that is rather popular at the moment, and he does it very well. But he's somebody, I would think, who doesn't fit naturally into the narrative mode, and Richard Tillinghast, I guess, does. I'm trying to think of people who aren't usually singled out, but they're all narrative people too.

ES: Terry Hummer and Rodney Jones have those rhetorical flourishes.

Yes, they do too.

ES: Ellen Voigt is less narratively oriented.

Ellen, Yusef, and I are the only ones who are doing the true tradition of nonnarrative, Southern, imagistic, agrarian poetry. Take me as a Southern writer, please.

AV: Why is that so important to you?

Because I'm from the South. My whole family's from the South. My mother's from the Mississippi delta, my father's from Little Rock, my mother's family's from northern Virginia. We've been in the South for hundreds of years. My great-great-great-grandfather was the last territorial governor of Arkansas and the first senator from the state. I grew up a Southerner, and I will always be one.

AV: Do you see any similarities between your poetry and that of the poets of the Southern Renaissance?

I admire Ransom very much. Ransom is someone I had early on admired tremendously—still do. I think he's a wonderful poet. I don't find any real connection between my work and any of those people. I read them mostly after I had got going. I read Ransom during the two to three years when I was writing exclusively metrical poetry, trying to learn how to do that. For three years, I wrote nothing but rhymed and metered poems and discarded them all. Ransom is one of the great masters of the metrical line. Ransom, Frost, Hardy, poets like that; Stevens, of course. And I really liked his work. He was also a favorite of my teacher, Donald Justice, at Iowa. At the time most everything I knew was coming through Justice, as I'd never studied any poetry before. That was the first class I had had. And he got me onto Ransom, not by saying "go read Ransom," but by talking about him. So he would be the one I would feel closest to, if only because I enjoyed his work so much. But I don't feel as though any of them had any particular influence in my way of seeing things or my way of putting things down.

AV: My next question is about Warren. He's a self-described yearner who searches the self, the natural world, the stars for some sign of transcendental meaning. Could you compare your search for meaning with his?

I do the same, in different language.

AV: Would you say that this yearning is part of what it means to be a Southern writer?

Well, I don't know. I think that's part of what it means to be human. There may be more of a sense of that earlier on in the South and New England, as opposed to the rest of the country, because they were, they are, more religiously oriented. As I said, I grew up going to church all the time. And I think that past a certain age it becomes a matter of one's being, of how one sees oneself vis-a-vis the larger world and the larger world beyond the larger world. So, yes, that's Southern, but it's just human too.

AV: Could you distinguish between some of Dickey's work in the lyric mode and your own?

7. AN INTERVIEW BY ERNEST SUAREZ AND AMY VERNER

I guess I wouldn't think that Dickey and I were at all alike. I would be much more like later Mr. Warren than I would be like Dickey. I like the poems in *Buckdancer's Choice*, *Helmets*, *Drowning with Others*, and even *Falling* I have a certain fondness for, but the *May Day Sermon to the Women of Gilmer County* was where he lost me. That's when he really sort of drew back, at least from my point of view, from what makes poems tick, which is a certain concentration and application of language, and his language got otherwise, which served him well in *Deliverance*. *Deliverance* was a wonderful story, a terrific book. But that was the kind of language he was moving toward in the *May Day Sermon*. He was starting to preach, and before that he was praying. There's a big difference between preaching and praying. So, I like the earlier work better.

AV: Has Faulkner influenced your work?

Faulkner was the only person I'd ever read until I got out of east Tennessee and went as far away as North Carolina. One of the reasons I read him was because my mother used to date his brother Dean, the one who was killed in the plane crash, when she was at Ole Miss in 1931–1932. Faulkner was a famous writer and such a cause célèbre, and she thought a lot of him. So I heard a lot about Faulkner and Eudora Welty, who was her other favorite Mississippi writer, and I read both of them. I read *A Curtain of Green* when I was still in high school, and I read all of Faulkner before I got out of high school. I didn't understand it, but I read it all. I read Faulkner and classic comic books. It was a great education.

AV: Have you gone back to him since?

I haven't. No, I never have. It's sort of like trying to go back to Thomas Wolfe. I tried to go back and read *You Can't Go Home Again*. It was, to me, totally unreadable; it's like rereading Lawrence Durrell. I had loved *The Alexandria Quartet*, and I once started reading *Justine* again, with all that terribly poetic prose. I couldn't do it. I don't think I would feel that way about Faulkner, but I haven't ever tried. Faulkner is a great influence because I read him when I was so young. I read him early on and probably got the idea that there is no language that's too much language. Then at the other end, maybe that's why I liked Hemingway, because I had had so much Faulkner, and I craved some simplicity and serenity. Faulkner is a big influence in the perception of things, if not in the execution of things.

ES: Black Zodiac seems like a self-conscious address of your career-long technical and philosophical concerns. Did you conceive of the book in this way?

I did; indeed, I did. I thought I would be as straightforward and honest about what I had been trying to do, and was still trying to do, as I possibly could. That's why *Apologia Pro Vita Sua* is the first poem, and *Disjecta Membra* is the last. It's part of the last trilogy which begins with *Chickamauga* and which will end with *Appalachia*. My concerns continue to be the same concerns, but I could see *Black Zodiac*, *Chickamauga*, and *Appalachia* as a unit, and a reevaluation. It took me five years to write *Chickamauga*, and it took three years and four months to write the other two. I sort of got into a frenzy. And once I started confronting what I knew I wanted to say...

ES: You wrote them concurrently?

No. But it took three years to write two and five years to write one. Of all the three trilogies, the latest is the most plotted in its movement. It mimics the same movement of *Hard Freight*, *Bloodlines*, and *China Trace* in the first trilogy. *Chickamauga*, *Black Zodiac*, and *Appalachia* are possibly too thought out, but there is a madness in the method. And, of course, a little bit of method in the madness. I very much wanted to say what was on my mind in these poems. In the journal form, for instance, people tend to say what they really feel. They do sort of "let it out." That's what *Zone Journals* was about, being as honest as I could about my relationship to the landscape and the world, and what was going through my head vis-a-vis each, at any given moment. *Black Zodiac* has the same sort of cathartic idea behind it. *China Trace*, *Zone Journals*, and *Black Zodiac* are the three books in the three trilogies that have the most truth-telling about them, I think, and I probably like them the best for that reason.

ES: They're the strongest books.

I think they're my three strongest books, but perhaps that's because I was trying to do more and say more in them than in the others. Not that I wasn't trying to say something in the others as well, but, you know.

ES: When will Appalachia *appear?*

It's coming out in November 1998. I have to write a little coda to it, and then, eventually, I guess, in a couple of years, the final trilogy, as yet untitled, will come out. Then the three trilogies, at least in my mind, will have the overall title of *Tennessee Waltz*.

ES: In the poem Meditation on Form and Measure, *you write "measure is verbal architecture // and form is splendor" [NB, 91]. Explain.*

"Measure is verbal architecture" is explainable in that the sound of words is something that's pleasing to the ear. People call it music, but it's not music. Any musician would say that it's not music. It is a measure. It is a measured kind of movement that helps you feel the motion and emotion of the poems and moves the lines toward their desired end.

ES: When you're working on sonic patterns, what is your approach? Is it intuitive?

It does seem to be intuitive. I work line to line, line to line. Since I don't do a narrative thing, you watch it as it hits your ear and you watch it as it hits your eye, and you see it and hear it take on shape and pattern. I do write in syllables. I count them all. And my two standard measures are the seven- and the thirteen-syllable line. Shorter lines group around seven, three, five, and nine syllables, and the longer ones group at thirteen, fifteen, seventeen, and nineteen. At nineteen it starts to get a little long. I do it because I know that English is not a syllabic language; it is an inflected language. Therefore, within certain syllable counts you will get certain sound patterns, just because of the nature of the language. If I organize the lines syllabically, the accentual patterns seem less predictable to me somehow. They seem more of a normal speech pattern, somehow just above speech, but speech. So if you move that around, then the combinations start to get, certainly not symphonic, but, at least, polyphonic. It's the line movement. I would say there are fewer possibilities within the strictly iambic pattern than in another sort of accentual pattern that's done on a syllabic base where the back and forth is more varied. Still you get, always, behind my lines the ghost of the iambic pentameter, as it's just the nature of the language. Particularly if you have the longer lines. I seem to be working consciously and intuitively at the same time. After a period of time, I have settled upon a way of writing that I find pleasing to my ear. It took me about twenty-five years. After a while, the sound patterns become intuitive with the syllable count. You sort of know what you're going to get. The trick then is to vary the timing enough with the dropped lines, the shorter lines, the longer lines, to get the polyphonic sound, as if it were *without* a predestined kind of containment. And I find that pleasing. But it's not lawless. The rules are the rules of the ear. But after thirty-five years one starts to trust one's ear. If you don't trust your own ear, who's going to?

ES: Your poems often use images of resurrection, but there's usually no metaphysical transcendence. Instead, there's a return to earth. In some poems, there's even a physical return to dirt. As you say in the poem Sentences, *"Heaven, that stray dog, eats on the run and keeps moving" [CM, 121]. Transcendence doesn't seem available. In other poems, like the poem* January" *[CM, 124], you describe a type of reincarnation. Do you have a system of belief?*

No. I have a system of nonbelief. I would love to be a believer. But I'm not. And that's why everything always ends at the stars, at the heaven of the fixed stars. In fact, that's the coda I'm working on now. It's called *North American Bear*, and it's seven poems. The great bear, the big dipper and that's as far as it gets.

ES: You're drawing near the end of the third phase of this project that you've been working on since 1971. Can you compare the new book, Appalachia, *with* Black Zodiac *and* Chickamauga?

Well, it's shorter, if nothing else. They're all one-page poems. It mirrors, to a certain extent, *China Trace* in the trilogy of *Hard Freight, Bloodlines,* and *China Trace*—which is to say, it makes an upward movement at the end. I sort of wanted to write a *Par-*

adiso, but apparently I'm not capable of writing one, or I don't have the necessary evangelical ingredients to write one. Therefore what I ended up doing was writing a sort of ersatz *Book of the Dead*. As you know, the Tibetan and Egyptian books of the dead are rather like guides, verbal amulets, little mantras, songs, whispered into the ear of the dying person to help him, the true believer, get across to where he is sure he is going. And I thought, well, I could do something like a secular Appalachian book of the dead. And so I have about six poems called *The Appalachian Book of the Dead* in this book. Also "The Appalachian Book of the Dead" is referred to in several other poems. And the movement of the book, of the imagery, is, I guess, relentlessly outward and upward. So in the same way that *Country Music* was a trilogy that was a kind of small-time *inferno*, *purgatorio*, and *paradiso*, *Chickamauga*, *Black Zodiac*, and *Appalachia* are a small-time *inferno*, *purgatorio*, and *paradiso*. *Purgatorio* in the *Divine Comedy* seems to me, in some ways, the richest of all of those three books in that it is a combination of scraping the inferno off your shoes and having your eyes on the prize at the same time. I feel that way about *Black Zodiac*. It seems to me the richest of these three books, although it couldn't exist, in my scheme of things, without the other two. Then again, everything is independent as well as interdependent in these trilogies, as I try to set them up. So that is the mirror I'm working on between the first trilogy and the third trilogy. The second trilogy, *The World of the Ten Thousand Things*, is a kind of palimpsest for the overall three. If I were taking all three trilogies to be an *inferno*, *purgatorio*, and *paradiso*, then the middle one would be the purgatory—the world, the dust, the things of this world.

ES: When you say that the third phase of this project is an ascension, what exactly do you mean by "ascension"?

I suppose it's, more than anything else, a figure of speech. Unlike the pilgrim Dante, I don't get into the celestial elevator and go up. The movement of the book, the concerns of the book, the horizons of the book, the outlook of the book, all tend to move from horizontal to vertical as opposed to, say, *Chickamauga* and, for the most part, *Black Zodiac*, which move from vertical to horizontal, downward instead of upward.

ES: What do you mean when you say that?

I mean what the book is grounded in, what the concerns of the poems are. The concerns of the poems in *Appalachia* seem to be more "otherworldly." Even though they may start here, they become "otherworldly." There are poems in there based on the lives of the European mystics of the Middle Ages. Those poems tend to be more concerned with their relationship to what's not there rather than what is, and trying to bring what's not there into terms of what is visible in the visible world. That's why I say it's probably really a figure of speech because it's a yearning on my part, more than anything else. It's a deep yearning, a deep desire for something that's beyond one's control and one's grasp, and beyond one's comprehension. This is nothing new, obviously, but it is the movement my whole project has been tending toward all these years.

7. An Interview by Ernest Suarez and Amy Verner

ES: I think it's more than a figure of speech because there's an emphasis and a reach.

Well, I hope so, of course. I don't have the sure footing of belief, that good ground for steady walking—I don't have that. But I do have emphasis, I do have reach, if that counts.

ES: What will you do next?

I don't know. I hope to write some more poems that won't be quite so obsessive about this sort of idea. Maybe it will drive me into prose. Who knows? But I hope not to stop. I hope to have an old age. One, I hope to have an old age. Two, I hope it's like Mr. Warren's and Thomas Hardy's, in that it's productive.

ES: In the sixties you wrote a short poem called The New Poem *[CM, 17]. What was that a reaction to?*

Oh, that was a reaction to a couple of things. One, it was a reaction to the idea that everything in the sixties was going to be different and make our lives different and was going to change everything. Two, it was a reaction to poems about the Vietnam War, that somehow they were going to make a difference. And they weren't going to make any difference at all, you know. At least in this country they didn't make much difference. And everybody was always talking about writing the "new poem." "I'm going to write the new poem. This is the sixties, everything is thrown out, we need the new poem." There was a lot of new stuff going on, there certainly was, and, as it turned out, a lot of productive stuff that was eventually assimilated. All the surrealists—the American surrealist movement that blossomed in the sixties—were eventually assimilated into the new body of American poetry and made it richer. Still, there was no new poem that was going to change everything. It would not be able to help us. So it was a youthful sort of gesture. It became the most anthologized poem I ever wrote.

ES: It's true. In many anthologies that's the first poem that they have listed by you, but it's certainly not a poem that's typical of you.

No, it's very atypical. It was in a book called *The Grave of the Right Hand*, a book written during a ten-year period where I was trying to figure out what I was going to do, and what I was trying to get started on. I tried all different kinds of things, and that was one of the things I tried. It was the "political" poem, but it was an antipoem.

ES: How do you see yourself in relationship to the "poetic movements" that evolved in the fifties and sixties—Beat, Black Mountain, Deep Image, and others?

I find myself outside all of that. I started writing poems very late, when I was in the army, over in Italy. I was twenty-three when I tried to write my first poem, and then later, at twenty-six, I got into the University of Iowa by mistake because no one read the manuscript I sent. So I just enrolled and started going to school. That's when I first started writing seriously. The Deep Imagists were coming on about that time, and the Beats had already happened, had already written their best work by the early sixties. The Black Mountain school was still going on, but even though Ezra Pound, the great hero of the Black Mountain school, had been the original cause of my writing poetry (because I had read a poem of his that I liked), that was not my interest.

ES: Did you know Charles Olson?

No, I never met him. I didn't know anybody, actually. I mean, eventually I came to meet people as I got older, but when I was young, I didn't know anybody. I went from Iowa back to Italy as a Fulbright student and so, again, in the mid-sixties, was away from whatever scene there was. Then, when I came back, I started teaching right away. So there really wasn't any time to go out and be part of a scene. If I'd have been ten years younger, I wouldn't have felt the need to get a job because I would have been raised in the sixties instead of in the fifties. If you were raised in the fifties, after you got out of school, you got a job. In the sixties it didn't matter; nobody had a job who didn't want one. But I went to work teaching and stayed there the whole time, and I've been treated very well by the academy.

ES: You've claimed that the best lyricists in the sixties were James Tate and Bob Dylan. I'm especially intrigued by your mention of Dylan.

I think Dylan's a great songwriter; I don't think he's the poet that people try to make him into. I read somewhere that the British critic Christopher Ricks is doing a big study of Dylan as the major poet of the period.[3] I don't feel that way, but I do feel he's the best songwriter that we have in this generation. There's no doubt in my mind about that, and I love the lyrics of his songs, in the same way that I love the lyrics of Tate's poems. They seem to be inventive and surreal in a way that was empowering and energizing in the sixties. Both of them were, each in his own discipline.

ES: Who are the living poets with whom you feel the biggest kinship?

Charles Simic is the one I feel the closest kinship with. Of course, he's a very imagistic poet. He and I have a lot of the same things our poems are about as well. Mark Strand is an old friend and someone whose work I've admired for almost forty years. I like Jim Tate, whom we just mentioned. I like Louise Glück. I like C.K. Williams, Jay Wright, Frank Bidart, David Young. I'm just talking about people I like in my age group. There's such a huge generation below me, with Jorie Graham, David St. John, Larry Levis, who just died, all of these people, really wonderful poets. And above, I was always a great admirer of Merwin, James Merrill, Donald Justice, but I feel closest to, and I think it is natural to feel closest to, people you sort of came along with and went through all the things with, and that would be Tate, Simic, and Strand.

7. An Interview by Ernest Suarez and Amy Verner

ES: Are you going to write any more essays?

Probably not, unless I have to. I don't know why prose is so hard for me. Probably because, as I said, I'm such an impressionistic kind of writer. But I might do some. As I said, if I ever finish this project, maybe I'll be forced into prose because I don't have anything else to say in poems. I hope not. Which isn't to say that prose itself doesn't have anything to say. It's just different, isn't it?

ES: From reading your poetry, I think that you would have a gift for short stories. They could be like a Fellini movie.

Fellini has been a big influence on me, I think. I never really thought that much about it, but the way he puts his movies together is the way over the years I kind of put my poems together. Episodic is not quite right. It's episodic in film and it's, well, I suppose it's slightly episodic in the poem too, but it's not a linear episode; it's a linguistic or imagistic episode. A group of things that come together to form a whole. And Fellini was the great master of this, as well as being the most visually interesting person. I started seeing his movies at the very same time that I started writing poems, in 1959, in Italy with *La Dolce Vita*.

ES: My all-time favorite film.

Yes, mine too. I've seen it eight times. I love it. Greatest opening scene—the shadow of the cross going up the side of that building—great movie. It's a great movie.

ES: I've seen interviews in which you've talked about painting, but, given your emphasis on the visual arts, what about film? We've just mentioned Fellini. Are you drawn to film?

I used to be. Like everyone, I used to watch a lot of movies. Now I'm almost always disappointed in movies. Every time I go to one, I'm disappointed in it. And I don't know why that is. Is it my advancing age, or the slackness of the movie? My guideline is, as soon as I see a fireball, I know it's a movie I'm not going to like. I did see *As Good as It Gets* the other night; I thought that was good. And I liked *Wag the Dog*. I thought Dustin Hoffman was just fabulous. The last movie I really loved was *The Commitments* some years ago. I like Woody Allen. I like all of his movies, some better than others, but I think he's terrifically talented. I liked *Deconstructing Harry*. I love that musical he did last year, *Tell Me That You Love Me*, whatever it was called.[4] Fabulous movie. And I liked *Pennies from Heaven* some years ago with Steve Martin. That was great. But, for the most part, I don't see movies much. Or at least not as much as I used to.

ES: Has film had an influence on your poetry?

Structurally, I think Fellini has, I hadn't ever really thought about it until right now, but I would guess so. Not only because I saw his films at that formative stage in my writing, but also because they were Italian, which was also very important for me. That was where everything happened to me—I started reading poetry, I started writing poems; the landscape of Italy entered me and has never gotten out. And the culture, the popular culture as well as the more serious culture, has been important to me. And Fellini and Antonioni and Mario Monicelli. All those people from the fifties and the sixties, those directors. I'm glad you brought it up.

CHAPTER 8

An Interview by Andrew Zawacki

AZ: Black Zodiac *was published very quickly after* Chickamauga. *Have you been more productive than usual in the last three or four years?*

CW: I did have quite an intense spell between the end of *Chickamauga* and the end of the book I've just finished, *Appalachia*, during which time—I think it was about three years and four months—I wrote two books. That's sort of an unheard-of situation for me. It took me five years to write *Chickamauga* and then it took three years and four months, as I say, to do *Black Zodiac* and *Appalachia*. Since *Appalachia*, which was finished in August of 1997, I haven't really written anything; we're now in January, January 19, 1998. I attribute that, I hope, to the finishing-up of a long project that I'd started back in 1971, when I got the idea for a series of books. I didn't know it was going to take twenty-seven years, but I think the wind kind of went out of my sails when I finished the last two books. I got speeded up toward the end, because I felt that I saw the end in sight, and I wanted to make sure that I got it done. Part of the impetus, also, is psychological, because my old friend Larry Levis had died at the age of forty-nine, dropped dead of a heart attack, and I said, "Jesus, I'd better get this thing finished; you never know." So that's part of it. The other part is that I had in mind what I wanted to do. The only other time that I had a writing spurt like that was years ago when I did *Bloodlines* and *China Trace* in a quick spurt of time—not quite as quickly as *Black Zodiac* and *Appalachia*, but then again I feel as though I knew what I wanted to do this time, knew how I thought I could do it, and always at my back I'd hear...

In Black Zodiac *you speak of "journal and landscape" as "discredited form" and "discredited subject matter" [NB, 72]. Why do you feel that the journal form specifically has been discredited?*

Originally published in Verse *16, no. 2, and reprinted in* The Verse Book of Interviews, *ed. Brian Henry and Andrew Zawacki (Amherst, MA: Verse Press, 2005), 18–29. The interview was conducted at Wright's home in Charlottesville, Virginia, on 19 January 1998.*

Well, perhaps I didn't choose my word as accurately as I should have. I thought of the journal form being discredited as a conveyor of serious literary ambition. Usually the journal form is thought to encompass shut-in women, old guys trying to make sense of or justification for what they've done or haven't done in their lives, and so on. What I was trying to do was to make the journal form and the idea of a serious look at landscape, which is thought of as a kind of Sunday painterly occupation—I was trying to make both of those into a serious vehicle for saying something that exists possibly beyond each. Since neither is generally thought of as a repository for poetic seriousness, but as poetic gesture, I wanted to take them both and see what I could do with them vis-à-vis ... this sounds pretentious, but the spiritual journey that I felt I've been on for the last thirty years, when I've been trying to write these poems. And I was trying to imbue them, or endow them, or at least inject them with the kind of seriousness that I thought they could contain and could regenerate in poetry. One never knows whether one has done that or not. It's the sort of thing that everyone tells you not to do: don't write a poem about the sunset, and quite properly so, because you can't beat the sunset. Well, probably one shouldn't write serious poems in a journal form, or write landscape that is imbued with something beyond the landscape. But since you're not supposed to, that seemed to be a good reason to try to do it. And since I like looking at landscape, and since my mental faculties seem better equipped for notation and observation rather than flow-through narrative, I thought perhaps these are good vehicles for me to try to get in and drive, and so I did.

Do you keep a journal, and have the journal poems grown out of journal entries? The reason I ask is that you've written that a poet's life consists only of those things not good enough to go into his poems. Has that somehow put an extra burden on the journal poems?

I think writing itself puts an extra burden on anything you try to put down, just because of the fact that you're putting it down, and once you've put it down, it's ineradicable to a certain extent. I don't keep a journal. I used to keep a little book of notations that weren't even interesting enough to be called pensées that I collected in *Halflife*; it was sort of a commonplace notebook, just things I would think of from time to time, and I did that for about ten years or so and then got tired of it; I thought it was rather pretentious and what I was saying wasn't very interesting really. So I don't keep a journal, and the journal poems do not come out of or exist previously in any kind of journal form. And I don't do them any more: I did that series of *Zone Journals* and *Xionia* as both a technical experiment in the long line and the idea that you could get anything into a journal form and get it in there accurately and unrandomly if you organized it right. So even though they are journals, they are journals perhaps conceptually, but they are poems technically and actually, which is to say that they partake of the beginning, middle, and end of a poem, rather than a journal where everything is kind of in the middle. They take as their structures the seasonal changes, which is maybe not a brilliant structure, but at least it's workable. They allow, it seems to me, so much more of a possibility for inclusion of material. As I said before, they seem to fit the processes of my mental capacities, which are notational and schematic and impressionistic, as opposed to logical and mapped-out. The idea of a journal—it's sort of like Scott Fitzgerald in the fountain outside The Plaza—the idea of the journal seemed like a good idea at the time. Anything that you've stopped doing seems sort of old-hat, but I think that the way the journals operated, and the way they contributed to the structural assembly of my poems, continues to this day. Which is to say that the poems I'm writing now, and the longer poems I wrote in *Black Zodiac* and the one in *Chickamauga*, *Sprung Narratives* [*NB*, 21–9], partake of that idea I generated in the journals. And one always likes to think that one is doing something that either hasn't been done before or hasn't been fully explored before, and at the time I thought that the idea of the poem as journal, rather than the journal as poem, hadn't been really explored as far as it might have. Of course journals have been explored and poems have been explored, but trying to get a finite poem into a kind of infinitely open form, which a journal is, I found seductive. One of the reasons I don't write prose or a memoir or that sort of thing is because—at least as far as my project has been for the last twenty-seven years, these series of books, series of trilogies that I've been doing—to me, anything that's been interesting in my life or that my life has generated has wormed its way into the poems in one way or another. The husk, or the narrative shell of that, would be what I would then go over and try to fill in with artificial material if I were going to do some kind of narrative about it. The heart of it, or for lack of a better word, the soul of it, is all contained in the poems. And again, that's another way that the journal poems were interesting, because I could say things in a journal that one would never let oneself say perhaps in a poem quite so openly. Because you could always say, oh well, this is a journal, people admit everything in their journals, why not be more open in this poem? Anything that I've had to say about my life, that was of any interest to me, has been said in my poems. And God knows if it's not of any interest to me, it won't be of any interest to anyone else, so I, you know, sweep the husks away and chew on the kernels.

There's a fairly explicit struggle in Black Zodiac *as to whether memory redeems or not. What is your hope, however skeptically you check it, for the role of memory in language or poetry?*

It's the case of the disillusioned lover. For years and years I thought memory was the golden ladder to heaven, and it may still be. But as I get older, memory tends to become memories, and memories are not memory. Memory is a tactile, tensile thread along which our whole lives have passed; memories are little snapshots that are pleasing or displeasing, but you have to work very hard to make them into something whole. The painter David Hockney has a process with photography where he takes snapshots, hundreds of snapshots, of a really banal or everyday scene or event, and then puts them together to make a narrative out of it. He calls them "joiners." They are actually layerings: he layers these photographs together to re-create the narrative that was there, and by re-creating the narrative, he lets you look at it from different points of view, and it's a fascinating visual experimentation. Now, what he's done is taken the snapshots and made the event into something whole again, with different refractions. I suppose one could do the same thing with memories and make them into memory, which is, as I say, the line that runs between the beginning and the end. So I am of two minds now that I see there are different ways to do this, and so I often think, well, maybe I shouldn't be doing it this way, maybe I should be doing it some other way. So when I say it's best not to remember at all, I mean it's best not to just have isolated snapshot kind of memories; I don't mean that it's best not to believe in the efficacy and the inevitability of the line of memory that connects us to our past and to our future. I guess when I feel that I've fallen into the memories pit, that I have then tried to reconstruct it in the way that Hockney reconstructs a photograph, in the ways that Paul Cézanne reconstructs the visual scene through the nonlinear approaches that he used to make his narratives and his representational paintings. But it's probably a battle that's of no interest to anyone but me, but when I'm writing a poem, it is supreme interest to me, because I'm trying to make something out of something, which is harder than making [laughs] something out of nothing, actually, because the somethings that you pick have to end up being the something that you see. Whereas if you make it up out of nothing, you have no obligation to anybody; otherwise, you have a great obligation to yourself, which is always the worst obligation to have and the one that's hardest to bring to fruition.

Regarding that obligation to oneself: in Black Zodiac *you write, "Before you bear witness, / Be sure to have something that calls for a witnessing ... / Don't shine what's expendable" [NB, 110]. Is this a personal issue, or does it also have historical or aesthetic components? Is it being shrugged in contemporary American poetry?*

Yes. One always likes to think that one occupies a certain high ground, be it an imagistic high ground, a narrative high ground if you write narrative, a technical high ground. What you don't want to occupy is the moral high ground, because the moral high ground is so full of people that there's no high ground there, because everybody thinks he has the right answer, and nobody does of course. If you have it for yourself you're lucky. I guess what I was talking about ... I was talking to myself—I never talk to anybody else. One, I found it fruitless. Two, the best advice I ever got was when I was fifteen years old and a man named Jim Perry at the little school I went to in North Carolina called Sky Valley (there were eight of us in this school one year; it was a farm, and they had a school one year)—he said, "People are always going to believe what they want to believe, you can't tell them anything." And he was right. So I talk to myself in my poems. I speak to myself, I give myself instructions, I try to carry them out. Any kind of injunction, any kind of nudging, any kind of moral password that I give in a poem, is to myself alone, and I don't pretend to speak for anyone else. One has to keep oneself alert, one has to try to keep one's own standards. If one's own standards aren't higher than what one perceives the standards of the rest of the situation are, then one is in trouble. That's why the moral high ground is always so crowded [laughs], because everybody thinks he's got this answered, but of course they don't— you do, right [laughs]? So I said yes because yes, I feel that way, but only personally.

I would never dream of telling anybody out loud what they should do. Like everybody else, I tell everybody what they should do, under my breath.

*How is it, given the fact of your work, let alone its thematic concerns, that "the unexamined life is no different from the examined life" [*Black Zodiac, *in* NB, *125]?*

Well, that's kind of a tongue-in-cheek statement, I guess. I meant only that your life is your life, and whether you examine it or don't examine it, it rolls along, or it doesn't roll along. If you spend your life examining your life, as I do, obsessively, and probably ridiculously so, then there's no such thing as the unexamined life. Therefore, the unexamined life is the same as the examined life. One doesn't go about saying: I'm now going to examine my life and see what this comes to. It's a daily process, I think, if you write out of your life, as most people do. Even Eliot, as we found out, wrote almost exclusively out of his own life. So since there's no such thing for a writer as the unexamined life, then like all statements, it's both a true and a false statement. It was probably a little cuter than I meant it to be when I put it down.

*In one of your newer poems, you say that "the dream of a reclusive life, a strict, essential solitude, / Is a younger hermit's dream" [*Reply to Wang Wei, *in* NB, *166]. Was that your dream once, and how has it changed?*

Yes, in my fantasy life I have dreamed of the perfect reclusion being the best way to think and to write about what one was thinking about. As one gets older, that becomes less and less of an attractive option, and more and more of a possible necessity. Any time it becomes a possible necessity, instead of a choice, anything starts to lose its luster a little bit. My ambition now is to be what John Ashbery once termed himself to be, "a well-known recluse about town."

How often do you return to Italy now, and why?

For some years, I didn't go back at all. After my son was born in 1970, I didn't go back for fifteen years, until 1985, because I really didn't want to go around with a kid on a backpack, that sort of thing, because Italy was still an aesthetic continuum for me. In 1985, Mark Strand and his family and I and my family rented a house in northern Italy, and we went back for two months. My son was fifteen at the time, and so that was OK. Since then, my wife and I have gone back almost every year. It gets shorter and shorter each year, because I like less and less to be away from home, as it turns out. It used to be I wanted to go for two years, then it was two months, now it's two weeks. I go because it still remains the start of everything for me, as far as writing, looking, thinking. I have a very good friend there, Gaetano Prampolini, who has a little house in the town of Spello in Umbria, and we go visit him usually every other year, and then we go somewhere the intervening year.[1] I like to go eat the food and look it the landscape, and I like to see Gaetano [laughs], I guess that's the reason, more than anything else. Also, the world is divided into two kinds of people: those who want to go somewhere new every time they go somewhere, and those who want to go back to the same place. I want to go back to the same place. Monet wanted to go back to the same place. Bruce Chatwin always wanted to go somewhere different. Also, Italy is the only country except England where I speak a little bit of the language, so it's easier to get around.

You've spoken of the inclusiveness of the journal and of the long line. Have you ever considered returning to the prose poem, which you abandoned after The Grave of the Right Hand, *as an equally inclusive strategy?*

I've thought a lot about the prose poem and going back to the prose poem, and I thought for years that just to effect a kind of, if not perfect, at least not imperfect, circularity, I should end this project, the coda, with five prose poems, the way I started [laughs]. But the reason I haven't is because somewhere along the line, no pun intended, I became married to the idea of the line of the poem, and it's a marriage which I don't want to break up. I got to the point in extending the line, after *China Trace*, that there didn't seem to be much purpose in then pushing it one more step and going back into prose, because I had come all the way from prose. Ultimately, I guess I agree with what Eugenio Montale, whose work I translated some thirty years ago, said about poetry. He said that all poetry rises out of prose and longs to return to it.[2] Like all great writers, he didn't explain that image, but I think what he means is that it's in that tension of trying to go back to prose that the poetic line gets its vibrancy and its electricity. But once it goes back into prose, then it becomes just prose, even if it's good prose, it becomes just prose, and, in that case, something lesser. Once I accepted that fact, I never really wanted to go back to the prose poem, although I too love the prose poem still, and it was a great ... it was a great what? It was a great opening for me when I first tried to do them many years ago, and I still have a great affection for them, and I like to read them, and I like to see them, I like to see what other people are doing with them. It's just that I feel that if I went back to the prose poem, I would be going back to something rather than forward to something. Maybe it's like saving the best thing on your plate till last, because you think it'll taste better. Maybe someday, but at the moment I'm too much under the sway of that comment by Montale to ever try to do it.

You've translated Montale and Campana. Do you translate much any more, if not for publication, then as an exercise between poems or between books?

That's how I got into translating in the first place, when I couldn't write my own poems. Again, I bring up my friend Strand. He and I were in school together, and this was what he said, "Well, if you can't write your own poems, why don't you try translating? You speak a little Italian." So that's how I got into it. Then I translated Montale and got very deeply into that, and I did do Campana back in 1984, after I finished *The Other Side of the River*. I didn't know what I was going to do, and so I translated Dino Campana. Boy, was it a lot of work, and I realized that I was not quite up to this endeavor any more. My Italian had deteriorated to such an extent that I was looking up every word, instead of every other word. Since then I haven't really done much. I translated five poems by a guy named Franco Buffoni, whom I met at a Montale conference in 1996 in Florence. He was a nice fellow, and he said, "Hey, if you ever want to translate any of my stuff...." He sent me a little thing that had five poems. So I tried that. They were really quite easy to translate, or should have been, and they were quite difficult for me, so I realized that I've got to give this up.[3] The reason I did Campana was he was one of the two important early Italian influences on me, Montale being the other. There was no stylistic influence by Campana, it was just his legend as the Italian Rimbaud, the *poet maudit* and all of that sort of thing, and so I thought I'd translate him, and it was fun. But as Minnie Pearl used to say when she was finished playing: "We're through playin' now." I'm through translating now, I think.

The last year has witnessed the deaths of many American poets: most recently Larry Levis, as you've mentioned, Denise Levertov, James Laughlin, William Matthews. Before that, Amy Clampitt, Alien Ginsberg, James Dickey, Jane Kenyon, James Merrill.... Do you have a sense that there's a generation of American poetry waning?

That's actually a hard question to answer, because I never thought of it in generational terms. Were I in my twenties, I would think about it in generational terms. Now that I'm sixty-two, it's for the most part friends who have died. I knew most of those people, I'd met them all, several of them were very good friends of mine. It's true that the generation above me, the generation of Merrill and Levine, Justice, Hollander and Merwin and Kinnell, all of those people—a huge generation born in the twenties, is now entering their seventies, and they are going to be dropping out as time goes by. One of the reasons I don't think in terms of generational loss is because my generation seems somehow caught between the generation of those born in the twenties and those born in the forties, which is another huge generation that's coming on behind us. Those of us born in the thirties, there are very few of us. Mark Strand once said, "Charles, we're a generation of three: me and you and Simic." Well, that's not true, it's just that we're all good friends and so he was joking. But in that joke is a kernel of truth, in that those of us in the thirties are kind of squeezed in. We don't really have a generation: we're either tacked onto the end of the twenties or tacked onto the beginning of the forties. If I were an ambitious young poetry climber, I would say, well, that generation is passing away and our generation is coming. But I can't say that, because I'm not sure we have a generation. But I do feel that there is, as there hasn't been perhaps for the last ten or fifteen years, a movement upward, a generation of movement, and I believe that people born in the forties are starting to muscle their way up. The thing about the generation of the twenties is that there were so many of them; it's going to be a long time muscling them out, as far as that sort of attitude goes. But yes, I guess I do have a feeling that there is a slight movement going on, although I'm not sure what the movement is, other than what I just said.

Your new poems include quite a bit of technological lingo: downloads, on-lines, print-

outs, meta-optics, and so on. To what extent does a spiritual poetry, in order to be legitimate now, need to accommodate this language of the time?

Part of the fact of using them is that I don't really know what they mean. I mean, I know how they operate, but I do not do computers, and I certainly don't do optics in any kind of scientific way. The words seem, when I use them, to have a specific reference to what I'm talking about, outside their sphere of influence, and so I do use them. It's not really an attempt to be "modern," as Hart Crane would have had it, when he had, you know, "a rip-tooth of the sky's acetylene" [*The Bridge*], that sort of thing, and would write about cars and trains and so on. I don't feel that I have to write about computers and what all of that business is going to signify to my life, or to you-all's life, I guess. But I don't want to try to avoid it either, so when it pops into my head, I use it, if it seems specific to the moment. I'm not trying to drag it in, I'm not trying to do it to show off, and I'm not trying to fit the language of the times into my poems, because I think my poems use the language of the times. They just may not use as many scientific allusions as other people. Because I'm not a scientific kind of guy.

In one new poem, you speak of "our landscape, / Bourgeois, heart-breakingly suburban" [A Bad Memory Makes You a Metaphysician, a Good One Makes You a Saint, *in* NB, *149]. Do you ever feel the heart-breakingly suburban is a kind of privilege?*

I was talking about my back yard, and the exterior life one lives; I feel that my interior life is anything but that. I think that there is a ... I don't want to say a school or a branch or a movement, but there are an awful lot of people who write, as my mother's friend malapropped all the time, "heart-renderingly" suburban poems, which is to say they're trying to make nothing out of something, and they too often succeed. That's another *genre* that I've taken on, the back yard poem, trying to make it more than just the back yard poem: "Sitting on the back stoop with a can of Bud Light watchin' my bird dogs and the john-boat leaned up against the garage...." I think there is too much outer suburban concentration these days. When I say that, you're right, it was slightly tongue-in-cheek, because I can be anywhere and write the same poem. I mean, I can be in the Taj Mahal or I can be, you know, down on the riverbank under a lean-to, and I'm still going to be writing the same poem, because my poem doesn't openly depend on where I am. That may spark the beginning of it, but it's not where the poem goes. I live a fairly typical American life. I have a house and a back yard. It's middle class. I'm middle class. I make no apologies for that. I don't know what else to do. Phil Levine's mother once cracked that he's the only person she knows who started out in the middle class and worked desperately down to the lower classes in his work. I've just sort of sat and spun around where I started. That doesn't mean that my mind has sat and spun in east Tennessee, or as it is now, in central Virginia. I don't know, I don't find any long-term disease in being middle class, it's what you do with what you've got. You can take the back yard and move it anywhere, just as long as it doesn't stay the back yard.

8. An Interview by Andrew Zawacki

You were enrolled in a creative writing program, and now you teach in one. What are some of the responsibilities of teaching creative writing? How much involves directing students, and how much is a case of what Thoreau said, that that government is best which governs least?

Well, I think Thoreau was right about his comment on writing classes in general [laughs]. It depends on whether you're teaching an advanced graduate group or whether you're teaching an undergraduate group. There's more "You shouldn't do this, you shouldn't do that" that goes on with the undergraduate, because they've been around it less. If you're lucky and get a good graduate group, you should just do the blocking for them and get out of the way, and that's what often happens. There are ... how do I say this? When I teach, I only talk about their poems. I don't talk about what they should *do* in them, where they should go next, unless they ask me—of course, I never know where anybody should go next. I don't even know where I'm going next. How can I tell anybody else where they should go next in their work? The question that's usually asked most often is: Should I try a long poem? Well, I say, sure, try a long poem, you know. If you don't like it, go back to writing short poems. Again, I'm talking about graduate students, because the battle that started out in the fifties and sixties to get writers into teaching courses has been won many, many years ago, and the students who come to graduate classes now know so much more than any of the students did earlier on, because they've been through many undergraduate workshops with good writers. There are just a few things that you can tell someone or teach someone: Donald Barthelme has said prayer was one of them, self-laceration was another, and "notions of the lousy" was a third,[4] and I think that's about all you need to be able to teach them. If you can teach them notions of the lousy, there's no other job you need to do. Almost everybody who gets into a graduate writing program is competent, or they wouldn't get in the program. Now, going from competence to occasional brilliance is a large step, and you don't get that many who can make that step. But that doesn't mean it's not fun to talk about their poems to see what they're doing, to encourage them—to let them imitate whomever they want to, because eventually if they're any good, they'll realize that's what they're doing and then they'll stop, and as they go along they will have learned something by doing the imitation. So I think the first time a poem comes up in a workshop and somebody says, "God, that sounds just like W.S. Merwin!" and "Jesus, that's Galway Kinnell!" or "Adrienne Rich already said ..."—so what? I'm of two minds, of course, about teaching in a writing program. I think there are too many people out there writing, but there are too many people out there doing everything, so I don't know that that's such a bad thing. The good stuff always rises to the top. The bad stuff will rise to the top too [laughs], so you have to be selective when you look at what's arisen. But I don't think anyone has ever been damaged by going to a creative writing class or workshop. I guess the one thing I really think is that you should try as hard as possible not to encourage people to write the way you do. I mean, if they want to, fine, they'll get out of it, but don't make them, and that's what happens in more cases than I think it should in workshops. And as Clint Eastwood said in *High Plains Drifter*: "It's what's inside them that makes them do that, teach that way."[5] So I say: go to a place that doesn't have that stuff inside of the teacher.

Does your wife Holly's work as a photographer have any impact on yours?

Not really. Holly is much more intellectually attuned to her art than I am to mine. Mine seems to be, as I've said before, more impressionistic, more notational, more language-oriented, more follow-the-image-and-see-where-it-will-take-you. Holly is much more conceptual: she gets ideas for these large series, which I find just amazingly beautiful and amazingly brilliant, because I can't do that, and we always love what we can't do, you know, if what we can't do is something that's good, and I feel that about her work. I have been influenced by a lot of the books that she has on photography. By looking at the pictures and seeing certain set-ups, in the early days I would write poems from certain photographs. There was one; I used a picture by an Italian photographer named Ugo Mulas, it's called "Bar Giamaica, 1953–54," which is a bar in Milano that I used to go to in 1959 and 1960, and I put my own people into the positions that he had his people in the same scene.[6] Manuel Álvarez Bravo, the great Mexican photographer—I've looked at his work from time to time, in the early days, and have not exactly used things from it but been influenced by his way of looking at landscape. But for the most part, not really. It's a different kind of enterprise, even though they're both imagistic, they're a different kind of enterprise. We seem to be working on the same spool perhaps, but at different ends of that spool.

The Wallace Stevens Journal *is publishing a special issue on apocalyptic language in Stevens. Is the encroaching millennium making its way into your work?*

Haven't thought about it at all, other than getting ready to call my next book *Millennium Falcon*.... No, seriously, I haven't really thought about it, except that I'm hoping that my third and last trilogy, which will be comprised of *Chickamauga*, *Black Zodiac*, and *Appalachia*, plus this illusory coda that I'm trying to write now, and which will be called, I think, *Journeyman*, will come out in 2001 probably—one of my favorite movies. So that's the only millennial concern that I have, other than to be as far away from Times Square on the first of January 2000 as I can possibly get. It really hasn't. My language has been apocalyptic since 1961. Why should I try the prophet now, for just the millennium? There'll be another one.

CHAPTER 9

An Interview by Troy Teegarden

TT: *When you put this collection of poems together,* Black Zodiac, *did you feel like you were going to win the Pulitzer Prize, the National Book Critics Award, and the Los Angeles Times* Book Prize? *I mean, you cleaned up on this one, didn't you?*

CW: (Laughs). Well, it was kind of a surprise to me, I must say. When you put any collection together you think you're going to win all of those prizes, right? But you're immediately disabused of that notion. Of course you don't think like that. I was just thinking that it's the next to last book in a long project, and I was hoping that it would be read. I'm kind of surprised that it's received as much attention as it has because it does seem to be a much more personal book than the one before it, a book called *Chickamauga*. It starts off with a poem called "Explanation of his Life" [*Apologia Pro Vita Sua*] and ends up with one called "Scattered Parts" [*Disjecta Membra*], again about my life, or the life of the character in this book. I thought it was a little close to the bone, and I thought people might not care for it. But I was disabused of that notion, too. I guess because people seemed to have liked it, or some people have.

Do you think the personalization of the poems is really what the hook is this time?

Maybe. That had crossed my mind after a while. The personalization had enlarged somewhat and was able to take in the people, which of course is what you always hope for. But I wasn't sure it was going to happen this time.

What were you doing when you'd found out you won the Pulitzer Prize? How did you feel?

Originally published online in The Metropolitan Review *2, no. 1 (Spring-Summer 1999), available at http://www.metroreview.com/Interviews_Wright.html. The interview was conducted by phone while Wright was attending the Sewanee Writers' Conference at the University of the South in Sewanee, Tennessee, in July 1998.*

I was up in my attic room where I usually am. NPR called me and said, "Can we interview you?" and I said, "What for?" and they said, "You just won a Pulitzer Prize," and I said, "Well, nobody's told me." And nobody ever did until the next day when a telegram came from Columbia University. I said, "Let me call you back when somebody's told me something." Then I got a couple of phone calls, and I called them back.

That's pretty good. You find out from the people who want to interview you about it, and you don't even know, yet.

(Laughs). I know, that's true. Well, I did know that I was a finalist. You know those things get around. And so I knew there was a possibility, but I had been a finalist four times before, so I wasn't much impressed by that. I wasn't about to say, "Oh yes, let's talk about it" until I heard from somebody a bit more officially. By the end of that evening, it was feeling of frustration because the phone rang solid for eight hours. I had to take it off the hook to go to the bathroom once, I remember, and I had to take it off to go to supper. One is pleased that people are so congratulatory. There's no real feeling. You just say, "Well, this is going on," and you sort of go with it. I'm pleased, of course. How could you not be pleased by all of that, hoping the attention will focus on the book and on the work and on the past work? That's the only thing that prizes are good for—to bring your work to the attention of people who might consider it or read it.

You mentioned your past work. When do you remember writing your first poem? Do you have any explicit memory of it?

I remember the first one I ever read. I'm not sure I can remember the first one I tried to write, although I think it was an imitation of the first one I read, and that was back in March of 1959 when I was in the army over Italy. I read a poem about Lake Garda in northern Italy where I was stationed.[1] It was sitting where I was sitting and looking out at the lake and the Alps in the background I was looking at, and I thought, "Wow, this is pretty good. This sure does sound good," not knowing at the time that it was written in iambic pentameter, which is why it sounded good. Then I think probably soon after that I was trying to write poems about northern Italy myself because that's where I was stationed. But I don't remember the first. I remember in college I wrote one poem in imitation of Dylan Thomas, but that's the only poem I'd ever written up until the time I got interested in poetry, which was, as I say, in March 1959.

What do you think are the best aspects of being a writer?

(Sighs) Boy, I don't know. You might have me on that one. (Pauses) I guess I would paraphrase Samuel Beckett and say that all one's writing is a failure because it never lives up to what you imagined it's going to be as you conceive it and as you are trying to do it.[2] But the best times are those when you fail best.

That's not a very optimistic view, is it?

I'm trying to be honest. Every once in a while you feel as though you've said what you thought you wanted to say, but after you go back, you say, "No, that wasn't quite it." The best times in writing are when you're in the process of writing, not when you finish it. It's when you're in it and the possibilities are myriad. And then you get the poem in shape, the possibilities dwindle of course. Then at the end there's just the one possibility the poem is about. That's never quite what you hoped it would be, but sometimes it's better than others and that's always good. I mean it's not like doing a business deal and you make the most money that anybody's ever made on buying or selling a building. It's not like that. There's always a faster gun in poetry.

When do you do your most productive writing? Do you have a certain time of day or any type of ritual you go through?

I used to, when I was much younger: write in the afternoons, which is very odd because most people don't. Now when I'm working on something, I tend to write whenever I can. I'll write in the morning, seldom in the afternoon, but morning and at night. After supper and before lunch is when I usually write. But when I am working on a poem or a project, I'm thinking about it all the time. Even when I'm not writing I'm thinking about it.

So you're walking around and then all of a sudden you come up with a line and just drop everything.

Well, you don't really drop everything. You either try to write down, try to remember it, or you try to remember what direction it's leading you in in the larger poem that you're working on. One often writes things down on scraps of paper.

Do you keep some kind of journal or just write ideas down on paper and stack them?

I don't keep a journal. I used to keep a little notational journal, but I've never kept a daily journal. I've never done it that way. Most of my poems are journals in a sense. They reflect my thoughts and my obsessions and what I'm concerned about at the time, and that usually works its way into my poems in a way. All my literary criticisms, my daily thoughts, everything works its way into my poems. My poems are fairly much an autobiographical movement of the way things have gone for me over the years.

One last question: Do you have any advice for other writers who are just getting started?

Read. Read everything you can. That's advice everybody gives, but it's the one true advice. Theodore Roethke said, "You want to write poems? There's the library, go in and go to work." You've got to know what's going on and what's happened before you can figure out what you want to do. I think it's a good line of work really. It's sort of a dying art. It's certainly not a hot one. All those things appeal to me about it. If you love language, you've got to love poetry. Poetry is language that sounds better and means more. What's better than that?

CHAPTER 10

Through Purgatory to Appalachia: An Interview by Martin Caseley

MC: *"Emily Dickinson had a stationary psyche ... Whitman's is ambulatory"* (Halflife, *22*)—*where would you place yourself on this axis?*

CW: That's a bit more difficult to say now than it was when I wrote the comment some twenty years ago. The comment in the old days was that I wanted to be E.D. on Whitman's road, i.e., to have a kind of restrained and structured compression within a larger, more expansive frame. I often used the image of the spider's web—an endlessly (theoretically, at least) expandable structure composed of small, interconnected, inter-webbed and discrete parts. Today, I'm not so sure I want to be on that road at all. I guess I'd like my expansiveness to resonate within a more cloistered area. I guess I'd want to be in E.D.'s room. But upstairs, in the cupola, with a 360 degree view, the landscape and everything in it a constant surround, so I could take it in without it taking me in. Subsumed, not consumed. You know, be part of my own process shot, swept up in the hurly-burly tumbling around my still, small voice of calm. Like that. My end of the axis is contemplative now, but what is contemplated isn't.

You have written very eloquently about Ezra Pound[1] and his status as "the last Victorian"[2]—could you expand upon this comment, as it's a rather idiosyncratic view of him?

Rather than expand on it, I'd rather reduce it. I probably should have said Edwardian, as that was his time (but, then, he wouldn't have been the last one of those). I continue to think of him as someone from the nineteenth century, whose passions and oddities were more Victorian than what we have come to label Modern, though, as we know, he spent most of his life talking "modern." The Padrino, the Godfather. But always

Originally published in PN Review *27 (September-October 2000): 22–5. Also available online at http://www.pnreview.co.uk/cgi-bin/text/texeng.cgi?file=/free/pnr135/interviews/135in01.txt. The interview was conducted by mail between November 1999 and March 2000.*

with a Victorian accent. His passion for Provence was Victorian, his passion for the philosophers of the Generation of Light (Erigena, Richard of St. Victor, Grosseteste) was Victorian, his early English influence (Robert Browning) was Victorian, his language kept lapsing back into Victorian tics, his passion for China was Victorian, his personal life was often Victorian and double-sided, his idea of the epic—the good man as hero in the wash of history and world culture—was Victorian, and, at last, his legacy is Victorian—scattered and reduced empire, his poem a shambles of good and misdirection. Yeats wasn't Victorian, nor was Joyce or Eliot or Frost or Williams or Stevens or Ford. Only Uncle Ez, who threw, as I once said, his body across the barbed wire of the early twentieth century and ushered the aforementioned over into the new air of modern times. As all the while he continued to work ceaselessly from his rather confined and compromised position, giving directions, issuing orders, trying to keep the troops in line.

In Quarter Notes, *you explain very eloquently the epiphanic effect Pound's* Blandula, Tenulla, Vagula *had on you in 1959, in setting you off on a poetic journey [QN, 94–5]. From then, you have worked within the lyric form: has your writing consciously set out to explore the boundaries of this form at all? I know you have written about the desire to explore a longer "two-step" line in your poetry.*

It has, actually. Of course, I started at the wrong end, reading *The Pisan Cantos* when I lived in Verona in 1959. I hadn't a clue as to what poetry was, much less a lyric subspecies. It wasn't until I got some schooling, as it were, that I began to see where it had started from—let's say Sappho—and where it had progressed to—let's say Pound/Eliot/Olson—in its progress and distortions (I'm talking about the early 1960s now). So I started over, short, compact lyrics—syllabics, accentual-syllabic stuff, "received" business, at first squeezing it tighter and tighter, and then loosening it as the lines got longer and the structures fuller. Eventually ending up in the *Journals* (published in England country as *Zone Journals* by Stride in 1996), which was about as airy and expansive a structure as I could work in and still call the process "lyric." I think one should push the lyric until it cries, "Uncle." The long line was an attempt to push the poem as close to prose as I could while still keeping it poetry. I have very consciously rummaged around in the lyric envelope, nudging its edges, seeing how much one could fit in before it became a non-container and just another pass-through. To come around to the original characters in your question, I guess I'd say that, at the end, Pound had lyric moments in his so-called narrative, and I have narrative moments in my so-called lyric.

You describe Pound's Cantos *as a "non-narrative epic" [QN, 35], and rate Crane's* The Bridge *very highly [QN, 166]—can your work be described in similar terms, given the submerged structure of trilogies you have written?*

Well, I hope there is a connection, or continuum, or at least a series of bridges that hooks up and holds together my three trilogies. I see them as so joined, but I'm not sure others will. Which is all right, as all the books were written individually, and written to stand on their own, though I consciously worked on them to move from the hardpan of childhood (beginning with a poem called *Dog Creek Mainline* in *Hard Freight* [*CM*, 36]) up to the whispers and hard light of *The Appalachian Book of the Dead*. That is an unbroken movement to me, though not always a straight line sort of thing. I wasn't using *The Cantos* or *The Bridge* as a map or overlay. I suppose I smelled the smoke of Dante's fires in the air, but I never saw their lights. My construct is certainly non-linear and non-narrative, and tends, I think, to be circular. I would hope it (the structure) might resemble, at its close, the peripheries and interiors of a fabled island rising out of the sea that one might look for. But it more probably resembles the coral reef that surrounds the island—undeniably there, but submerged and, in the proper light, glittering. Another comparison, more terrestrial, might be Venice, connected by bridges. You can only get it whole when viewed from above. O well.

What organizing or underlying theme is expressed by the several poems entitled The Appalachian Book of the Dead *in your latest volume? Can you explain this a little for English readers unfamiliar with your work?*

During the course of the past thirty years, a rather large—indeed, perhaps, grandiose—project began taking shape in my work: a trio of trilogies is how it turned out, *Country Music*, collected work from the 1970s, *The World of the Ten Thousand Things*, work from the 1980s, and now *Negative Blue*, collected (selected) work from the 1990s. Three trilogies, each mirroring the other in structure and design, both within each trilogy and overall in the three books. *Appalachia* was not only the last book in the last trilogy, but it was also the last book of all three of the trilogies. I felt I should write a kind of Paradiso, or half-way house at least. The trouble was that everything the trilogies talked about refuted the idea, much less the actuality of a Paradiso. Besides, I wasn't really capable. So I hit upon the idea, at least to my mind the good idea of an ersatz Book of the Dead. Like the Egyptian one and the Tibetan one, it would be whisperings into the ear of the true believer, little verbal amulets, mantras, chants for those who *knew*, as the author did not, where they were going and why. As a structural theme it references back to the first two books of its own individual trilogy, but to the larger context of the two preceding ones as well. All in all, a "grand" design that I hope remains hidden, as each volume, and each trilogy, is independent and singular in its own way, though linked and locked in all down the line—at least in the mind and intentions of their creator.

Do you feel that the desire to create a "longer and more conversational" line is an exclusively American concern? In Quarter Notes, *you cite Pound, Williams, Olson and Justice.*

Well, I doubt that it's "exclusively" an American concern, but it certainly seems to be a predominant one. Whitman, obviously, set the game, and he set the bar as well. And at a pretty lofty level. We've all been jumping ever since. It's kind of our national pastime. Long Line. Baseball and Long Line. I don't know. Perhaps it keeps us from thinking we're still colonized. I'm surprised the Irish haven't tried it.

Black Zodiac seemed to me to be marked by a keen sense of mortality—death-haunted, even—would you agree?

Yes. It's the purgatorial book of the last trilogy. And you can't go through purgatory unless you're dead. It's the most tortuous of the three books, I'd say. Certainly compared to *Appalachia*, where The Appalachian Book of the Dead comes into play, and the relative quietness of syntax and subject matter takes effect. *Chickamauga* is an odd little inferno, really never getting past the anteroom of limbo, hellish enough for some people. It's a doorway, not a tunnel, to *Black Zodiac*, which suffers the purgatorial clear-out of all confessions—self-torture, self-mutation. Death-haunted, perhaps, but a way-station on the trail to a ghostlier X, a deadlier zone.

There is a playful element in some of your recent poems which reminds me of late Auden (wordplay/illusionary conversational tone): is this entirely incorrect?

Interesting segue here. Although I didn't have him in mind at all, one always hopes one's chops will catch the masters' ears. And he is certainly one of those. I never took anything from Auden except a profound admiration, amazement, and love of the way he used words. (I once, in 1964, was offered, from his vacated house on Ischia, all the books he had left when he transferred his summer residence from Italy to Austria. Unfortunately, they were almost all merely volumes he had selected for the Yale Younger Poets series, books I already owned. But I almost took something from him!) Like Yeats, he grows in stature in my eyes as the years go by. And in my ears as well. As I say, there is no influence there, but we all tend to loosen up a bit in our work as we get older, to let more light and air in. There may be some of that. And there's this—when I lived in Rome, 1963–65, I wrote nothing but metered and mostly rhymed verse, trying to learn how it was done. And at the end of my stay, I threw it all away, all two years' worth. Auden (along with Larkin) was one of my major models during this time. Possibly, thirty years later, some of that has risen to the surface. Cream does. Dead bodies do.

There are several admiring references to Philip Larkin in Halflife, *and to* The Less Deceived *in particular, which I found quite surprising [*Halflife, *106, 153, 154, 173]. You may be aware that Larkin's English reputation has see-sawed, particularly since the publication of his letters. What exactly did you take from him, and what, if anything, do you continue to take from his work?*

In my earlier days, back in the 1960s, for instance, I took Larkin's work as one of the paradigms (I think that's the current buzz word) of what the clear, clean, metrically accurate, emotionally resonant lyric poem could be (Donald Justice was another, as was Auden; two out of three were English). If I seem to mention *The Less Deceived*, it was because that was the book available in the first half of the decade, the time I began trying to write with some direction, when I was taking in everything I could lay my hands on to see what might fit for me. When *The Whitsun Weddings* appeared (I first found it in 1964 in the British Library in Rome), I switched my attention to it. As I gradually settled into my own poetic costume, over the years I ceased borrowing his things. But the memory of that early time is warmed back up any time I open one of his books. Each poem, to change the metaphor (or simile), is like a glowing room. As for what I take now, it's mostly a memory of one afternoon in 1983, in Oxford, looking up at a window in St John's College, Kingsley Amis turning to Edmund Keeley, our mutual friend, and me, along for the day-long crawl, and saying, "That's how Philip and I got in and out when we were late." That casement had all the shine of Juliet's window at that moment. As for the published letters, I thought them fascinating. We all have our sins, and I don't excuse anyone's, especially my own. But I think he wrote the best poems in England during the second half of the twentieth century. Nobody else, to my way of thinking, can lay a glove on him. He was to the second half what Auden was to the first, the best guy around. And, like Auden, he left us some permanent poems. A list of my candidates upon request.

Robert Graves seems to be tersely dismissed in one of the poems in Appalachia *[After Rereading Robert Graves, I Go Outside to Get My Head Together, in* NB, *186]. Is this a passing reference to* The White Goddess, *or are you in reaction to Graves' theories of the Muse?*

I *was* re-reading *The White Goddess* when I wrote the poem, and enjoying it, actually, especially the early Battle of the Trees. The poem is primarily in reaction to his theories of the Muse, though in the end, of course, it glancingly bows to them. Like Keats's, however, an awkward bow, and a partial one, partially unkept.

In other places, you have spoken of the monastic impulse behind poetry, and of wanting your work to be like "visionary frescoes on the walls of some out-of-the-way monastery" [QN, 81]: is there any connection between Graves and these ideas in your thinking?

None, really. One (Graves) is pagan, of course, the other meta-Christian. The one (Graves) was a spur-of-the-moment, one poem reaction to something I had been reading. The other is, for better or worse, a life-long obsession and artifact. In the good old days—say AD 200–400—in the switch-over from one religious venue to the next, there probably was much more of an actual connection. Let's face it, the Roman gods (not to mention their Greek ancestors) had a very seductive element to them. Propitiation even turned a head or two. But for me, there wouldn't have been enough ascetic deprivation in it, somehow. Give me my wall, put on my smock, I have a monastery in me. I'm afraid I'm drawn to absences—what's missing is always more sensuous and alluring than what's there.

At the beginning of Halflife, *you state "theory comes after the fact, it is not the fact"* [Halflife, 3], *and oppose this to the line of poetry: is this still your opinion?*

Actually, yes I do. That petulant little rant about the Line and Poetry and Language was, not surprisingly, tangentially aimed at Language Poetries and their attendant pedantries. A side-swipe on the way to, I hope, a larger truth—which is that poetry, if not Platonic, is surely numinous. And luminous. And exists outside the realm of theory. And prior to it, not successive. No Deconstruction first, then deconstructed poems (Language Poetry). No Post-Structuralism then de—as it were—structured poems (Language Poetry). It's a cart-and-horse, chicken-and-egg sort of thing. In the old days, poems happened and then people set about writing criticism to justify their existence. None of this writing poems to justify the tenets of critical theory. Death of the author is one thing, death of the poem is another. And lately I've been mulling over the re-discovered bone patterns of my new stance, the Death of the Reader. It will put everyone in his proper place, and everything in perspective.

You have commented that Christianity is "something to work against" [Halflife, 110], *and yet poems like* Ostinato and Drone *[NB, 169] and* It's Turtles all the Way Down *[NB, 170] in* Appalachia *seem to imply that your thinking has moved on. Is this true?*

I don't know that "moved on" is the term. Perhaps it is. Moved around, more likely. I don't know why, but there's something comforting in thinking one doesn't have to be extra-terrestrial in order to come to terms with things. That's part of the lure of the Orient, I guess. Also that it's dabble-friendly, in ways that the Occident is not. When you try to get out from under something—a rock, let's say—you're in the open, and susceptible to targets of opportunity. Your rock, however, forever remains your rock. Even if you can't roll it away. My main mojo is Christian, but that is *what* it is, a mojo. It's not a map. And I'm a magpie. Whatever shines. This is always a difficult subject, of course. One tends to be like a glider in one's spiritual life. When the proper hook and line comes along, one is seized and lifted up. Ultimately, of course, one has to cut oneself loose and ride the thermals and undefiable dogmas of gravity. And finally come to rest. It's the glide that's glittering, the unalterable law of descent. The more one's thinking moves on, the more it stays the same.

In the poem Quotations *[NB, 160] there seems to be a deliberate looseness. It reads almost like one of your "Improvisations." Bearing in mind your comments on rhetoric in* Halflife, *this sounds like a fairly deliberate design. Would you care to confirm or strenuously deny this hunch?*

It is loose, and, indeed, it is on purpose. I had always, for almost thirty years, wanted to make a poem out of pieces of other poems, but so that it didn't sound, to me, as though it *were* just other poems. As though it seemed to have, if not coherence, a time line and a line of march of its own. This is as close as I've been able to come, going from an illusion to a comment in the first section, to a partial quotation in the second, to a third section made up entirely of another text, and then a final section where it's about half and half, and references back, at least in overall suggestiveness, to the points of the other three. Probably a silly enterprise, but it was all very structured and very calculated on my part and is, by necessity, on the surface seemingly loose to the point of apparent arbitrariness, but underneath, in the structural joints and joists of intention, very related and interwoven. It's easy to quote, but difficult to make a quotation over into your own image. I'm still thinking about it, as I haven't got it quite right yet.

Followers of "title-ism," the movement invented and spearheaded by yourself and Charles Simic, will relish some of the newer poems, such as If This is Where God's At, Why is That Fish Dead? *[SHS, 16] and* If My Glasses Were Better, I Could See Where I'm Headed For *[SHS, 19]. Are there any others we should look forward to?*

The poems you mention are from a group of ten fourteen-line poems, gathered under the rubric *Millennium Blues*. Many of the titles represent a spike in the ongoing graph of Titleism. They may also represent one in its heart. It's hard to tell. I'm always vamping at the edge of that envelope. Even as we speak. So to speak. Watch this space.

Chapter 11

An Interview by Willard Spiegelman

Night Rider

Winter blue moon, light like a wax-thin slice of *finocchio*,
So grainy, so white.
It's 1999, last night of January,
Everything order and form out back, everything in its place
Ready for praise—which I give—in its ghost and disguise.

Still, something is calling us, something not unlike unbeing.
The lure of the incidental calls,
                      immensity beckons.
All who have turned from memory, all who have not turned,
One by one we are called,
                  one by one we are chosen—
The fire here is the fire there, ash, and the sure-fire end of ash.

O Something, be with me, time is short.
Our days are like slipped stitches,
                      the cloth is wide and deep.
Our prayers go unanswered, if prayers they are, our whispers unheard.
No earth, no heaven.
Thus are we summoned, we who have not understood this.

That which was broken away from you will be restored,
That which time took, that which earth borrowed, will be returned,
It says somewhere in a book.
It also says, the shadow of light is within us.

Originally published in The Literary Imagination *2, no. 1 (Winter 2000): 104.*

It also says, the tomb of the body is forgetfulness.
Not too much thought of endgame today, however, blue
Crack in the east, blue
                crinkle and dip

Of Piedmont toward Tidewater,
Central Virginia suddenly sunlight and loose glass
As February's kaleidoscope turns once, then turns again.

But always, like the distant susurration of surf
Heard and half-heard in the burning ear—
I am the undefiled and incorruptible one;
I do not exist, as everything mortal exists in me,
Sunfall like water sheen in backwash across the yard.

Nothing prepares the brain
                        for the heavy changes in the heart.
Nothing prepares the soul for metaphor's sleight-of-hand.
Nothing prepares the left hand—luminous twin—for the sins of the right.
Nothing prepares the absence of pain for the presence of pain.
Nothing prepares what is for what's not.

One gets tired.
The sun goes up and the sun goes down and one gets tired.
When evening comes, the doves will settle down in the holly tree,
The story goes. When evening comes,
                        the winds will be black,
And treetops, even without their leaves, will start to sway.

Meanwhile, let's tinker around some with the afternoon,
Its lack of smell, its half-broken and unmended trees,
Its text of appearances
                    that belies the world as we must read it,
Slowly now, uninterruptedly,
More shadow than light, more shade than dark on the clean page.

Moon partial tonight,
                a Tuscan bean in a non–Tuscan sky,
A promise of what's to come.
Not much to say to what is,
The dark almost absolute down here,
                        lack of familiar things,
A promise partially kept.

Even so, I think it's all incomprehensible,
Everything that we look at.
Much easier, I think, to imagine the abyss, just there,
The other side of the hedge,
      than to conjure the hedge,
The trees, and time like a puddle of water and not a stream.

Below me, red-clay Rivanna, river of Lethe
I cross and re-cross each day.
The world, I think, was made by mistake.
         Perishable, mortal,
It is like us, its children, pale and predictable.
Unlike the abyss, such black, such immortal water.

———

Still night, unholy night, dark of the moon,
        pagan stars
A twice-splattered narrative
Retracked in their intervals like secret thoughts through the black sky.
We all have our ways of telling things,
Great chunks of dead flesh broken up into lines of poetry.

We all have our ways of keeping the Buddha alive
As he comes forth, a common pilgrim, out of the thick forest.
We all have our ways of directing the sacrificial horse
Back to the place of sacrifice,
      as if he'd appeared
By chance, though guided, the Indians say, like Buddha imperceptibly.

And there's his arrangement in the sky.
And here's his arrangement on the ground,
         pleasure of the without,
Brittle and secondary February bloom stalks,
Trees leafless and shadowless
Just under Orion, just west of the Pleiades.

———

Snuff end of February, no moon and
        cold tongs to the touch,
Year of the Rabbit, 15 degrees.
Crunch, crunch goes grass like broken head hair,
Our breath like Apache smoke signals
         —they come, they come—
From one yard to the next. But they don't come, Lord, they don't.

> If I had, as Robert Johnson says, possession over Judgment Day,
> No stone would rest unrisen,
> And life, which promises only that we will desire
> Only the things we can't have,
> Would be rolled away,
>   cool dark of cave mouth first exit,
> Crocus heads gazing quietly at the distant southern hills.
> As one absorbed in looking around,
>   each time I've looked, each time it's new—
> Each time I said it, I got it wrong.
> In front of me, two plus two, behind me, two plus two.
> If I could do what I thought I could do, I would leave no trace.

WS: *You seem to be veering with a bit of wariness toward the millennium, don't you agree? This poem [*Night Rider*] rehearses so many of your perennial concerns, themes, and techniques that I am tempted to call it a summary as well as an introduction to "Charles Wright." What would you say to someone reading you—this poem, in this journal—for the first time?*

CW: Well, I guess I'd say that the poem is representative, or at least indicative, of manners, matters, and motions I have come to believe are important to me (and, I guess, by extension, my work). And which I try to give tongue to. I hope it would show what I think is my trademark system of sound patterns, lineation, and verbal structure. I suppose I would say they should read the "dropped" lines as extensions of the lines they are dropped from, with a rather pronounced caesura. I suppose I would say that the sound pattern runs from stanza to stanza throughout the whole poem, and not just within each isolated stanza. And I suppose I would say that the concerns the poem is confronting, which it talks about, are, as you suggest, continuing ones for me, and are likely to remain so. When one imagines one has the beast in view, it seems silly and sloppy to suddenly go in another direction.

As for the millennium, I'm not sure what you mean. It's true the poem seems to lug out toward the end of something, but I'm not sure it's the millennium. One religion's millennium is another religion's lunch. The end is not an abstraction, no matter how much we would like it to be. And no matter how much they keep telling us it is. And as for veering warily toward it, I veer warily toward everything, particularly things with double consonants.

But in the end I'd have to agree with you, I suppose, that *Night Rider* has the trappings, at least, of a summation of some of my more recent, and more sticky, concerns. It certainly doesn't encompass *everything* I've worked through over the years, but a right smart amount. As to what I would say to someone, I guess I'd say to look upon it as an outpost, not an empire, and don't despair.

As befits your subject here you seem also to be returning to some biblical cadences, in phrasing and imagery, that for some years had been absent in your work. At the

11. AN INTERVIEW BY WILLARD SPIEGELMAN

same time I can't I help thinking that the opening of the poem, with its night scene, and the presence of spectral, ghostly pallor, recalls your Homage to Paul Cezanne *[WTTT, 3–10], almost twenty years back, which some people think of as your greatest poem.*

Odd you should say that. About *Paul Cézanne*, I mean. As I'm looking quickly at it here—and trying to remember just what I had in mind with *Cézanne* so many years ago—one could almost make a case for the first section of *Night Rider* here as a reprise of what I was trying to get at in the whole eight sections of *Cézanne*. So maybe I'm getting a bit better at squeezing things down. Or perhaps I'm merely getting less imagistic and more didactic, more one-dimensional. I hope it's not the latter, of course, but when you work the same ground, you're bound to turn up some old spuds. No help for that, I'm afraid. *Cézanne* is one of the few poems of mine that I continue to have an affection for, I must say. I was trying to get at something through formal technique that can't be reached in that way, and it was a great learning experience for me. Which is why, perhaps, I keep trying to get at the same subject matter in other poems in different ways, so many years later. I had had (and continue to have, I guess) a mild love affair between the technique of lineation in poems and "lineation" in painting, and was hoping to marry them off. It didn't quite take, but it was torrid for awhile. Finally, as Mark Rothko said, vis-à-vis his own work, it wasn't about painting; it was beyond painting.[1] I'd have to echo that as far as poetry is concerned. It's beyond poetry. So I backed off match-making and returned to the book.

Which you also bring up, right? Though a different Book. I'm not so sure that what you are talking about is so much "return" to some of the cadences—I suppose Bibliocentric—I've laundered and used before, as it is a reemergence of them in a more visual incarnation. Which is to say that I think they are always lurking just under the surface of everything I write. From time to time they rise up out of the ground like an underground river, or stream, say, that's been following my steps everywhere I walk. Early Episcopalianism is a dark and deep water. Someone asked me recently how I could bear not being Jewish. I told him I already had plenty of guilt and didn't need any more. He laughed and asked what I attributed this donnée to. I answered, tongue again in the vicinity of my cheek, early Episcopalianism. And so he let me off the hook. Some things just burr up and stick with you forever. These cadences, so-called, are what I started with, and I guess I'll ride that horse till we both drop. Or till I do.

The poem begins, like so many from your recent trilogy of short poems, with mere phrases. Why does it often take you a while to develop full sentences with subjects and verbs?

I think the idea of phrases (which I myself wouldn't call "mere") comes initially from a rhythm I hear in my head. A sort of, often, staccato tonguing, if you will, that then eases, or segues, into a calmer, quieter, longer run. Or it doesn't segue in that direction, but continues its, I hope, melodic abruptness. In any case, it comes from rhythmical effect, and substitutes, at least in my mind, for subjects and verbs. Which is to say, the proper distribution of fragments and phrases, rhythmically charged, can become, at least to the ear and to the senses, grammatically grounded full sentences of a kind of virtual grammar and syntax.

Do you see individual items first, and actions only afterwards? Do you want to produce some equivalent to a painted or filmed "scene," relying on distinct or small images?

It also may be that I do see, and think of, individual items first and "actions" later. Again, however, I would say that the proper distribution of things and items, the right ones in the right order, becomes its own action. And it also may be (in fact, I'm sure it plays a large part) that what I was talking about just a moment ago—about the Cézanne poem and its attempts to apply painting techniques to verbal "planing" and lineation—does have a great deal to do with the process. I think I do still see the poem as lined and layered, built up piece by piece into a kind of seamless whole, not so much like a wall, but an iconostasis, a screen of images, in the perfect poem, each line is an icon. Naturally, I haven't come close to that yet, but my application and my tendencies are always in that direction.

Is this what you might acknowledge as your "Imagist" tendencies? Or your inheritance from Ezra Pound, whom you have long cited us your first major poetic influence?

I guess, yes, I would say that all this devolves, or smokes up, from my lifelong "imagist" tendencies (small *i*, however), and the notion that no idea in itself is as strong as an image presented which contains that idea. Or the idea of that idea. If that's an "Imagist" tendency, so be it. I don't place myself in that long gray line, but I may ghost in and out of it from time to time.

I have, indeed, in a younger, more naive period, cited Pound as my first major poetic influence. At least from a writer. And, boy, have I been hoisted on that halyard ever since. I read Pound forty years ago. He was the first poet I ever read seriously, and I haven't had much to do with him since (though I did teach a seminar at UC Irvine on him about twenty years ago). I wasn't sophisticated enough at the time to keep my mouth shut, to, as Robert Frost advised, leave no tracks. In any case, sure, I learned a lot from him. I'm proud to have learned from a great poet and not someone popular from the generation above me, as is so often, and unwisely, the case. And from whom one has to go about unlearning over the years. I've said what I have to say about Pound—the great poet gone wrong, botching his own work, unable to keep his public mouth shut (as Eliot did, as others did), a small-time Lear ranting and temporarily insane in the cages (where, ironically, he wrote some of his most beautiful stuff), all that—and I suppose my imagistic tendencies are an inheritance from Pound. If so, I thank him again and cross to the other side of the street. I continue to think of him as one of the major America poetic presences of the century, along with Williams, Stevens, and Frost. Old loves rise up from the dark every so often, but it's best remembered that the dark is where they live now. Whatever it was I got from him I got decades ago, and have since assimilated or subsumed into my own manner. Whatever that manner is. I thank him for early advice, I thank him for opening the poetic impulse in me that until I read him had found no outlet, but I carry no torch.

Speaking of Pound, in what ways do you think that you have moved away from him in the past forty years? Are you aware of being influenced, now by your contemporaries or even (as the years go by) by your somewhat younger colleagues? Mark Strand would seem an obvious stylistic parallel and Jorie Graham, for all of the obvious differences between the two of you, might be someone from whom you might claim to have learned something.

Well, the first part of that question I think I've just been talking about. As far as I've always been concerned, there hasn't been that much to move away from. I've never cottoned to his subject matter, for instance, or his grandiosity or his public posturing. I have honored him, and read him, and revered him for the purity of his lyricism, for his humanity and poignancy in *The Pisan Cantos*, and for his generosity to other writers, and the iron belief he had in the sanctity and transubstantiational qualities of literature. And culture in general. I probably got the idea for the "dropped" line from him, though I have made it rhythmically and visually different from him and his—his, for instance, almost always seems to be two individual lines, or more, while mine is always a continuation of the line it's dropped from, the line that precedes it, a giant caesura, if you will, a change in pitch, but the same tune—it's all the same long line. I probably picked up my fondness for the seven-syllable line from him (though more likely that comes from Thom Gunn and Donald Justice), although the lines I admired were usually eight syllables. And I got, no doubt, my slight education in the value of quantity in the free verse line, the length, duration, and vital importance of vowel sounds, and the importance of the sound of syllables themselves, from him and his insistence on the "musical phrase" (whatever *that* is), which probably rises out of the virtual impossibility of applying classical quantitative meters to stressed English verse, but whose attempt has been made, of course, by some. And by some very recently, in fact. By the metrical magus Donald Justice, to be exact. The watered down versions, the sensibility to the sound patterns and play-offs, in free verse do offer aural possibilities strictly stressed verse lines don't. I probably picked up some of that from him. But to answer your question, I've moved away as much as possible. He is just one piece of a mosaic of influences. Every writer has a mosaic of influences. Different pieces, perhaps, but each man his own mosaic. It can't be otherwise. Unless you're the guy who said the first word, and that's no one I know.

    I don't, actually, feel I'm being influenced by my contemporaries now, though, of course, I have been in my earlier days. Strand, for one, when I was a student and he was my friend, my much more advanced friend, at Iowa. And Donald Justice, who was my teacher at Iowa, was an early influence, Charles Simic's methods, especially his beautiful way with images and his belief in, and practice of, strong lineation, haven't been an influence, but something I've long admired. James Tate's incredible imagination and linguistic acrobatics for over thirty years have been a source of deep pleasure and deep amazement to me, but not an influence exactly. These days I seem to be influenced, if at all, by older things, masters I go back to—Stevens, Yeats, Celan, Eliot, people like that—and read, not just for pleasure, but also for wisdom.

I wish I could say I have been currently influenced by some younger person or persons, as I think it would be very healthy, but, alas, I don't think I have been. You mention Jorie Graham. I wouldn't mind, as you say, laying claim to some influence there, but it's not so. I have long admired both her intelligence and her work. But her recent work seems to be going in a direction I am probably not prepared to follow. There is a dramatic construct to the new poems I've seen (from the book *Swarm*) where she is the central speaker and the broken fragments and utterances serve as a kind of summing up, or, even, summoning up, of large notions in a fin-de-siècle, twentieth-century style. A kind of performance for the page, out of *Medea* or Robert Browning. Fascinating, as her work always has been from the beginning, Ovidian in its metamorphoses, but a stage I don't see myself or my work in or on. Too set in my ways, probably. But she's top dollar, and endlessly protean in her work.

Amplifying the last question, I am tempted to wonder: How does a "mature" poet continue to grow, to change, without unnecessarily repeating himself? Many of your readers—both fans and somewhat impatient critics—might accuse you (or thank you) for treading the same paths, with the same tonalities, over decades. How would you characterize the development of your poetry?

How sweet and evasive that question is. In other words, why do I keep on repeating myself, imitating myself? Well, who better to repeat, who better to imitate when he has finally figured out what he wants to say, and how he wants to say it? I said earlier that if you work the same ground over a period of time, you're bound to turn up some old spuds. What I didn't say was that, if the ground has been used properly, you're going to grow bigger and better stuff. Unless, of course, the weather turns on you, and then you're in an act of God, and helpless. How, indeed, to continue to grow and to change and not just repeat yourself, but to dig deeper, to see how far down you can get? Ah, the answer to that question brings the priest and the doctor in their long coats running over the fields. Actually the received wisdom is "curiosity," and I am sure there is a great deal of truth in that. New exits, new entrances. But the same building, I would add. Especially if you think you've got the right address. Go on in. Go on further in. Go on further in differently.

What I hope has happened to my stuff is what I mentioned earlier, that I'm able to say in a shorter space, and to say more exactly and precisely, what I've been trying to say all along. One hopes the rhythms haven't gotten stale or slack. One hopes the tones and pitches are more acute and accurate. One hopes the music is more diversified and delineated. One hopes that the thing said is the thing said differently and more distinctly. One hopes the work is disassembled and put back together likewise. To refer back to a previous question, I would hope I have taken my old themes and preoccupations and made them new in ways that aren't boring and aren't repetitive. Both to me and to my imagined, but probably imaginary, reader.

11. AN INTERVIEW BY WILLARD SPIEGELMAN

*As so often in your poetry, the landscape in this poem [*Night Rider*] offers both hope and evidence of failure. When you look outward, in your backyard, or wherever you happen to be, are you simultaneously enlightened and frustrated? Or perhaps you are aware of a sequence, rather than a simultaneity, of emotional as well as artistic responses to what lies outside the self?*

First, I'm usually delighted just seeing what I see, delight in its being there and delight in the seeing. Then if I drift into a deep seeing, so to speak, a contemplative way of looking, I guess I begin to be, if not enlightened, at least lightened. And if I become that, then I can become othered. The state of becoming enlightened is a line I have yet to cross, I think. In Kingsport (Tennessee) where I grew up, the state line was on the other side of the Holston River, just a little out of town. Virginia was the state. Enlightenment is like that, just across the line on the other side of the river. So what I have is a sense of wonderment and discovery, constant rediscovery, of the magnitude and multiple tables of the natural world, the possibilities of available entrance into it, and what might be just behind or just beyond it, and then the almost constant frustration, to use your word, of being unable, incapable, or not assigned, somehow, to avail myself of such entrances. Either through personal ineptitude, generic ineptitude, or natural inability. Or impossibility, I guess I should say. Outside the self is the other self. A bright day in the weeds or a dark night in the soul, it's still other and still otherwise, sequential or simultaneous. Outside that other self is enlightenment and golden ladders. A twice-torn journey, a hard trip. As for the last part of the question, most of my emotional responses to things and ideas turn inevitably "artistic" as I try to make sense of them. Not, however, a numerable or patterned sequence of events or mini-responses. If anything happens, it seems to happen at once, or "they" seem to happen simultaneously and I reach for a pencil and a place to stand.

Thwarted or half-suppressed religious impulses lie close beneath the surface of much of your work. I have the sense from Night Rider *that the religious obsessions (including fear of death, concerns about an afterlife, a willingness to believe in a "soul," however that map be defined) of your youth are returning to you in late middle age. Is this so?*

Yes, that's so, somewhat to my surprise. Time, I suppose, the great provocateur. Also an increasing sense of I guess ease in what I've always been trying to get a handle on (which is to say, there is no, I've finally discovered, handle to get on, so there seems little reason to feint and juke and try, as it were, to run around it—running into it is, perhaps, a preferable way) and coming to terms with, so why not just sit it out in the open and talk to it. It won't talk back, as I've discovered, so camouflage and wily evasions no longer seem as necessary, though sometimes they still seem prudent.

With what provocations, and with what poetic consequences does this occur?

This is a squishy area for me, and always has been, as far as poetic consequences are concerned, the area of, for lack of a better word, "spiritual" things. As I say, I have been riding this horse ever since I began writing poems, though I often disguised it as a bird or an automobile. In other words, I think I told it true, but, boy, did I tell it slant. After 60, you begin to straighten things out a bit. Each passing year, for me, it has gotten straighter and straighter. To the point now where the horse has been rode hard, but he's not put up wet any longer. As St. John of the Cross advised long ago, I seem to have found my true road, so, to make the final mix in the metaphor, I've closed my eyes and begun to walk in the dark.

Much of the "weariness" in this poem reminds me of many of Wallace Stevens's characteristic maneuvers (this is especially true in the third stanza and its gorgeous depiction of winter's inevitable beauties). Have you been reading him in new, different, or deeper ways recently? Your last stanza, with its line "...we will desire / Only the things we can't have," is especially Stevensian (cf. "And not to have is the beginning of desire"). Do you agree?

People are always trying to pin Wallace Stevens on me. Which is all right, as he is not the tail to my donkey. Though I do read him, and admire him more and more the older I get. He's one of the poets, as I said earlier, I go to the shelf for at night when I feel like a drink of poetry. But I still don't—or haven't—read him in a systematic or nefarious way, i.e., he's not a house I've burgled very often. Just the odd plastic flamingo or wooden duck from the lawn over the years.

Still, the little repetition riff in what you call the third stanza (and I would call the third section) is most probably Stevensian—at least it's the sort of maneuver he would do from time to time. I find I do it from time to time, though not thinking, or (more importantly) knowing it came from Wally World. Maybe on one of those nights I went to the bookshelf I had a couple of drinks too many from *The Collected Poems*. As usual in such cases, I hadn't meant to, if I did, and didn't want to as well.

I suppose one of the reasons I like to read Stevens now (and Yeats and Celan) is that there is in them a kind of acceptance of the *stanchezza profonda*, the deep exhaustion, at the center of things which most of us come in contact with as we get older, I don't mean a physical tiredness (though there is some of that), but the spiritual weariness we bump up against in middle-age, a weariness, I might add, we never really grapple with and certainly never conquer, but which we acknowledge and give its due. So I suppose if that's "a new, different" way of reading Stevens, when I read him, I confess I have done that. But, as I say, I do it with almost all the older masters I tend to read now. Hardy, for instance, recently. Donald Justice has expressed this common failing and inevitability very beautifully in his later poems.

As for the "desire" line of mine in the last section, I have no inkling that that was/is Stevensian. Of course, if you're looking, everything sounds like Stevens. He did touch all the bases, you know. He went all the way around.

One (perhaps) debt to Stevens is your use of the fifteen-line, three-stanza, unit. What makes you decide upon one kind of organization for it poem instead of another?

11. An Interview by Willard Spiegelman

Odd that you should add-on a question about Stevens and technical details. Especially the fifteen-line, three-stanza unit, since that's been my favorite. Or was in my earlier, surely pre-Stevensian (if I am now, as you hint, in my Stevensian mode) days. It was my go-to form way back in my *Hard Freight*, *Bloodlines* time. I felt very comfortable with it, and in it, rather like—as I once said—a basketball player who feels most comfortable shooting from a certain spot on the floor. I *love* the fifteen-line poem and can say, categorically, that mine has no reference to Stevens. It, in my case, seems to have evolved, like the duckbilled platypus, to a condition of ease and *Dasein* that nature intended me to have whenever I needed it.

As for organization of my poems, at least stanzaically, however the first group of lines arranges itself, however many the number of lines, that's my pattern for the rest of the poem. Unless the poem seems to call out for an arbitrary stanza base, i.e., differently numbered ones. This tends to happen if the thought patterns break down in smaller units, such as two- or three-line groups. I seem to have a lot of four-, five-, and six-line stanzas, for some reason. Perhaps that's as long as I can keep a stream of thought in my head. I *am* addicted to stanzas, however, and hardly ever, if ever, have just a block of lines down the page. That looks ugly to me, and rather suffocating, without breathing spaces or air vents.

As far as long and short poems go, it depends if I think I've got more to say on a given subject, or a different approach to a subject that dictates length—although I have arbitrarily set certain lengths to poems, usually temporal rather than spatial. For instance, *The Southern Cross* some years ago was a designated six-month poem: I wrote for six months and that was the "structure" of the poem (guided a bit by me, of course, toward the end, and ending). *A Journal of the Year of the Ox* was a yearlong effort, January to December 1985 (again, steered a bit the last month or so, and "plotted" somewhat throughout the body of the poem). The shorter poems tend to last until what I can see morphs into what I can't see. And then to the end of that.

Most often, the poem itself makes the decision. I hop along until I catch up and bring the thing to a halt. It's seldom that I plan and carry through a flow-through organization of an entire poem. I'm usually just along for the ride.

This poem is like a smaller version of some of your longer journal poems. It moves from late January through (early?) February to perhaps some unspecified later date, and from the chill of winter to something like the promise of spring, with crocus heads "gazing quietly at the distant southern hills." Do you want your readers to have a sense of progress, through time, to some hope for rebirth and—if not Christian resurrection—new growth?

Yes, I do. I don't have the notebook here in which I actually wrote the poem, but it would have the completion date in it. Still, it ends toward the end of February, as that's when the crocus start up in Charlottesville—mid- to late February. I am addicted to the seasons, as is very evident. It's a structural wheel I can't seem, like St. Catherine, to get off of. And as a structure, it suits my temperament as well as my purposes. Especially as I approach late middle-age, I have an almost visceral reaction to, and appreciation of, the changes and the portents each carries on its back and inside its body of mythology. Autumn was always my favorite, the romantic favorite, until recently. Now spring holds the field, and the constant tiny chant and drumbeat of "begin again, begin again," succors me in. Most of my poems, I find, are about progress of some sort, some sallying forth, some step-by-step slog through the mud of time. Christian resurrection is not in this picture, however, although no doubt the idea of all that came from mythology's backyard. The seasons have been at the heart of the heart of the beast since the beast first drew breath. And that breath was Primavera's wing draft. Rebirth, new growth, the old man's mantra. You bet.

Like many other critics and general readers, I have remarked (in print) on your mastery (like Tennyson) of melancholy in its manifold moods. And yet I think it's clear that most readers derive enormous pleasure from your poetry, appreciating your eye for natural beauty, for the enormous possibilities for hope in the world. Does Charles Wright, man and/or poet, not find similar happiness in the ten thousand things of this world?

The things of this world are my only happiness. I include in such things, of course, the wriggling and squeaks I give forth, like a caught mouse under a cat's paw, in my writing and non-attainments about the toothed and long-tongued mouth of the other one. As I once said in a verse, "what gifts there are are all here, in this world" [*Italian Days*, in *WTTT*, 93]. I am a melancholy man by temperament, I fear, and my forays into it in my work are not so much "literary" as personal, especially when I am concentrating on metaquotidian things. It's the things of this world that hold me in thrall, however, and set the mind to music and the heart to whatever happiness it is that the heart uncovers. And also one has to remember that a penchant for melancholy, a substantive and sustaining melancholy, becomes a thing in itself in the long run, tactile and rubbable, and becomes a living and generative part of the world of the ten thousand things.

You acknowledge at the end of the poem, with some frustration, that every time you "said it" you "got it wrong." Surely this is the prime motivation of any creative artist: if you ever thought you got it right you would either stop writing or just die, wouldn't you?

Yes, I would.

We (and you) should be grateful for the chronic dissatisfactions that creep into your poems, as both provocation and subject matter.

I build a little altar almost daily to the wrinkle-browed, scowling and sullen god of Dissatisfaction who is my pimp and protector. No creeper he. He rushes in, as they say in another context, where angels fear to tread. As you say, if I ever "got it right," I wouldn't know what to do with myself. All my poems are brief chants and off-key hymns to God D. The next step would be E, of course, and that's for Enlightenment, and we've already talked about that a while ago. I suppose if I ever got it "right," everything in place and each word snug and sure, when the last period was placed the Rapture would set in, kick in, and all that would be left of me would be my loafers smoking under my desk. Do I want that? Hmmm. To a writer, Dissatisfaction is next to Godliness. One must nurture it and keep its altar clean and constantly find and put forth new offerings for its consumption. And I am, as you suggest, forever grateful to it, both as provocation and subject matter, for its presence and over-shadowing in my life and writing. Which are, of course, the same.

You would "leave no trace," you say in the last line. Your poetry has always been concerned with traces and tracing: lines, vestiges, ghostly hints, sketches—many synonyms come to mind. Such tracing might explain in part your tendency, which I mentioned earlier, to use verbless phrases, instead of full sentences, at crucial junctures in your poems. Does tracing, rather than fleshing out bespeak a desire to keep things light and tentative? A fear of filling things in? Of being stopped in your tracks? I think, as well, of your own written appreciations of artists like Cézanne, Morandi, and Mondrian, all of whom are deeply concerned with the relationship between inside and outside, between getting things in and keeping them out, inclusion and exclusion. Can you comment?

Keeping things apart, leaving things out, blank canvas, blank page spaces, not quite completing what is obvious, completing what is not obvious, the idea of knowing what comes next and then declining to say it, or fill it in, determination to keep the circle from touching—one works, as I once said, in the synapse, in the electric field between what is and what isn't, between the beginning and the beginning. It's not so much a desire to keep things tentative as one to keep things from touching, from becoming complete and becoming final. One wants to feel the kinetics, the possibilities, always the what's-left-to-do. If you know what it is, and you know where it goes, the longer you can keep it out, the deeper it will go once you put it in. Exile's the ultimate synapse—from there you can go anywhere. Cézanne, Matisse, Morandi, and Mondrian—negative transcendence, what you take out is stronger than what you put in. There are no Gods, there are only saints.

Where to now?

~~Disneyland~~. ~~Disneyworld~~. Dollywood.

CHAPTER 12

An Interview by Ted Genoways

All my poems seem to be an ongoing argument with myself about the unlikelihood of salvation.
—Charles Wright, Halflife [37]

TG: *Talk a bit about what drew you to poetry.*

CW: Well, I had no interest at all until I graduated from college and realized I wouldn't be able to write prose, because I had tried to write stories and they had all ended up purple: you know, no storyline and action, no definition of any kind. And I can remember sitting in the Bachelor Officers' Quarters at Ft. Holabird, Maryland, and being very proud of myself one evening, because everyone else had gone to the bar and I sat home drinking wine and reading a book of Chinese poems—translations I had found somewhere. And I don't know whether I liked the poems so much or whether I liked the idea of myself staying away from the riffraff and reading a book of Chinese poems as a twenty-two-year-old second lieutenant. Right after that, I remember going to New York on leave for the weekend and buying—since I was interested in poems by that time (in the abstract)—a copy of *The Selected Poems of Ezra Pound*. When I went out to California to the language school, I didn't have time to do that sort of business. I was studying every night for hours and every weekend, but I still had Pound's *Selected Poems*, and I took that to Europe. When I got to Italy, the book of Chinese poems, somewhere in the mists, got lost.

    In March 1959, two months after I got to Verona, where I was stationed, a friend of mine had borrowed—when he found out that I had it—the *Selected Poems* of Pound, and he gave it back to me. I told him I was going one afternoon to Lake Garda, and he said, "Read this poem, *Blandula, Tenulla, Vagula*, because you will be sitting at the end of Sirmione Peninsula on Catullus's supposed villa." And I did, and I thought it was fabulous. And it didn't have a storyline; it was a lyric poem. It worked by accretion—it described the landscape; it had interior questions that were unanswerable, the

Originally published in Southern Review 36 (Spring 2000): 442–52.

rhetorical questions one tends to ask in one's life. I thought this was pretty much it, and from then on I got very much interested in trying to write poems. Or what I thought were poems. I didn't know what a poem was. Of course, I'd taken English courses in college, but I never paid much attention to poetry ... but I started hearing something, and I continued to hear it as I moved through the rest of the *Selected Poems*.

There was an old bookstore on Villa Mazzini where Vanni Schweiwiller published fine-press books. *All'insignia del Pesce d'Oro*: at the sign of the golden fish. That was his logo. Pound was so weird at that time—just one year back from St. Elizabeth's and living up in Milano—that he would let Schweiwiller, who had a little press in Verona, have the first editions of his poems; then they would go to Faber & Faber, then to New Directions. This little bookstore had these editions of the cantos, of odd poems and translations, and it also had commemorative items. So there was access to some Pound material. That was basically how I came to it, and that was the only thing I knew about poetry—which wasn't enough, of course, but it was a start. I got a tune in my head. And from there I went to Iowa, where I was never officially admitted. I just sort of walked in and started taking classes. No one knew any different, because there were two teachers [Donald Justice and Paul Engle], and each thought the other had taken me in over the summer. It was very loosely run in those days. I think it was actually much more interesting, and I can say that, because I've taught in the current one. I realized from the first day that *The Selected Poems* of Ezra Pound was not going to get me very far in the workshop, and so I had better start reading something else.

When you got to Iowa, you began schooling yourself in and writing a lot of formal poetry.

Yes, well.... It was mostly during the three years afterward—two in Italy and then the third year back at Iowa—that I was writing in pentameter and rhyme and meter, trying to get that under some kind of control. At least get a handle on it. I did experiment with that some at Iowa in the first two years, but since everybody else was doing syllables, hey, why shouldn't I? I didn't know anything; I was doing whatever was happening.

I was very lucky to be there during the breakup of the fifties glacier of strict formalism that Iowa had had. There was still enough of that ice around so that I could find out what it was about, but people were leaning toward freer movement in their lines. Syllables were a halfway house. People had been trying to write some free verse, of course, but it was still OK, and even applauded, to write formal meters too. At the same time, people were doing prose poems. It was a good time; a lot of things were going on.

The syllables you began writing, those that appeared in The Grave of the Right Hand, *are all either five-syllable or seven-syllable lines. And your lines still have odd syllable counts.*

Well, except for every once in a great while.

What is the appeal of the odd-syllable line?

For one thing, I like numbers. I graduated from high school in '53, college in '57, and my laundry number in college was 597.... There are all these odd numbers. But mostly it was to keep it out of any kind of normal progression, which is to say that if you have even numbers you're more likely to fall into tetrameter or pentameter. Easier to keep it out—but still have the ghost of it—with the odd, because you get an extra little syllable. The seven-syllable line is still my ur-line even now, thirty-five years later. And my seven-syllable line will stretch to thirteen, another one I like, or fifteen or seventeen, sometimes nineteen, and then back down to as low as three or five. But the seven-syllable line is the one everything starts from—either goes forward from or stays back from. I suppose that's because once I started doing that I really heard it in my head, and I can't get it out. Sort of like someone learned pentameter and then did other things, but when they come back without thinking to what a line of poetry sounds like, it always sounds like pentameter. Well, I didn't have that; I had the seven-syllable line, and it's close enough to formal meter that it pleases my ear. It makes a musical sound, and even if you stretch it and shrink it, you have this background of formal meters to overlay your conversation on. Not chitchat, but a conversational tone that keeps it from being, you know, "What hast thou, O my soul, with paradise?"—the first line of *Blandula, Tenulla, Vagula*, which I thought was so gorgeous at the time. Still OK, but a little Victorian. Pound was, as we all know, the last great Victorian. He threw his body over the barbed wire, and modernism ran up his back and over into no-man's-land. He was there, looking, but he still got hung up on the wire the rest of his life. Without him modernism wouldn't have gotten there, but I'm not sure he ever really caught up. He was a great Victorian, just like Hopkins. That has nothing to do with what you asked....

But it's interesting, because both Pound and Hopkins seem to have so profoundly influenced your work.

I guess it's sound patterns. I like sound. That's no secret; and Hopkins was so idiosyncratic and so odd, inimitable, that you can really enjoy him—or dislike him, I suppose, if you're William Carlos Williams and think he's taking everything the wrong way—but you can enjoy him without guilt and without fear. Pound is somewhat the same way. I haven't read him in twenty, twenty-five years. Everybody reads someone a lot in the beginning, and whoever pulls you in sticks with you. And you hope somebody good pulls you in and not somebody bad—somebody you can't get rid of. So, yes, I was pulled in by an occasionally great poet, someone who's very interesting and helped shape the way we look at things in this century. I would rather have been pulled in by Pound than by Eliot, even though I admire Eliot's poems, and I especially like *Four Quartets*. But I would much rather have been initiated by Pound, because I think the possibilities for exploration are larger. At least in my case, Pound would be expansive and Eliot restrictive. But I didn't have a choice—I just happened upon Pound; that's the way it went. I feel fortunate.

The statement at the beginning of Appalachia *bills it as the completion of a "trilogy of trilogies."* Hard Freight, Bloodline, *and* China Trace, *together with a prologue from* The Grave of the Right Hand, *became* Country Music; *then* The Southern Cross, The Other Side of the River, *and* Zone Journals, *together with the epilogue* Xionia, *became* The World of the Ten Thousand Things; *and now* Chickamauga, Black Zodiac, *and* Appalachia *complete the last trilogy. What do you see each of those sequences as doing, and how do they work as a whole? You describe it as a sequence.*

It's an odd sequence. All three trilogies do the same thing, and they have essentially the same structure. Past, present, future: yesterday, today, tomorrow. That's just the guiding—well, it's not a thought—the guiding sound bite behind the first trilogy, which actually went that way, I think. Then I wanted to technically alter the way I was writing the line in the next group, and I went on other explorations. For instance, I tried to do more narrative in *The Other Side of the River*; I did longer poems in *Zone Journals*. And I wanted to bring in other kinds of business, like raising the diary form to a higher level of artifice. I don't know exactly how to say that, but I wanted to make it a more serious form, and I wanted to see what one could do with it in poetry and still have it be entries. So all that was behind the next group of books, but they're still structured the same way. There's the past, the present, and the future, but larger. And so is the last one. I still don't know the name of the last trilogy, but that's on top of the second trilogy, so you get an inverted pyramid. It's the same pyramid but larger each time.

So, to answer your question, they're all doing the same thing, which is a kind of radar echo, I suppose, of the *Divine Comedy*. You know, I don't even like to bring those words up, but—the way James Merrill had three books in *The Changing Light at Sandover*, and the way Pound was trying to write one, the way a lot of people do—that's the thing the sonar is coming back from that you can never see and never approach.

That's why I said *Appalachia* is not a paradise, because I seem to be incapable of writing one. Though mentally, perhaps, certainly spiritually, it's become a book of the dead, because I can give a pep talk to those who might be true believers, which is what most books of the dead are, the Egyptian books of the dead. That's why it's the last one, and, I guess, why it was written so quickly in terms of my usual production. *Chickamauga* took five long years to write, and both *Black Zodiac* and *Appalachia* together took three years and four months. I saw the end in sight, I saw the conclusion of what I was trying to do. And when I didn't do anything for months and months and months, I realized I really was at the end. I wasn't just kidding myself. I had had something I was trying to do, and I did it, and that was it. Now I can sort of shut up again, I hope.

That's a real glaze-over, because there are lots more things that go together to make up each individual book, and each poem is individual—they don't depend on

12. An Interview by Ted Genoways

what precedes and what follows—but they are enhanced, I think, in the overall thing. And I do think that this last trilogy is as much one as the first was. I suppose the middle one would be the least "trilogeic," in the sense I've been talking about, but since it's more about the present—you know, "the world of the ten thousand things"—that seems only fair. Naturally, it should be the least structured.

And Appalachia *seems to be a conclusion not only to this trilogy but to all of them. There are references throughout to your earlier books.*

There are things in *Appalachia* that go all the way back to the first trilogy, particularly *China Trace*, because that's its mirror book. That's on purpose, not because I didn't know what else to say. That's why I said the trilogies are all doing the same thing, only differently, more expansively.

Some of these poems seem even to look like the earlier poems. There are a number that are completely left-justified, with none of the trademark drop lines.

I don't know why. It's just the way I was hearing it. Maybe once I sped up and saw the end, the lines moved faster. What I've been working on since *Appalachia* is this thing I started in March, and I'm still ... I have a couple of stanzas, each about six lines, and one or two of them will be dropped. I do know that every once in a while in *Appalachia* there seems to be a spate of them with not too many dropped lines. I don't know why that is.

How do you decide how the poem will move across the page? How do you decide between a drop line and a line break, for example?

I don't have a program for the way I use them. It's the way I hear them. If it's coming together and springing, then I'll drop it down. If it needs to have a little push, I'll drop it. If it seems to be breaking under its own weight, then I'll drop it to the next line. If it doesn't, I let it go. I don't have any program: "Out of every five lines one or two must be dropped." It's not like that.

No, but there is an amazing sense of structure in your work—which is surprising, when so much of it seems to be an argument against narrative.

Not really. Do you mean professionally or in my own stuff?

In your own stuff. I don't think you're being dogmatic. But there is a tension between your resistance to narrative and this overarching architecture—in each individual poem and in constructing a twenty-seven-year cycle. And so many of your books move forward in time, in strict allegiance to chronology. Explain the difference, in your mind, between structure and narrative, and between chronology and narrative.

Overt narrative tells a story. Covert narrative also tells a story, but in a different language. Everything has a narrative to it; don't get me wrong. It's just that I'm no good at storyline. My story is always underneath, always covert. Chronology perhaps is a way of helping move that mole under the ground, and you watch his little pile behind him as he goes. Structure, of course, is my substitute for storytelling. I guess I'd like to be like Robert Frost and spin yarns in beautiful blank verse, but I can't do it, so I have to make up my own prosody. Out of a deficiency I've tried to make a positive thing. And I talk about it so much that people think, "Even if I don't like it, at least he knows what he's doing." But structure long ago became paramount to me in forming my poems, because narrative is not going to hold it together. So the way I layered impressions, images, the observations, is key to covert, unspoken narrative, but it was there inevitably. At least I hope it was there, holding it together, because something has to. You can't just put it in a box and say, "There's a structure." That's what the New Formalists try to do. The Old Formalists *built* that box, you know? There's a big difference. So I was trying to build my own box in a different way. That's why I have this juxtapositional way of putting things together. That works in poems; it would be disastrous in prose. And it is, which is why I don't seem able to do essays or that sort of thing, because my mind just doesn't work in those terms. I can get a thought from A to B, but I go circuitously. I can't go straight to it. I think I'm going straight to it— I'm trying to—and the storyline gets you there, but as I say, it's always hidden. Like a punji stick underneath the trail. Sometimes you stumble on it, sometimes you don't. All I can say in answer to that question is that I perceived in my poetic makeup a huge deficit and deficiency, and I've tried to make something out of that void.

And others are embarked on similar projects. What sets your work apart for me—and David Young points this out—is your sense of humor [QN, 124–5]. It seems when you're up against the most serious matters in your poems, you're at your most self-effacing. It's not looking directly into the face of the divine....

It's checking out the belt buckle. As I should. That's true. It would be foolish to take one's self as seriously as one's subject matter. I'm really glad that David Young recognized this, because everybody is always saying, "This guy is so morbid, so somber," and I never thought of it that way. I thought I was talking about serious things, but never in a way that would be ponderous or turgid. In one's secret self, one comes up against these things; you have to face them, but you also have to realize that you're just a song-and-dance man. So you had better sing as best you can and shuffle off to Buffalo. And that's it. But you don't want to not go in and do it.

I don't know. It's hard to talk about that. It's all so much larger than all of us. You have to be careful how ponderous you can start to sound, or no one is going to take you seriously. You can't sound like Ecclesiastes all the time.

In Appalachia, *the poem* Star Turn II *opens with the description of the night sky. There are a few comparisons, but after it's compared to a sequined dress, there's this drop line: "—hubba, hubba—" [NB, 182].*

12. An Interview by Ted Genoways

My favorite line in my entire works. I knew it from the second I wrote it.

But it's not the sort of interjection we expect to find in contemporary poems, especially not those tackling the sorts of issues you're taking on.

Yes. The seriousness you're trying to describe is there, but there is also a little levity to make it easier to take. I think "hubba hubba" is witty—actually, I think it's funny. Most of my stuff tries to be witty. For instance, there's the line "'Sainthood the bottomless pity' someone said" [*NB*, 180]. Well, I said that, because I thought it was sort of witty and it had to do with what I was getting ready to say. It's a serious thought, but it's also humorous. I'm not as funny as Jim Tate, for instance, who is amazingly and continuously funny. As Woody Allen once put it, "Too much seriousness is a bad thing." So I try not to have too much seriousity.

You've spent twenty-seven years creating your poetics and writing this trilogy of trilogies. What are you going to do with next twenty-seven years?

I really don't know. Obviously, I'm going to keep writing poems. This spring has been kind of crazy, but I hope everything will settle down and I can get back to work. I obviously will not have this same path or trajectory in mind, so ... it's hard, it's impossible to change what you're thinking, but I've got to come at it in a different way from the journey this project seems to have been on—from the early poems in *Country Music* to the last poems of *Black Zodiac* and *Appalachia*. At least I see a definite arc—a movement with different weaves to it—but the arc is always the same: from the past to the impossible or possible, the improbable or probable future. And that's good. I did that. Now I've got to figure out how to be interesting to myself with the accouterments that I have accrued over the years. And not write the same poems. We've all got maybe four or five ideas in our heads our whole lives. We know that, and we all write basic variations of the same handful of poems, because those are what our interests are. If you don't write what your interests are, it will be a piece of fluff—or worse, a piece of something else. And so I have my concerns and my interests, and I'll, have to figure out a way to reshuffle them and keep on writing poems. I can't turn into an essayist, because I can't keep the thoughts straight. If I'd had a life, I could have written a memoir. I never got a life; it's all in my poems.

Or all you're willing to show.

Well, yes.

One can't help but notice that you've appeared uncomfortable at times this spring, especially at the Pulitzer reception.

Well, one wants one's work to be paid attention to, but I hate personal attention. I just want everyone to read the poems. I want my poetry to get all the attention in the world, but I want to be the anonymous author of *Black Zodiac*. That's impossible to do, I know. Some people love the spotlight; I like the shadows. I like the spotlight on my work, because that's what's important. It's better looking and younger and wealthier and more articulate. No, I never have liked the spotlight. I have friends who love it and are great at it. Not me. The attention for the book is wonderful. I'm not sure it's gotten me more readers, but I've got more buyers, and that's good. So keep those cards and letters coming to the bookstores. Not me.

CHAPTER 13

An Interview by Morgan Lucas Schuldt

MS: *When you take a good long look at American poetry today, poised at the start of a new century, a new millennium, what do you see?*

CW: Too many people. Too many people who say, "Well, I guess I got a flair for this. Got all 'A's in class, why not try it?" Too many flares, not enough fire. MFA programs are becoming (have become) like Law School—"May as well go there; nothing else to do." There are almost as many poets as lawyers these days. When the revolution comes, we won't know which ones to kill first. Truthfully, though, I see a wide and waving plain of competence. A few gulches and draws. But the mountains are so far in the distance, I can hardly make them out. Still, I'm the wrong person to be answering this question, I'm afraid, as I see all this from my window. I'm not out there amid the alien grain. I'm back in my back room, hoping for something to visit me, rather than vice-versa.

> It's difficult for the cream to rise
> When all the milk is homogenized.

Is there poetry that still needs to be written? Or perhaps better put, is there anyone still haunting us from the literary past with whom poetry needs to contend?

"To contend with" is not a figure I'd use myself. There really isn't a competition, no matter what Hemingway always said. It's not the Olympics. "Come to terms with," perhaps, in light of what's been done and what's not been done, and what is left opened up to us. Paul Celan, Ezra Pound, Franz Kafka, great ghosts we need to séance with.

Originally published in Sonora Review, *No. 43 (2002): 74–80. The following interview took place by post between February and April of 2002.*

> Yeats and Auden, come on down,
> Take us back to higher ground.

Language—its meanings and frustrations, its spiritual and metaphysical approximations—seems always to have been important to you. In a decidedly different way, language and its failures are also the focus of our current avant-garde. Aside from theory, what, if anything, does Language poetry offer?

The quick quip is, a vacuum to fill. But not only is that unfair, it's inaccurate as well. My problem with Language poetries is insoluble, as what I don't like about it is, it turns out, its expressed aim (or one of them)—no "whole," no completed "meaning," no arrival point in its linguistic destination. The voyage itself is the destination, what goes on within its own boundaries is the interest and end-game. I agree that these are interesting stations. But they are only stations. The destination is the cross, and all that that implies. One of their purported foremasters, Ezra Pound, said, at the end, his structuring of the *Cantos* was ultimately wrong. He intended the poem to go where the winds took it, "in periplum," as he put it. Unfortunately, his ship never came in. He couldn't "make it cohere." "That's no way to make a work of art," he said, or words to that effect. My problem with Language poetries is that they work entirely "in periplum," the concentration on phrase and sentence, with no landfall in sight or mind, being the sought-after end result. That's chasing your tail, to my way of thinking, not making a circle, a whole.

The lack of wholeness bothers you then?

Philip Johnson said about architecture, "You can't not know history."[1] You must know the rudiments of meter and structure in English verse. In your heart you know this. As in their hearts, surely, the Theorists know they have to learn about reasoned discourse, about the how and why of a text and what it means, not just its collapsible parts and points. Surely they know the season will change. Surely they know you can't ice skate forever. When the water comes back, you've got to face the dragon, and Grendel, and Grendel's mom. Poets have to know the same thing. Form and Structure and their attendant fire. Architecture. History. Rhetoric is the antipasto of the gods. There is much to admire in Charles Bernstein's and Ron Silliman's work, and in Michael Palmer's especially. But their aims, linguistic and political, don't entice me. At least not now. I think their best hope is to be absorbed, like Surrealism, into the accomplishable fabric of perception and writing. What they don't want is to become like Dada, a dead end, to be brought out like a stuffed goose from time to time by academics, to be looked at and explained. Things have beginnings and ends.

> Pound and Williams, guard the gate,
> Call the roll and set them straight.

So the rhetorical dazzle of Language poetry doesn't impress you?

13. An Interview by Morgan Lucas Schuldt

Poetry comes, for lack of better words, from the heart (the "foul rag-and-bone-shop of the heart," as Yeats had it),[2] and from the soul—neither a place you can put your finger on, but a place you can surely put your foot in, if you don't watch out. It is a matter of "soul making," as John Keats said.[3] It truly is *not* a matter of arrangement, of performance, of presentation, or rhetorical dazzle or surprise, though all of those matters may be part of it. It is *not* the distractions, but the focus. It is not the undercard, but the main event. There is always an emotional half to the equation, but the other half is always craft—you have to be able to say it your way. It's the only time that two plus one makes two—language is half, technique is half, and emotion is half. An emotional value is always involved. Distortions and side events are often interesting and entertaining, but they are *not* the stillness and fathered attention at road's end. It's not a question of paper, or type-writers, of white space or of dark space—it's a question of what's in your life, and where you want that life to lead you. You've only got one, and you can fill it with whatever you want. You're free and American. But if it is poetry that you want, then don't look for language games, intellectual rip-offs, or rhetorical sing-alongs. It's too often been a matter of life and death to those who really cared. You've got to know, in your heart of hearts, that Keats is right, that it is about soul-making, that it does matter, and that it can make you or break you as a person. It is the main event, as I say, and ancillary to nothing. It's either Atonement or At Onement, but it is one of them.

There are those who complain that, as opposed to, say, our European counterparts, American poets confess too much, that our individual pasts have become too precious to us—too much of the "I" in poetry. Why does autobiography continue to occupy the attention of so many poets writing today?

Whitman, of course, is one obvious and towering reason. *Song of Myself* is the American poetic national anthem. The lingering presence and dark aura of the Confessional Poets from mid-century 1900 (especially Plath and Sexton among women writers) and a certain ease of informational access. One could go to Rilke's unfortunate statement that "everyone has a subject matter, his childhood," or something like that.[4] And the fact that every workshop instructor in every MFA program (or, more likely, undergraduate class) repeats it into the waiting and, for once, open ears of his students. And that's probably the crux of the thing—every student in every writing class is told to "write what you know." And that's all they know. They'd probably be better off being told to write what they don't know and to make it their own. But they learn that down the road if they're any good. And if they aren't and don't, they'll continue to spin their wheels in their own driveways. And if that driveway's in suburbia (as it usually is), the ubiquitous smell of burning rubber will keep on troubling our sleep. We all need the shield of Perseus to look at the Gorgon slant-wise and second hand.

> Walter, Walter, tell me true,
> Are all these I-poems really you?

In Quarter Notes *you've stated how "there is no great art without great style," and that "all major writers are great stylists" [104]. By extension, how much does great style involve great risk?*

Zen master Ch'ing Yuan wrote, "Before I began studying Zen, I saw mountains as mountains, rivers as rivers. When I learned some Zen, mountains ceased to be mountains, rivers to be rivers. But now, when I have understood Zen, I am in accord with myself and again I see the mountains as mountains, rivers as rivers."[5] Great poems are egoless. All well and good to write about "grand" things and "grand" concepts. But you must translate them so that when you're finished, they fit in your back pocket. So that they are iconized and objectified. So that they are apprehensible. Samuel Beckett says it definitively—"Fail. Fail again. Fail better."[6]

Is poetry risking enough these days?

Well, of course it is. The last great frontier of poetry is complete unintelligibility, complete opacity. And there are many working that horizon as we speak, so to speak, silhouetted against the skyline like the Seventh Seal. That, of course, is linguistic risk. Personal risk is something else, as in, say the cases of Crane, Sexton, or Berryman. Poetry was just the spar they held onto before their fingers got numb and they had to let go. Listen, everyone who writes takes risks on his own terms, and within his own poetic convention. What's risky within the formal, iambic tradition (Eliot, say, and Berryman and middle Lowell) is no risk at all to someone working in Language poetries or the prose poem (Russell Edson, for example, or Killarney Clary). Every time you try to do something you've never tried before, you take risks. Depends on how high the stakes are whether or not others see it as "risky." One needs to have a portable comfort zone. Also, you need to remember which one is Daedalus and which one is Icarus. We all take them. Some of us push the envelope, some of us lick its flap.

> Andre Breton and Tristan Tzara,
> One is our boy, the other's Samarra.

Time and again you've spoken eloquently about the epiphanic effect of Pound's Blandula, Tenulla, Vagula. *That day in 1959 seems to have become one of the great stories in literary history, mythic even. After forty years, does that day feel somehow fated, lucky, coincidental? Perhaps some combination of the three?*

Probably a fated coincidence. After four years of arduous service in the Army of Conformity at college, I was hair-triggered for something to happen. But lucky as well, in that my arrival in Italy coincided with Pound's repatriation, his connection with Verona (among other things, his books were printed there), and my having bought a copy of his New Directions *Selected Poems* in New York just before I shipped over because I thought it was a cool thing to do, "intellectual," you know. And lucky beyond belief to have been assigned to a unit that had three such interesting guys as Harold

Schimmel, a poet, George Schneeman, a painter, and Peter Hobart, an art history major from Yale, all of whom helped educate me in ways that college never had. And beyond all that to have discovered poetry through reading a major contributor, a great innovator, etc. I was ready to be turned out. Just happy it turned out to be someone whose work really counted.

> Chew tobacco, chew tobacco, spit on the wall,
> Charles Wright, Charles Wright took the fall.

With the publication of Negative Blue, *just last year, you ended a massive, lifelong undertaking, completing your trilogy of trilogies. What can we expect from you in the years to come? Ready to try your hand at playwriting or fiction?*

Hey, I still feel like I'm trying to break into show business. As an old song-and-dance man, I've got a couple of turns left to show. New book this past April, 2002, *A Short History of the Shadow*. So goodnight, Mrs. Calabash, wherever you are, no prose for me.

> Beauty is Truth, Truth Beauty,
> Rooty-toot-toot and a rooty-toot-tooty.

CHAPTER 14

Oblivion's Glow: The (Post) Southern Sides of Charles Wright— An Interview by Daniel Cross Turner

---

> *Those without stories are preordained to repeat them.*
> Charles Wright, Polaroids *(2002)* [SHS, 33]

DT: *What would you say is most Southern about your poetry? How do you relate your work to this tradition?*

CW: It's hard for me to relate to that tradition because I don't write narratively. Although I've tried, I just can't do it. I don't have that particular gene in my DNA that lets you tell a story. I guess I'm mostly a Southern writer because of the place of my birth, west Tennessee. My mother's and father's families are all Southern. So, by geography and definition, I'm a Southern poet. I went to school in the South, and all of

This interview, which originally appeared in storySouth, *Summer 2005, was conducted in two parts: the first portion took place at Wright's home in Charlottesville, Virginia, on 11 April 2003, and the second came from written responses from his cabin in Troy, Montana, on 26 May 2003. Turner's headnote contained the following reflections on Wright as a nontraditional Southern poet: "On the surface of things, Charles Wright would seem at odds with most of what has traditionally defined the Southern poet. The Southern emphasis on storytelling is missing from Wright's doggedly non-narrative verse, since there is only the faintest trace of a story line present in his poems. He does not use religion in a conventional way either, for he is quintessentially concerned with the question of nontranscendence in an age of 'postbelief,' as he puts it succinctly in* Polaroids *(2002). As for the Southern marriage of memory to place, that time-honored tendency to root memory in the soil itself, we are almost as likely to find Wright imaginatively wandering in Italy, California, or Montana as in the South. Even when his poems are set below the Mason-Dixon line, there is often as much a sense of placelessness as there is of place in his abstract and repetitive, peopleless landscapes.... Though he is bound to the past, he does not practice a wistful or unreflective nostalgia; in fact, he self-consciously exposes the Southern penchant for nostalgia in* Nostalgia *(2002). Presented with the traditional checklist of these stock motifs of Southern poetry and culture, Wright confessed wryly, 'I'm out on all counts.'"*

that. And I feel myself as a Southern poet, but apart from the tradition. I'm trying to think of current poets who would be on the same side of the main narrative track—people like Yusef Komunyakaa or Ellen Voigt, who's sort of narrative, but not as narrative as most of the guys are. Donald Justice tangentially—he was my teacher—but he also is much more narratively inclined. There aren't many of us who are doing the associative, imagistic progression in their poems, although as I get older, I get more garrulous and more snippets and little bits of narrative tend to creep in. I wish I could get more in, but I just don't seem able to. I'm much more impressionistic and cinematic, I think, in my presentation than narrative.

No need to apologize. You seem to be doing quite well with your nonnarrative style.

[Laughs.] No, I don't apologize for a moment. It's just that mostly I'm not considered a Southern writer because I don't follow the tradition, the five things you mentioned, and because I lived out of the South from the age of twenty-one until forty-eight. What else would I say? There's a very famous—maybe I've said this before—Czech photographer named Josef Sudek. He had only one arm. He was a great photographer and he used this big view camera and he did landscapes and still lifes and things like that. He was once asked why there were no people in his pictures. He said, "Well, I don't know. There are always people there when I start, but by the time I get everything done and take the picture, they've all gone." And that's sort of the way my poems are. I think of them as being populated with people who are whispering stories in my ear which I then launder in my own way and present, and by the time the poem gets presented, all the people are gone and nothing's left but the whispers. Once the people go, there goes your narrative.

Good riddance.

[Laughs] Yeah, I kind of think that. I mean, there are plenty of people doing narrative.

And it seems that your work makes an important intervention into the tradition of Southern poetry precisely in inverting or ignoring or resisting that checklist, which has become quite conventional by now.

I think that by default perhaps my defects have helped to turn some of my stuff into a positive. For a while, I was the only one doing that in Southern poetry. If you can make your defects into positive things, I guess you're all right.

I was intrigued by what you described a moment ago as your "cinematic" poetics. Could you say something more about this aspect of your practice?

I'm not really sure. I haven't thought about it a lot, but I think that I have probably been more influenced by the Italian movies that I saw in the late 1950s and early 1960s than I have allowed myself to previously acknowledge. I was looking at some of my poems just the other day, and I realized that the openings are always immediate. There's no sort of lead-in—they just jump into the poem. And that gesture—that's the movies. I'm a great fan of Fellini and Antonioni and Mario Monicelli, and all those Italian directors of the 1950s and early 1960s. I saw their movies with great passion back when I was younger, and that was about the time when I was trying to learn to write poems. I'm sure that there's been some influence that I haven't even thought about, but the more I mulled it over the other day, the more it seemed apparent to me that this sense of immediacy, direct presentation, rapid movement from one image to the next, owes something to the quick cut and the jump cut of the movies. Fellini, of course, has a terrible Romantic and excessive streak that I adore, and of course, you always try to keep that down, but some of it keeps seeping through. I can't have kept all of that out of my poems, even though the subject matter is different. Well, not entirely ... he writes and then shoots a lot about memory, and he's got people in there, but I bet he could shoot it without people if he wanted to.

Like Fellini, your poems are intensely visual, reveling at times in instances of spectacle, but also kinetic, as you noted. You use painting a great deal, but your poetic images are rarely static—they're moving *pictures.*

Yeah, I've always thought painting had been an influence, and I've talked about it until the cows come home over the years. It's just in the last month or so that I've begun thinking that maybe it's more the movies that have influenced me. I was thinking about it because I don't go to movies anymore. I find the movies very unsatisfying nowadays. I know the minute I see a fireball I'm not going to like the movie, and most movies have fireballs in them now. [Laughs] And I was thinking about when I did love the movies, Truffaut and Godard and those French as well as Italian directors—I guess I have to say the European directors, since that's where I was during my twenties, in Italy. And I began to think it probably had quite an effect on me, even though I hadn't thought about it.

Would you talk a bit about your memories of growing up in Tennessee and North Carolina?

I was born in Pickwick Dam, Tennessee. My father was an engineer for the TVA, which was government work, and he was glad to get it. And we moved around for about eight years to various dam sites, Knoxville and Hiwassee Dam, North Carolina, until 1942, during the Second World War, when we went to Oak Ridge, Tennessee for more government work. So the first ten years of my life—I was born in 1935—through the end of the War, we were fairly peripatetic, moving around. And since we were in government housing—in Knoxville, we weren't, we lived in a regular house—and my father was in government work, I guess I didn't feel the Depression as much as someone like Donald Justice, who writes agonizingly about it. His father was a carpenter, and Don is ten years older than I am, so he was of an age to react to it in some ways that I guess I wasn't because the Depression stopped at the beginning of the War in 1941, more or less, and I was six then, so I didn't really feel the effects. And I don't know that my parents did, since my father was always employed during that time. I have no memories at all of Pickwick Dam—we left there when I was either six months or one year old—then moved to Corinth, Mississippi, across the way, then Knoxville, Tennessee, then Hiwassee Dam, North Carolina, which I remember very well and with great fondness. It's just a two-road town for the dam site and a thin, old bridge which I remember well. Then we moved to Oak Ridge during the War, where everyone wore badges and you had to come in and out of gates. We lived next door to a two-star Admiral, who was working on the Manhattan Project. And my father was working on the Manhattan Project, not as a scientist, but as a civil engineer. He was in charge of one of the two buildings where they did all the work. He never talked about it. I don't know what being in charge of the building meant, but that's what he finally told me he did after I badgered him about it. He did tell me once that he bumped a three-star general off a plane going to Denver, so God knows what he had in his pocket. After that we moved to Kingsport where I really grew up after age ten. My father had a small construction company. His partner was a man named Tom Rentenbach, who was supposed to leave his construction company in Knoxville to join my father's firm in Kingsport. About a month before Rentenbach was supposed to come, he got the job to build Neyland Stadium, so he never left Knoxville.

Those are some interesting overlaps between your personal history and the general history of the South, from the TVA to the Manhattan Project to Neyland Stadium. I was particularly interested in the intersections between the TVA and the South. What are your feelings about how the TVA changed the South?

Well, it put food on our table, so we liked it. But it seems everybody else, Robert Penn Warren and Andrew Lytle and all those, thought it was terrible socialism. Andrew Lytle lost his family farm and land, which is now under water, so I understand how those people might feel. But, of course, there was no electricity in that area of the country when the TVA came in. My father had been working for Louisiana Light and Power in the swamps of Louisiana and southern Mississippi before he was hired by the TVA. As it turned out over the years, my father was really a socialist, which I didn't know at the time. I'm sure he was really in favor of this, bringing something good to people who didn't have anything. So I basically think that the TVA was a good thing. I know that people don't like the government interfering in their lives for the most part—until they need the government to interfere. I'm sure my father had no second-thoughts whatsoever. He once said that when he first moved to Pickwick Dam, it was such open country that he could take his gun and his dog and go from the house to the building site and get his limit of quail in the morning on the way to work. You can't even find a quail anymore, unless you go to some plantation down in South Carolina or southern Georgia. And this was in the mid-1930s. No electricity and lots of quail.

That's the old South.

That's the old South.

How do you feel such experiences influenced your poetry?

As I got older, they influenced my poetry more. In the early days, I was just trying to write poems or poetry, whatever that was. I didn't know what it was, so I would get some abstract subject matter. When I wrote a poem called *Dog Creek Mainline* (1973) [*CM*, 36], which was the turning point for me halfway through my second book, I realized what I wanted to write about: my life. I wanted to try to figure it out and I've been doing that ever since. So I have to say that my early experiences—or let's say reflections from images of echoes from my earlier life—have been a profound influence on my poetry. My poems often come out of the stories from my life. This came to a head when I wrote a book called *The Other Side of the River* (1984), where I tried hard to do some narrative and wrote some narrative-esque poems. After I had written that book, I said, "Well, I've done that. To hell with that. Let's go back to what I like to do, which is the impressionistic stuff." And that was the end of my poems about my childhood too because then I moved back to the South, to Virginia. I finished that book in California, where I had been living for seventeen years. Once I moved back to my home area, I never wrote another poem about my childhood, which at the time I thought was weird, but now it makes perfect sense to me because I was thinking about it all the time, thinking back to my past. Once I came back to the South, I didn't—I just didn't do it.

In fact, you wrote a poem, Tennessee Line *[NB, 16–17], which describes precisely that process of thinking back on your Southern identity from a remove in both time and space. The poem shows you out in Monterrey, California, reevaluating the influence of the Tennessee line, both literally and figuratively, on the making of your self.*

Yes, I used to write about it all the time. As Ezra Pound said, things have ends and beginnings. Once I came back here, that was the end of that. So I just sat in my backyard and wrote a couple of books about the landscape.

Yes, you're arguably the most concerted landscape poet at work in Southern poetry today, though you go about it in an extraordinary way. Your poems seem consumed with the idea of place, but you exhibit a very different sensibility about this subject than most of your poetic contemporaries. There's a sense of abstraction to the point of placelessness when you write about Southern sites.

Most other Southern poets are much more interested in the history of the place, or the history *in* place. I am more interested in it as *I* look at it, as *I* see it. Again, this is where the painting motif and the cinema motif come in because I'm interested in the surface of it as I see it and what's possibly behind the surface that I don't see, whereas they see the history in the place, and it's not so much what they see but it's what was there and what it meant to people. I'm more interested in what it may mean to me. So it does tend to break down into abstracts because place or landscape substitutes for ideas and reactions more than it has to do with things of the present and things of the past. There is some difference in how I perceive what landscape means to me and how narrative poets explain what landscape or nature means to them. I usually see landscape as a screen for abstract ideas of what's behind the place; narrative poets tend to see it as a long tunnel into the past or a long, well-lit hallway into the past. And that's fine too. We simply look at things differently. I can't imagine Mr. Warren, for instance, looking at a landscape and having the same reaction to it as I would. For me, it is abstract and that's where—for lack of a better word—the spirituality comes in. I find a spirituality in landscape instead of a history in landscape. It's not something as simple as "Nature is the great church of man." I don't mean that. I mean that the landscape translates and reinterprets. It's a kind of string of associative feeling that runs through most of us. The Southern narrative tradition looks at landscape as history, a door into the dark, as it were. I tend to look at landscape as revelation, a door into the light. When I look at the landscape, I see what's not there. Of course, my eyes aren't so good anymore. [Laugh] I may not be seeing the right things.

Two of your volumes from the 1990s, Chickamauga *and* Appalachia, *seem to gesture toward that kind of deep-structure narrative history that you disavow:* Chickamauga *as hallowed Civil War battlefield,* Appalachia *as the South's most economically deprived, yet culturally distinct subregion. Given that these places have so much history condensed in them, why did you choose them for the titles of volumes in which you explore most intensely this sense of landscape as a form of abstract revelation? Despite the titles, the volumes present a vision of landscapes drained of history.*

The poem *Chickamauga* shows a pretty abstract idea of history. I took it as the title of the book because that's where my great-grandfather was wounded out of the Civil War and I wanted to have some connection, some familial connection with that particular volume, since I had the Dante trilogy in mind. *Black Zodiac* was the second book, which would have been the purgatorial part. *Appalachia* was the final book, the book of the dead, since I couldn't write a *Paradiso*. The reason *Appalachia* was called *Appalachia* was because *Chickamauga* was called *Chickamauga*, which is to say that each title has four syllables. *Black Zodiac* also has four syllables. These are silly reasons, but it had something to do with it. Also, *Appalachia* is the exact opposite of what one might think of as a paradisal place, but, growing up in it, I loved it. I tend to think of western North Carolina, eastern Tennessee, southwestern Virginia, that part of Appalachia, as containing heavenly aspects, which I know is not true for most people, but they were for me. This again comes back to all the landscape business. You think about what's behind it, but you're left with what you can see. I always wanted to have a book with a Southern title, so I picked *Chickamauga* and on the front of the book there's a picture my wife took of me saying "Chickamauga."[1]

That seems a perfect instance of a "postsouthern" moment, as you invoke the sancti-

fied place-name of Chickamauga in a parodic manner. You empty it out of its narrative history, reducing this storied past down to a mere four syllables.

Yes, I think so. I wasn't interested in history in that way. Poets like Fred Chappell, David Bottoms, and Dave Smith are more involved with that kind of narrative history. All of those guys are storytellers. I'm a listener.

How would you place your poems of an abstract, peopleless South in relation to Wallace Stevens' ethereal vision of the South in poems like Anecdote of the Jar, The Idea of Order at Key West, In the Carolinas, *or* Some Friends from Pascagoula? *Does it make a difference that you grew up in the South instead of just passing through, like Stevens?*

Wallace Stevens was a major carpetbagger. A really swell-looking bag, and nothing but beautiful things inside. But a carpetbagger nonetheless. No one has ever had a finer bag, and patterned beyond the normal imagination. My own unreconstructed pieces are of little note in comparison, and certainly of a more primitive nature. Though primitive does have its own kind of beauty, and its own kind of integrity, and a strength to stand its own ground. And it *is* my ground, if nothing else. Still, his magic, foreign-looking bag.

How do your Southern landscapes compare to your Italian landscapes? Or Montana? Or California? Either in memory or in your poetry.

In memory, all my landscapes are the same. In reality, too, come to think of it. Different trees, different hills, but always the same iconostasis, always the same groping for grace.

In Sprung Narratives *(1995) [NB, 21–9], you describe older Southern roadways that have been bypassed by a newer system of highways:*

> The valley has been filled in
>   with abandoned structures
> New roads that have been bypassed
> By newer roads
>   glint in the last sun and disappear.
> As twilight sinks in
> Across the landscape,
>   lights come on like the light next door... [NB, 28]

What is the significance of the recurrent images of these seemingly "lost" highways (US 11, US 23, US 52, US 176, etc.) in poems like Lonesome Pine Special, The Southern Cross, Lost Bodies, *or* Gate City Breakdown, *all from* The Southern Cross *(1981)? Why do you return, time and again, to these remembered* road*scapes?*

I was referring there to a simple four-lane highway between Kingsport and Bristol, Tennessee. It took them years to build it, and when it was finished it was already outdated. I meant it as a part of what is past or passing. I continue to refer to the older highways—U.S. 11, U.S. 23, U.S. 52, etc.—because those were the ones I drove on, those were the ones that linked my life to "elsewhere." They were my youth, my (by now) treasured and glittering youth. You'll see. The highways aren't lost, my youth is.

In your experience of the Southern highways, what was the effect of these roads on the changing of Southern culture as you witnessed it?

The same as a lump of butter melting in a hot skillet. Of course I wasn't there to witness this disappearing and clarifying act. I left the South in 1957 and didn't come back to live there until 1983. By then, it had all congealed into a *fait accompli*, as we used to say in Kingsport. Interstates and television—Hello, Nashville, goodbye.

There seems to be a broad shift in your poetry from the rambling, open space of the rural highways to a more stable, confined—yet resolutely metaphysical—suburban space, where the echo of traffic on the nearby bypass is a faint reminder of the movement, speed, and pace of the highway. Just as your persona has become increasingly static as you reinvent your "I" voice as a wry and reflective kind of lawn-chair philosopher, your poems themselves have become more compact, compressing much of the sprawl of your mid-career highway poems. What accounts for this shift in your poetic interests and style?

Advancing age, most likely. Also, there was a conscious attempt, after *Country Music* (1982), to lengthen my line and my scope of experience, hence the technical spaces and lengths in *The World of the Ten Thousand Things* (1990). Just as consciously, the poems in *Negative Blue* (2000) attempted a combination of those impulses in *Country Music* and *The World of Ten Thousand Things*: compression and extension—long lines and vistas in a compact space, the idea of Emily Dickinson beside Walt Whitman's road. Also, one tries to convince oneself that the older one gets the less time it takes to say what one has to say. I attribute this canard to the miscalculation of hope over experience, and a certain amount of truth.

How has the sense of memory changed from your earlier poems to your later poems?

I'm not as interested in it as I once was, and it's not as interested in me as it once was. Neither is as important to the other as we once were. It's darker now, and objects are not as clear as they once were: they do not appear larger in the rearview mirror any more than they actually are. Ultimately, memory tells you only what you want to hear. Bad advice.

Can you gauge the influence of Christianity, and of the Episcopal church in particular, on your life and poetry? To invoke Flannery O'Connor, are your poems "Christ-

haunted" in terms of form? That is, the ecclesiastical, psalmic, almost vatic quality of your rhythms seems to bear the traces of Christian spiritualism, yet your poems tend to thematize a sense of nontranscendence, of the severe limitations of traditional belief in an age of "postbelief."

God-haunted perhaps, but not Christ-haunted. Christ-haunted would be the extreme Christian poets—Hopkins, Herbert, Donne, Merton, Lowell in his Catholic period. I don't fit in that company. The ritual call and response of the American service, the cadences of the King James Bible, early country music, the looney "spiritualism" of the Sky Valley Community in my early teenage years all certainly played a part in the pastiche of my life and poetry. So yes, a tangential Christianity. I remain, however, a God-fearing non-believer, though Christ doesn't really enter in to it.

You once commented that you write out of a "negative sublime," placing yourself between—or, more properly, beyond—both Wordsworth's egotistical sublime and Keats' negative capability. To me, this sense of a self-negating sublimity seems to derive from the insistent and accumulative power of your poetic rhythms. Although you are not a strict formalist, the ghost of meter pulses through your verse, lending it a sublimely negating force. Could you say something about your conception of the relation of sound and sense in your poems?

Good sounds make good sense. At least we hope so. Pure style is pure meaning. At least we hope so. Negative transcendence is a virtual reality. How you say it, in the end, becomes what you have to say. Or vice-versa. Though others will say otherwise, you have to dance to the music.

What do you see as the future of poetry?

Oblivion. But oblivion, like Wallace Stevens' bag, has its own warm glow.

CHAPTER 15

An Interview by Louis Bourgeois

LB: *Do you think there is a true tradition of Southern poetry beyond the role of the Agrarians in American Literature? That is, do you think there is a descending tradition of Southern poets going back to Poe? If so, what kind of impact do you think Southern poetry has had on American literature?*

CW: Actually, no, I don't. There are no major poetic figures in American literature from the South until that generation, except Poe, of course, and he was in essence, a French poet, and an American prose writer. Until John Crowe Ransom and crew, there are really no high-profile Southern poets. Conrad Aiken, perhaps. In ways similar, I mean, to the fiction tradition, which we all know is deep and pervasive—from Mark Twain on. In the immediate view there are Donald Justice and James Dickey and Archie Ammons, and a good many younger (younger than they, I mean) writers who might help begin a true tradition. Still, the "Southern" tradition is narrative, of course, and I don't know if the poetry tradition is, or should be, the same. Perhaps it should not be, to counter the fiction flood. A little boat atop the dark and fearsome waters of Lake Faulkner, going wherever it pleases, singing against the wind. It will probably continue to have the same impact on American literature that it has always had. None. In any case, tomorrow is another day.

Have any Southern poets had an influence on your early development as a poet? For example, did the Agrarians play a role in your poetic training to the extent Wallace Stevens, Ezra Pound, and the T'ang Poets did?

Donald Justice, my teacher at the University of Iowa, was a major early influence. The influence on my actual writing was subsumed rather quickly, the influence on my thinking about writing and about poems more "wide-spread" and longer lasting. The

---

This interview, originally published in Carolina Quarterly 56 *(Spring-Summer, 2004), was conducted through correspondence during the spring of 2003. A revised version, printed here, appeared in* VOX *1, no. 2 (April 2006): 50–6.*

only Agrarian whose work had an early, tangential effect on me was Ransom. I loved reading his poems, and learned a great deal about writing meter from him. As well as Justice (and Auden and Frost, a couple of guys from the northern South). I think he is, like Justice, terribly underappreciated in what his work has meant to the generations of younger writers who came along after him. As compared, say, to Warren, Tate, and Jarrell. It's a different tradition, really, more compressed, more lyric, less heavily narrated, more deflective, less "ambitious" on the surface, but at least, if not more so, underneath. Perhaps they should be the beacons for the up-coming, less narrative poets who will come forth out of the darkness.

Do you see yourself writing in a Southern tradition of poetry (assuming that such a tradition exists)? For that matter do you, at this point in your career, see yourself as a Southern poet? Are there any contemporary Southern poets who interest you?

A lot of this question has its answer in the two previous ones. I guess it's fairly obvious by now that I see myself in the "tradition" (a tradition, by the way, that I appear to be starting just now) of Ransom and Justice, as opposed to the more visible and established tradition, say, of Warren, James Dickey, and Dave Smith. Other poets in this line would, be people like Ellen Bryant Voigt and Yusef Komunyakaa, while writers in the other, more populous line would be people like David Bottoms, Fred Chappell, and most everybody else.

Of course I see myself as a Southern poet. That's where I'm from. But I don't see myself as exclusively so, or seamlessly contained therein. Anymore than Ransom and Justice were. The South is only the base. But it is the base. Frost saw himself as a New Englander, though born in San Francisco, and Pound as an exile afloat on the debris of Western civilization, though he was born in Idaho. Eliot saw himself as an Englishman, though born in Missouri. They were all more inclusive than their origins. I would hope for the same thing.

There are a lot of contemporary poets who interest me. I've already listed several from both "lines." Wendell Berry is another obvious example. Dave Smith is a major figure. Robert Morgan. I like Henry Taylor's work a great deal. Andrew Hudgins. William Harmon. The list goes on.

There seems to be a great deal of formal continuity in your work from at least The Southern Cross *on. Could you comment on the expansion of your line after* China Trace?

Well, as I've said before and elsewhere, I have tried to compress my line and my poems into a handful of matter, to squeeze everything down to its essence as much as I could, like a black hole gripped down into a ball. After that, I wanted to open my hand and let the line and poems expand as far as they could toward prose, without becoming prose. I worked through longer concepts (*The Southern Cross*) [*WTTT*, 42–55], narrative-based poems (*The Other Side of the River*) [*WTTT*, 78–81], and on toward the diaristic and quotidian reportage of *Zone Journals*. Always pushing the line in its conversational quality toward the break-off point of prose. I thought that *Zone Journals* was as far as I could, or should go. Then in the third and final group of poems contained in *Negative Blue*, I tried to combine the two efforts—a longer line with a condensed subject matter. And that's what I've been working on the past dozen years or so. Or so I flatter myself. At least one thing is sure—I've stretched the line out so much that it will probably never be able to snap back to its shorter incarnation. And that's fine with me. Longer line, bigger fish.

Walt Whitman also used a fairly expansive line. How much have you considered his line, and do you think it has had any effect on you or your own work?

Like every other red-blooded American boy, I considered his line a great deal. Like Muhammad Ali, *Song of Myself* is the greatest. His line is, of course, a self-contained unit for the most part. A Winnebago for the open road. Long and loping declarative objects and sentences. Who hasn't heard the hoof-beats of that great horsepower. Still, my not-so-secret love was Emily Dickinson. And so I tried, again not-so-secretly, to smuggle her on board for the long ride. And there we are, rolling along in our Long Line Special, gist and pith with their faces pressed to the window glass. C.C. Rider and the Heartbreaker.

You have written or stated in the past that The Grave of the Right Hand *is your least favorite of your books. Yet, it is one of my personal favorites (I love the rhythmics of that book and the overall mystical quality of it). I am particularly intrigued by the poem* To a Friend Who Wished Always To Be Alone *[GRH, 16]. To me, it is a poem rooted in the tradition of Deep Imagery. Could you tell us a little about this poem? Was it born out of real experience? Or was it just a state of mind you captured on the page, a totally imagined experience?*

Bill Martin was a college friend of mine, from Louisville, Kentucky. In our dorm, he had the only single room. He rarely partied with the rest of us. He somehow seemed to have more serious and self-set aspiration for himself and his future than the rest of us. When we graduated in 1957, he was commissioned a 2nd Lieutenant in the Army, through ROTC, and elected to go Regular Army instead of the standard two-year obligation. On his way to Ft. Benning, Georgia, to report for duty, he was killed in a car crash, age 22. The poem was written in the early 1960s. We all have friends or acquaintances of great potential and possibilities whose lives were snuffed out all too early. He was the first I knew to whom this happened. It had a real effect on me, and I did what I could to remember him. I made the poem all one sentence so it could be thought of as a continuum, like a fountain of water slowly turned off and extinguished. The poem is a totally imagined experience; Bill's part in it was not. How it relates to Deep Imagery is for you to say, not I. Such ideas were much in the air at the time of its writing, though I didn't think this poem partook of them. Perhaps I was wrong.

Age-old question: To your mind, are poets made, born, or something else?

Something else. You can "learn" to write poems, but you can't learn vision and talent, ambition and grace. You can't learn imagination. You can learn music, but you can't learn where it comes from. You can't learn instinct, you can't learn the gift or the go-between.

Do you think prosody classes should be mandatory for poetry writing programs? In other words, before a student graduates with an M.F.A., do you think he or she should have so many required hours in form classes? Do you think he or she should be required to write several forms (i.e. sestina, sonnet, villanelle, etc.)?

Yes, you can't not know history.[1] If you're not going to write in the historical meters of English language verse, you'd better know what they are, and why not. The forms aren't that important, but the meters are (each of the three forms you mention, of course, are foreign—the sonnet is Italian, the other two are Provencal). Forms are optional, form is not. Received meters are three of the possible four we have to work with. Free verse is merely one of the four. You've got to know them all. I don't know how many required hours you need, but a prosody class should be SOP [Standard Operating Procedure]. If you are foolish enough to jump out of an airplane, you'd better be sure the parachute works. If not, the fall may be swift and spectacular, but the end is soon in sight.

I get the sense from Pound and Eliot that they thought it essential that a student of poetry should know a dozen languages before that student would be "qualified" to write poetry. Perhaps I am exaggerating, but I was wondering what you thought of the study of foreign languages for students of poetry writing. More simply, do you think a poet can be any good if she doesn't have a working knowledge of at least one language other than her own? But then there is Cioran who says that one should write only in one language. What are your thoughts on the subject?

The intelligent student should know as many languages as he can. That being said, I'm not at all sure that that's any foundation for writing a poem. It's a good foundation for translating poems, which exercise is one the great teachers of how poems are put together and how your own might benefit from it. A poet can certainly be a good poet even if English is the only language he knows. Providing, of course, that's the language he's writing them in. How many languages did Keats know? How many did Philip Larkin know? Still, knowing another language gives you the power of knowing that something is out there, beyond the gates. Even if you don't know it well, you can see the different landscapes, and smell the different aromas. I certainly wish I knew more than the little of the one I do know. But even if I did know that one perfectly, I wouldn't write in it. I agree with Cioran—one should write only in one's own language. (Actually, I guess he didn't say that, he said in one language. He wrote in French, but he was Rumanian. Still.)[2] Others have done otherwise, but usually to lesser effect. But not always (see above). And, of course, Samuel Beckett is always the exception to every rule. But Paul Celan, who lived in the same city as both of them, and was Rumanian too, continued to write in German, his native language, until the end. Which, who knows, might have been helped along by that very fact. Joseph Brodsky wrote in English late in his career, with not too happy results. It's a long and rocky road, and you'd better have a good pair of shoes. Your own language is good leather, with a good tongue.

Is prose writing a strange or difficult experience for you?

Prose writing is difficult for me, for some reason. Not strange, just difficult. One must have a mind of summer to write prose—everything warm and oiled, no need to seek shelter from the storm. Apparently, I have a mind of late fall—the wind blows, leaves fall from the trees; the rain is cold and uncompromising. Things fall apart. The synapses stutter and stand back. No flee-flowing continuity, no logical avenues. You can't stop the leaves from falling, but one tries, one tries. Difficult, but not strange.

What do you think of the prose poem?

Actually, I like the prose poem a lot. The only poems I kept from my first book, as you know, were prose poems. The ultimate poem is probably a prose poem, the line extended and extended until it becomes a sentence and then another sentence, the sentence being thought of as a kind of super-line, venturing farther and further into the unknown. This, of course, only if the prose poem is conceived of, thought of and executed as a poem, and written down as a poem; then it can have the felicities and values of good prose along with the construction and constrictions of poetry. The sentences must be thought of, as I say, as sinuous poetic line, and not as a mere prose narrative. Well, I suppose it's a matter of intent and intuition. Rimbaud's *Illuminations* as opposed to Baudelaire's little poems in prose. I much prefer the former, and I think most good twentieth-century prose poems descend from it, and him. *A Season in Hell* seems more prose-like to me. Still, who knows? It's all just talk and theory and blah blah until the thing is written. Listen to the sound it makes.

Considering the prose poem and free verse, for that matter, what would you say is the fundamental difference between prose and poetry? How would you reply to a person who says there is no fundamental difference once one breaks away from formal meter? Does the difference between prose and poetry then become one of attitude, timing, sound, or something else?

I like what Eugenio Montale said, to the effect that poetry rises out of prose, and longs to return to it. It's in this longing, the desire to return to its original state, that poetry resides. Somewhere between conversation and communication and the condition of the song, some lyrical language in the in-between. Poetry says less and means more. One never breaks away entirely from formal meter. Good free verse is a formal kind of meter. It just doesn't employ received forms or received cadences. Good free verse creates its own forms and its own metrics. Actually, free verse probably aspires to a more formal condition than more "formally" oriented poems do. Received forms and meters are always looking to rough themselves up, the good ones, to vary their patterns in order to justify its existence. Formal values exist in both, as do their opposites. The difference between prose and poetry is one, as I say, of conception, sound patterns, and attitude. Listen to the sound the language makes. The difference is the difference between East Jesus and West Jesus. They both would like to join Jesus, but they are not taken in. One sings, the other plays, but Jesus is ultimately unswayed and unaffected and annexes neither.

Now that we are well on our way into the twenty-first century, what are your thoughts on the future of poetry in the English language?

Bleak. Unless, of course, you consider oblivion a good career move. But then I consider the future of almost everything I've ever cared for bleak, so don't listen to me. There will always be, as Philip Larkin says about churches, the odd ruin-bibber about, and there will always be poems written and poems circulated.[3] But poetry as a force, poetry as a viable genre for communicating emotional value among the tribe is probably doomed to a long and drawn-out extinction. I don't quite see a Fahrenheit 451 scenario, but more that than the present state. Still, I'm not Karnak, my crystal ball is just industrial glass, and I don't always have my spectacle on. Watch this space.

What do you think of neo-formalism?

Not much. I rather like the old formalism, where the writers were concerned with poems, and not just the forms. The Neos seem overly concerned with the vessels and less with the wine therein. The old formalists knew where the power was, and what conveyed it was merely a gift to the initiated. And everything flowed together. In any case, as Ezra Pound said about the Greek gods—the gods haven't returned, they never left.[4] The old formalists never left. Is Richard Wilbur gone? Is Donald Justice gone? Is Anthony Hecht gone? Please. Not to mention Heaney and the Irish mob. There is a certain stridency I find unappealing about the "claims" of the Neos. The older guys have still got the rubber to the road. Those thumbs you see out on the highway are all trying to catch a ride.

Notes

Chapter 1

1. Cesare Pavese, *Hard Labor*, trans. William Arrowsmith (New York: Grossman, 1976); *Dialogues with Leucó*, trans. William Arrowsmith and D.S. Carne-Ross (London: Peter Owen, 1965).

2. It was at this time that Wright began translating Montale's *Mottetti*, which were eventually published as *Mottetti = Motets* ([Iowa City]: Windhover Press at the University of Iowa, 1981).

3. During this time Wright was also reading Dante with Maria Sampoli at the University of Rome.

4. "For me a doughnut's value resides in the hole. You can gobble up the doughnut, but the hole remains" (Osip Mandelstam, "Fourth Prose," in *The Complete Critical Prose and Letters*, ed. Jane Gary Harris, trans. Jane Gary Harris and Constance Link [Ann Arbor, MI: Ardis, 1978], 324).

5. *Lion in the Garden: Interviews with William Faulkner, 1926–1962*, eds. James B. Meriwether and Michael Millgate (New York: Random House, 1968), 238.

6. According to Janet Malcolm, when Stein was being taken into the operating room for surgery she asked Alice B. Toklas, "What is the answer?" When Toklas didn't answer, Stein asked, "In that case, what is the question?" ("Someone Says Yes to It: Gertrude Stein, Alice B. Toklas, and 'The Making of the Americans,'" *New Yorker*, 13 & 20 June 2005: 148–165). Malcolm records another account of Stein's last words: "What is the question and before I could speak she went on—If there is no question then there is no answer" (p. 164).

7. Many of the entries that follow were included in Wright's "Halflife: A Commonplace Notebook," in *Halflife*, 20–39.

8. "Lack one lacks both, and the unseen is proved by the seen, / Till that becomes unseen and receives proof in its turn" (Whitman, *Song of Myself*, pt. 3, ll. 16–17).

9. Ezra Pound, "Vorticism," in *Ezra Pound*, ed. J.P. Sullivan (Harmondsworth: Penguin, 1970), 51.

10. Ezra Pound, *Gaudier-Brzeska* (New York: New Directions, 1974), 81.

11. Ezra Pound, "Vorticism," in *Ezra Pound*, ed. J.P. Sullivan (Harmondsworth: Penguin, 1970), 49.

12. Ibid.

13. Ibid.

14. Ezra Pound, "A Retrospect," in *Literary Essays*, rpt. in *Ezra Pound*, ed. J.P. Sullivan (Harmondsworth: Penguin, 1970), 41.

15. Ezra Pound, "Vorticism," 54.

16. The traditional definition of a sacrament; the phrasing is attributed to St. Augustine.

17. Joan Didion, "The Coast: Good-bye, Gentleman-Ranker," *Esquire* 88 (October 1977): 50.

18. A reference apparently to the second stanza of Wright's own *Holy Thursday:* "There's always a time for rust, / For looking down at the earth and its lateral chains. / There's always a time for the grass, teeming / Its little four-cornered purple flowers, // tricked out in an oozy shine. / There's always a time for the dirt. / Reprieve, reprieve, the flies drone, their wings / Increasingly incandescent above the corn silk. / No answer from anything, four crows / On a eucalyptus limb, speaking in tongues. / No answer for them, either" (*WTTT*, 14).

19. "Allen Ginsburg Talks about Poetry" [interview with Kenneth Koch], *New York Times*, 23 October 1977.

20. Leonard Michaels, *New York Times Book Review* (4 December 1977).

21. Allen Tate, *Essays of Four Decades*, 3rd ed. (Wilmington, DE: ISI, 1999), 446.

22. Tom Stoppard, "But for the Middle Classes"

[Review of *Enemies of Society* by Paul Johnson], *Times Literary Supplement*, 3 June 1977: 677.

23. Letter to his wife Clara, qtd. in Rainer Maria Rilke, *Letters to a Young Poet*, trans. M.D. Herter Norton, rev. ed. (New York: Norton, 1962), 99.

24. Letter 268 (to T.W. Higginson), in *The Letters of Emily Dickinson* (Cambridge, MA: Harvard University Press, 1958), 2:412.

25. Lawrence Gowing, "The Logic of Organized Sensations," in *Cézanne: The Late Work*, ed. William Rubin (New York: Museum of Modern Art, 1977), 56.

26. Ezra Pound, *ABC of Reading* (New York: New Directions, 1934), 92.

27. "Where talent is called upon, there imagination gives out" (Georges Braque, *Cahier* [Paris: Maeght, 1994], 28).

28. John Keats, Letter to George and Thomas Keats, 21, 27(?) December 1817.

29. Hart Crane, "General Aims and Theories," in *The Complete Poems and Selected Letters and Prose of Hart Crane*, ed. Brom Weber (London: Liveright, 1966), 220.

30. From Rilke's letter to Witold von Hulewicz, 13 November 1925, qtd. in *Sonnets to Orpheus*, trans. M.D. Herter Norton (New York: Norton, 1962), 133. For a slightly different translation see Rainer Maria Rilke, *Letters on Life*, trans. Ulrich Baer (New York: Modern Library, 2006).

Chapter 2

1. "A poet is, before anything else, a person who is passionately in love with language" ("Squares and Oblongs," in *Poets at Work*, ed. Charles D. Abbott [New York: Harcourt, Brace, 1948], 170).

2. W.H. Auden, *In Memory of W.B. Yeats*, pt. 2, l. 5.

3. Cf. John Stuart Mill: "Poetry and eloquence are both alike the expression or utterance of feeling. But if we may be excused the antithesis, we should say that eloquence is *heard*, poetry is *overheard*" (*Autobiography and Literary Essays*, ed. John M. Robson and Jack Stillinger [Toronto: University of Toronto Press, 1981], 348).

4. See the final photographs—*Untitled (1)–Untitled (7)*—in *Diane Arbus* (Millerton, NY: An Aperture Monograph, 1972).

5. Letter to Sue Dickinson Gilbert, October 1883, No. 868 in *The Letters of Emily Dickinson*, ed. Thomas H. Johnson (Cambridge, MA: The Belknap Press of Harvard University Press, 1958), 3:799.

6. Ginsberg claimed to have written *Howl* spontaneously, but it was written and edited over the course of 1955–56.

7. "Poetry is a verbal statement of emotional values; a poem is an emotional value verbally stated" (Ezra Pound, *The Confucian Odes* [New York: New Directions, 1959], xv).

Chapter 3

1. Eugenio Montale, *La Bufera e alto* (1956). Wright's translation was published as *The Storm and Other Poems* (Oberlin College: Field Translation Series 1, 1978).

2. Wright's translation of Dino Campana's *Canti orfici* (1914) was published as *Orphic Songs* (Oberlin College: Field Translation Series 9, 1984).

3. Kenneth Rexroth, "The Poet as Translator" in *The Craft and Context of Translation* (Austin: University of Texas Press, 1961); rpt. in *World Outside the Window: The Collected Essays of Kenneth Rexroth* (New York: New Directions, 1987), 189.

4. Jonathan Galassi, Wright's present editor at Farrar, Straus and Giroux, wrote the introduction to Wright's translation, *Orphic Songs*.

5. The distinctions come from Dryden's Preface to his translation of Ovid's *Epistles* (1680). See *The Works of John Dryden*, ed. E.N. Hooker, et al. (Berkeley: University of California Press, 1956–), 4:87.

6. Robert Frost, *Provide, Provide*, in *Complete Poems of Robert Frost* (New York: Holt, Rinehart and Winston, 1949), 404.

7. "A translation from language A into language B will make tangible the implication of a third, active presence. It will show the lineaments of the 'pure speech' which precedes and underlies both languages.... That such fusion can exist, that it must, is proved by fact that human beings *mean* the same things, that the human voice springs from the same hopes and fears, though different words are *said*. Or to put it another way: a poor translation is full of apparently similar saying, but misses the bond of meaning" (George Steiner, *After Babel: Aspects of Language and Translation*, 3rd ed. [New York: Oxford University Press, 1998], 67).

8. "Translation is a possible art and a necessary one, and I think that we do really want to know, insofar as it's possible, what Dante and others in the past thought and felt. The translator should try to understand how they thought and felt and try to completely suppress himself, or to put it the other way around, try to flow into that person he's translating and do it faithfully" (Galway Kinnell, interview in *American Poetry Observed: Poets on Their Word*, ed. Joe D. Bellamy [Urbana: University of Illinois Press, 1984]).

9. In a letter to Woodhouse (27 October 1818) Keats refers to "the wordsworthian [sic] or egotistical sublime"—which is Wordsworth's commanding sense of the poet's primary self (*Letters of John*

Keats, ed. Robert Giddings [New York: Oxford University Press, 1987], 157).

10. The three "journal" poems mentioned here appeared in *ZJ* and were reprinted in *WTTT*.

Chapter 4

1. W.H. Auden, *In Memory of W.B. Yeats*, pt. 2, l. 5.

2. "Poets are the unacknowledged legislators of the World," the concluding sentence of Shelley's *A Defence of Poetry* (1821; pub. 1840).

3. "'The unacknowledged legislators of the world' describes the secret police, not the poets" (W.H. Auden, "Writing," in *The Dyer's Hand and Other Essays* [London: Faber & Faber, 1975], 27).

4. The phrase is quoted by Heinrich Wiegand Petzet in his Foreword to Ranier Maria Rilke's *Letters on Cézanne* (New York: Fromm International, 1985), xxiv.

5. Theodore Roethke, *The Wraith* (New York: Anchor Books, 1975), 102 (l. 15).

6. Richard Wilbur, *The Complete Poems of Poe* (New York: Dell, 1959), 120.

7. Robert Lowell, *Skunk Hour*, in *Selected Poems* (New York: Farrar, Straus and Giroux, 1976), 96.

8. See n. 6 of Chapter 3.

9. The source of the quotation is uncertain. Cf. "The idea of God is a thing of the imagination. We no longer think that God was, but was imagined. The idea of pure poetry, essential imagination, as the highest objective of the poet, appears to be, at least potentially, as great as the idea of God" (*The Letters of Wallace Stevens* [Berkeley: University of California Press, 1996], 369).

10. "Form holds little interest for me. Content is everything" (*Required Writing: Miscellaneous Pieces 1955–1982* [London: Faber and Faber, 1983], 68). Larkin later dismissed the statement: "I'm afraid that was a rather silly remark, especially now when form is so rare. I read poems, and I think, Yes, that's quite a nice idea, but why can't he make a *poem* of it? Make it memorable? It's no good just writing it down! At any level that matters, form and content are indivisible. What I meant by content is the experience the poem preserves, what it passes on. I must have been seeing too many poems that were simply agglomerations of words when I said that" ('The Art of Poetry, No. 30," *The Paris Review* 84 [Summer 1982]: 20).

11. Wright apparently has this remark of Dickinson in mind: "If I read a book and it makes my whole body so cold no fire can ever warm me, I know that is poetry. If I feel physically as if the top of my head were taken off, I know that is poetry. These are the only ways I know it. Is there any other way?" (*The Letters of Emily Dickinson*, ed. Thomas H. Johnson [Cambridge, MA: The Belknap Press of the Harvard University Press, 1958], 2:342a).

12. The allusion is to the final line of Yeats's *Among School Children*: "How can we know the dancer from the dance?"

13. On the "egotistical sublime," see n. 9 of Chapter 3. "Negative capability" is a phrase from John Keats's letter to George and Thomas Keats, 21 December 1817, expressing his theory of poetic openmindedness: "I had not a dispute but a disquisition with Dilke, on various subjects; several things dovetailed in my mind, & at once it struck me, what quality went to form a Man of Achievement especially in literature & which Shakespeare possessed so enormously—I mean Negative Capability, that is when man is capable of being in uncertainties, Mysteries, doubts without any irritable reaching after fact & reason."

14. See n. 6 of Chapter 2.

15. On Ginsberg's account of how he sought to reproduce the feeling of inspiration he got from Cézanne's paintings, see his interview with Thomas Clark in *Writers at Work: The Paris Review Interviews*, Third Series, ed. George Plimpton (New York: Penguin, 1967), 291–4.

16. See n. 4 of this chapter.

Chapter 5

1. Robert Pinsky, "Description and the Virtuous Use of Words," *Parnassus* 3, no. 2 (1975): 134–46; rev. version rpt. in *The Situation of Poetry: Contemporary Poetry and Its Traditions* (Princeton, NJ: Princeton University Press, 1976), 111–18.

2. Charles Altieri, "The Dominant Poetic Mode of the Late Seventies," in *Self and Sensibility in Contemporary American Poetry* (Cambridge: Cambridge University Press, 1984), 32–51. Helen Vendler, "Travels in Time," *New Republic* 198, no. 3 (18 January 1988): 34–6; rev. version appears as "Charles Wright" in *The Music of What Happens: Poems, Poets, Critics* (Cambridge: Harvard University Press, 1988); rpt. in Andrews, 13–20; and in Giannelli, 29–35. Vendler, "The Nothing That Is," *New Republic* 213, no. 6 (7 August 1995): 42–5; rpt. in Giannelli, 68–75. Vendler, "The Transcendent 'I,'" *New Yorker*, 29 October 1979, 160–74; rpt. in *Part of Nature, Part of Us: Modern American Poets* (Cambridge: Harvard University Press, 1988), 277–88; in Andrews, 1–12, and in Giannelli, 115–25.

3. Wright quotes the passage from Cézanne in *Halflife*, 20, from Joachim Gasquet, *Paul Cézanne* (Paris: Editions Bernheim-Jeune, 1926).

4. That is, with *Country Music* and *The World*

of the Ten Thousand Things Wright has completed two-thirds of the three trilogies.

5. See *New Yorker* 62, no. 36 (27 October 1986): 40, and *New Yorker* 62, no. 24 (4 August 1986): 26–7.

6. Gaetano Prampolini. See his translation of *The Other Side of the River, L'altra riva del fiume,* ExCogita Editore, 2001. See also his translation of *The Secret of Poetry, Is,* and *Nostalgia,* in *La Luna, Pensiero* 12 [1999], and of *The Southern Cross* in *Testo a fronte* 16 (March 1997): 136–7.

7. Wright's second collection of prose, *Quarter Notes: Improvisations and Interviews,* was published in 1995 (Ann Arbor: University of Michigan Press).

8. Pinsky had claimed (see n. 1 of Chapter 5) that Wright's "mannerist" verse had completely abandoned statement and description.

9. Calvin Bedient, "Tracing Charles Wright," *Parnassus* 10 (Spring-Summer 1982): 55–74; rpt. in Andrews, 21–38, and in Giannelli, 126–41.

10. See n. 1 of this chapter.

Chapter 6

1. The source of the quotation is uncertain. In an interview, Wright remarked, as he goes on to say here, "All poems are about not dying" (*Halflife,* 82).

2. *Sunday Morning,* pt. 5, l. 3 and pt. 6, l. 13.

3. "The ancients said that poetry / is a stairway to God" (*Syria,* in *Collected Poems 1920–1954,* trans. Jonathan Galassi [New York: Farrar, Straus and Giroux, 1998], 345 [ll. 1–2]).

4. Theodore Roethke, *A Far Field,* in *Collected Poems,* 195 (pt. 4, l. 13).

Chapter 7

1. "And when one day one perceives that their occupations are paltry, their professions petrified and no longer linked with living, why not then continue to look like a child upon it all as upon something unfamiliar, from out of the depth of one's own world, out of the expanse of one's own solitude, which is itself work and status and vocation? Why want to exchange a child's wise incomprehension for defensiveness and disdain, since incomprehension is after all being alone, while defensiveness and disdain are a sharing in that from which one wants by these means to keep apart. Think, dear sir, of the world you carry within you, and call this thinking what you will; whether it be remembering your own childhood or yearning toward your own future—only be attentive to that which rises up in you and set it above everything that you observe about you" (Rainer Maria Rilke, *Letters to a Young Poet,* trans. M.D. Herder Norton, rev. ed. [New York: Norton, 1954], 46).

2. *QN,* 118.

3. Christopher Ricks, *Dylan's Vision of Sin* (New York: Ecco, 2004).

4. Wright apparently means Allen's 1996 film, *Everyone Says I Love You.*

Chapter 8

1. Prampolini, professor of Anglo-American language and literature at the Università degli Studi di Firenze, has translated and written about Wright's poetry.

2. "Verse is always born out of prose and tends to return to it" ("Seven Questions about Poetry for Eugenio Montale," in *The Second Life of Art: Selected Essays of Eugenio Montale,* ed. Jonathan Galassi [New York: Ecco, 1982], 335).

3. For Wright's translations of Buffoni, see *The Grotto, Santa Maria F.P.,* and *The Plum Coloured Sky* in *The Bitter Oleander* 3, no. 2 (1997), and *The Carmelite Sister* and *Forte d'Orino* in *Yale Italian Poetry* 2, no. 1 (Spring 1998).

4. Barthelme made the remark in response to a question by J.D. O'Hara in his *Paris Review* interview: "The Art of Fiction, No. 66," *Paris Review* 80 (Summer 1981).

5. In the movie, The Stranger says to Sarah Belding, "It's what people know about themselves inside that makes 'em afraid."

6. See Wright's *Bar Giamaica, 1959–60* in *WTTT,* 39.

Chapter 9

1. The poem was Pound's *Blandula, Tenulla, Vagula.*

2. "Ever tried. Ever failed. No matter. Try again. Fail again. Fail better" (Samuel Beckett, *Worstward Ho* [New York: Grove Press, 1984], 7).

Chapter 10

1. See Wright's "Improvisations on Pound," *Field: Contemporary Poetry and Poetics* 33 (Fall 1985): 63–70; rpt. in *Halflife,* 10–19.

2. Caseley apparently picked up the phrase from Wright's interview with Ted Genoways (p. 121 below).

Chapter 11

1. "The struggle is beyond painting, not with painting" (qtd. in James E.B. Breslin, *Mark Rothko: A Biography* [Chicago: University of Chicago Press, 1993], 323).

Chapter 13

1. "I try to pick what I like throughout history. We cannot not know history" ("Whither Away—Non-Miesian Directions" [speech at Yale University, 5 February 1959], in Robert A.M. Stern and Peter D. Eisenman, eds. *Philip Johnson: Writings* (New York: Oxford University Press, 1979), 227.
2. From the final line of Yeats's *The Circus Animals' Desertion*.
3. "Call the world if you please 'The vale of soul-making'" (John Keats's Letter to George and Georgiana Keats, 21 April 1819).
4. See n. 1 of Chapter 7.
5. Ch'ing Yuan's lines can be found in D.T. Suzuki, *Zen Buddhism: Selected Writings of D.T. Suzuki*, qtd. by Arthur Danto, *The Transfiguration of the Commonplace: A Philosophy of Art* (Cambridge, MA: Harvard University Press, 1981), 133.
6. See n. 2 of Chapter 9.

Chapter 14

1. The dust jacket has eleven photographs of Wright's mouth, but he was not pronouncing the word "Chickamauga" (Charles Wright to Robert Denham, private communication).

Chapter 15

1. See n. 1 of Chapter 13.
2. "A writer worthy of the name confines himself to his mother tongue and does not go ferreting about in this or that alien idiom. He is limited, and likes to be—out of self-defense. Nothing wrecks a talent more certainly than a mind too wide open" (E.M. Ciroan, *The New Gods*, trans. Richard Howard [New York: Quadrangle, 1974], 90).
3. Wright is referring to Philip Larkin's *Church Going*: "I wonder who / Will be the last, the very last, to seek / This place for what it was; one of the crew / That tap and jot and know what rood-lofts were? / Some ruin-bibber, randy for antique, / Or Christmas-addict, counting on a whiff / Of gown-and-bands and organ-pipes and myrrh? (ll. 38–44).
4. "No man can see his own end. / The Gods have not returned. 'They have never left us.' / They have not returned" (*Canto CXIII*, in *Cantos*, 807).

A Selected Bibliography

This bibliography is divided into sections: Primary Sources—Books; —Translations. Secondary Sources—Books; —Articles, Essays, Parts of Books; —Reviews (with three subsections: Poetry [with individual titles chronologically]; Translations; and Essays).

Primary Sources

Books

Appalachia. New York: Farrar Straus Giroux, 1998. French translation by Alice-Catherine Carls, forthcoming (Belval, France: Éditions Circé).

Backwater. Costa Mesa, Calif.: Golem Press, 1973.

Black Zodiac. New York: Farrar, Straus and Giroux, 1997. Braille edition, National Library Service, BR 11995. *Zodiaco Negro*, Spanish trans. by Jeannette L. Clariond. Valencia: Pre-textos, 2002.

Bloodlines. Middletown, CT: Wesleyan University Press, 1975.

Buffalo Yoga. New York: Farrar, Straus and Giroux, 2004.

Colophons. Iowa City: Windhover Press, 1977. Limited edition: 200 copies.

Country Music. Middletown, CT: Wesleyan University Press, 1982.

Country Music. 2nd ed. Hanover, NH: Wesleyan/ New England Press, 1991.

Chickamauga. New York: Farrar, Straus and Giroux, 1995.

China Trace. Middletown, CT: Wesleyan University Press, 1977.

Crepuscolo americano e altre poesie (1980–2000). Trans. Antonella Francini. Milan: Jaca Book, 2001.

Dead Color. Poems. San Francisco: Meadow Press, 1980. Limited edition: 285 copies.

December Journal. N.p.: Geary Press, 1990. Limited edition.

The Dream Animal. Toronto: House of Anansi, 1968.

Five Journals. New York: Red Ozier Press, 1986. Limited edition: 100 copies.

Four Poems of Departure. Portland, OR: Trace Editions, 1983. Limited edition: 500 copies.

The Grave of the Right Hand. Middletown, CT: Wesleyan University Press, 1970.

Halflife: Improvisations and Interviews, 1977–87. Ann Arbor: University of Michigan Press, 1988.

Hard Freight. Middletown, CT: Wesleyan University Press, 1973.

A Journal of the Year of the Ox. Iowa City: Windhover Press, 1988. Limited edition: 150 copies.

Littlefoot. A Poem. New York: Farrar, Straus and Giroux, 2007.

North American Bear. La Crosse, WI: Sutton Hoo Press, 1999. Limited edition: 136 copies.

Negative Blue: Selected Later Poems. New York: Farrar, Straus and Giroux, 2000. Exeter, Devon, England: Stride Publications, 2000. French translation by Alice-Catherine Carls, forthcoming.

Night Music. Exeter, Devon, England: Stride Publications, 2001.

The Other Side of the River. New York: Vintage, 1984. Italian translation: *L'altra riva del fiume*, trans. Gaetano Prampolini. Milan: ExCogita Editore, 2001.

Private Madrigals. Madison, WI: Abraxas Press, 1969. Limited edition: 200 copies.

Quarter Notes: Improvisations and Interviews. Ann Arbor: University of Michigan Press, 1995.

Scar Tissue. New York: Farrar, Straus and Giroux, 2006.

A Selected Bibliography

A Short History of the Shadow. New York: Farrar, Straus Giroux, 2002. Italian translation: *Breve storia dell'ombra*, trans. Antonella Francini. Milan: Crocetti Editore, 2006. Spanish translation, *Breve historia de la sombra*, by Jeannette L. Clariond, forthcoming.

Six Poems. London: Royal College of Art, 1964. Illustrated by David Freed. Limited edition: 20 copies.

Snake Eyes. Exeter, Devon, England: Stride Publications, 2004.

Southern Cross. New York: Random House, 1981.

Uncollected Prose: Six Guys and a Supplement. Salem, VA: Roanoke College, 2000.

The Venice Notebook. Boston: Barn Dream Press, 1971. Limited edition: 500 copies.

The Voyage. Iowa City: Patrician Press, 1963. Limited edition: 25 copies.

The World of the Ten Thousand Things: Poems 1980–1990. New York: Farrar Straus Giroux, 1990.

Wright: A Profile. New Poems by Charles Wright with an Interview and a Critical Essay by David St. John. Iowa City: Grilled Flowers Press, 1979.

The Wrong End of the Rainbow. Louisville, KY: Sarabande Books, 2005.

Xionia. Poems. Iowa City: Windhover Press, 1990. Limited edition: 250 copies.

Zone Journals. New York: Farrar Straus Giroux, 1988. Exeter, Devon, England: Stride Publications, 1996.

Translations

Dino Campana, *Orphic Songs.* Oberlin College: Field Translation Series 9, 1984

Eugenio Montale, *The Storm and Other Poems.* Oberlin College: Field Translation Series 1, 1978.

Eugenio Montale, *Mottetti = Motets* [Iowa City]: Windhover Press at the University of Iowa, 1981. Limited edition: 220 copies.

Horace, Odes 3.8 and 4.12, in *The Odes: A New Translation by Contemporary Poets.* Ed. J.D. McClatchy. Princeton, NJ: Princeton University Press, 2002.

Girardo Ansaldi's libretto, in David Daniel's *Alessandro Stradella's Oratorio San Giovanni Battista: A Modern Edition and Commentary.* Ph.D. thesis, University of Iowa, 1963.

Secondary Sources

Books

Andrews, Tom, ed. *The Point Where All Things Meet: Essays on Charles Wright.* Oberlin, OH: Oberlin College Press, 1995. Rev. in *Virginia Quarterly Review* 72, no. 4 (Autumn 1996): 118.

Denham, Robert D. *Charles Wright: A Companion to the Late Poetry, 1988–2007.* Jefferson, NC, and London: McFarland, 2008.

Giannelli, Adam, ed. *High Lonesome: On the Poetry of Charles Wright.* Oberlin, OH: Oberlin College Press, 2006. A revised and expanded version of Andrews, above.

Moffett, Joe. *Understanding Charles Wright.* Columbia: University of South Carolina Press, forthcoming (2009).

Articles, Essays, Parts of Books

News stories are marked with an asterisk.

*Adams, James. "McKay, Wright Win Griffin Poetry Prizes." *Globeandmail.com.* 7 June 2007.

Allbery, Debra. "Lives of the Artists: Line, Landscape and the Poet's Calling in the Work of Charles Wright." Warren Wilson College Audiotape, January 2000.

Albright, Daniel. "Noble Savages in Armani Suits: Recent American Art: Proceedings of the XV Biennial Conference Siracusa, November 4–7, 1999." *America Today: Highways and Labyrinths*, ed. Gigliola Nocera. Siracusa, Italy: Grafià, 2003. 51–65.

Altieri, Charles. "The Dominant Poetic Mode of the Late Seventies." In *Self and Sensibility in Contemporary American Poetry.* Cambridge: Cambridge University Press, 1984. 32–51.

Bediant, Calvin. "Coloring Nature Big and Wet, Dry and Varied, and Pushed Aside." *Antioch Review* 52 (Winter 1994): 15–33.

———. "The Predicament of Modern Poetry (The Lyric at the Pinch-Gate)." *Chicago Review* 51/52 (Spring 2006): 135–54.

*Biespiel, David. "First Sunday on Poetry: "Nostalgia" by Charles Wright." *The Sunday Oregonian*, 2 March 2003. http://www.atticwritersworkshop.com/firstSunday/march_2003.php.

Bond, Bruce. "Metaphysics of the Image in Charles Wright and Paul Cézanne." *The Southern Review* 30 (Winter 1994): 116–25. Rpt. in Andrews, *The Point Where All Things Meet*, 264–73, and in Giannelli, *High Lonesome*, 221–9. Also available at http://www.english.uiuc.edu/maps/poets/s_z/c_wright/bond.htm.

Boyle, Peter. "Tradition and Wisdom in Charles Wright's *Black Zodiac* and *Chickamauga*. *Verse* 15–16, no. 3/1 (1998): 102–8.

*Bratcher, Drew. "Charles Wright's Poetry of Place." *Washingtonian.com.* http://www.washingtonian.com/blogarticles/mediapolitics/capitalcomment/3436.html.

*Brickhouse, Robert. "Poet Charles Wright Elected to American Academy of Arts and Sciences." *Inside UVA*, 2 April 1995. http://www.virginia.edu/insideuva/textonlyarchive/95-04-21/1.txt.

A Selected Bibliography

Buck, Paula Closson. "A Deeper Disregard: Thoughts on Reading Charles Wright." Paper presented at the annual meeting of the Associated Writing Programs on a panel "Charles Wright at 70: A Celebration and Retrospective," Vancouver, BC, 31 March 2005. Typescript. 8 pp.

Butterick, George F. "Charles Wright." *Dictionary of Literary Biography Yearbook 1982*. Ed. Richard Ziegfeld. Detroit: Gale Research, 1983. 389–400. On CD-ROM, Version 3.1, 1997.

Cain, Stephen. "Two in T.O.: The Canadian Publications of Allen Ginsberg and Charles Wright." Paper presented at the conference of the National Poetry Foundation, University of Maine, Orono, ME, 28 June-2 July, 2002.

Carls, Alice-Catherine. "Charles Wright, poète da la transparence." *Poesie premiere* No. 12 (Winter 1998–1999): 3–24.

_____. "Charles Wright." *Le Journal des Poètes* 68, no. 8 (December 1998): 9–11. Translation of seven poems, with a brief biographical introduction.

"Charles Wright." *Contemporary Authors. New Revision Series*. Vol. 62. Detroit: Gale Research, 1998. 447–50.

"Charles Wright." *Poetry Foundation*. http://www.poetryfoundation.org/archive/poet.html?id=7560

Chitwood, Michael. "Gospel Music: Charles Wright and the High Lonesome." *Iron Mountain Review* 8 (Spring 1992): 23–5. Rpt. in Andrews, *The Point Where All Things Meet*, 241–7, and in Giannelli, *High Lonesome*, 186–91.

*Chollet, Laurence. "Poetry Set in Motion." *The Record* (Bergen County, NJ) (13 June 1993).

Conte, Joseph Mark. *American Poets since World War II, Fourth Series*. [*Dictionary of Literary Biography*, vol. 165]. Detroit: Gale Research, 1996.

Contemporary Authors: Autobiography Series. Vol. 7. Detroit: Gale Research, 1988. 287–303.

Cooperman, Matthew. "Echolocation and the Imperative of Landscape: Charles Wright's Late Appalachian Trilogy." Paper presented at the Twentieth Century Literature Conference, Louisville, KY, February 2001.

Costello, Bonnie. "Charles Wright, Giorgio Morandi, and the Metaphysics of the Line." *Mosaic* 35, no. 1 (March 2002): 149–71. Rpt. in Giannelli, *High Lonesome*, 304–24.

_____. "Charles Wright's *Via Negativa*: Language, Landscape, and the Idea of God." *Contemporary Literature* 36, no. 2 (2000): 325–46.

_____. "Introduction: Flame and Flux." *Shifting Ground: Reinventing Landscape in Modern American Poetry*. Cambridge, MA: Harvard University Press, 2003. 3–5.

_____. "The Passions of Charles Wright." Paper presented at the 1999 Association of Literary Scholars and Critics, 31 October 1999.

_____. "The Soil and Man's Intelligence: Three Contemporary Landscape Poets." *Contemporary Literature* 30, no. 3 (1989): 412–33. Material on Wright rpt. in Andrews, *The Point Where All Things Meet*, 145–54.

Crenshaw, Brad. "Charles Wright." *Critical Survey of Poetry*. Vol. 7. Ed. Frank N. Magill. Englewood Cliffs, NJ: Salem Press, 1982. 3147–54.

Cushman, Stephen. "The Capabilities of Charles Wright." *Iron Mountain Review* 8 (Spring 1992): 14–22. Rpt. in Andrews, *The Point Where All Things Meet*, 222–40; and in Giannelli, *High Lonesome*, 203–20.

Daniels, Kate. "Porch-Sitting and Southern Poetry." In *The Future of Southern Letters*, ed. Jefferson Humphries and John Lowe. New York: Oxford University Press, 1996. 61–71.

*Darbyshire, Peter. "Winners of Griffin Poetry Prize Announced." *National Post* 23 June 2007. http://communities.canada.com/theprovince/blogs/readthis/archive/2007/06/07/winners-of-griffin-poetry-prize-announced.aspx.

Davis, William V. "Bruised by God: Charles Wright's Apocalyptic Pilgrimages." Paper presented at the Swansea Conference (2000) in a session on "Walt Whitman and His Legacy." See *American Studies in Britain* 82 (Spring-Summer) 2000.

_____. "Making the World with Words: A Reading of Charles Wright's 'Appalachian Book of the Dead.'" *Latitude 63° North: Proceedings of the 8th International Region and Nation Literature Conference, Östersund, Sweden 2–6 August 2000*, ed. David Bell. Östersund, Sweden: Mid-Sweden University College, 2002. 255–70.

Devine, Kelly Anne. *Language Journal: A Study of Charles Wright and Deconstruction*. San Luis Obispo: California State Polytechnic University. B.A. thesis, 1997.

Dodd, Elizabeth, "'Looking Around': A Fidelity of Attention in Charles Wright's Transcendental Journals." Paper presented at the annual meeting of the Associated Writing Programs on a panel "Charles Wright at 70: A Celebration and Retrospective," Vancouver, BC, 31 March 2005. Typescript, 14 pp.

Finch, Annie. *The Ghost of Meter*. Ann Arbor: University of Michigan Press, 1993. 132–5.

Francini, Antonella. "Chronicle of a Long Fidelity: The Case of the American Poets." *Rivista di Poesia Comparata* Nos. 16–17 (1997): 11–16.

_____. "Crepuscolo americano: la poesia di Charles Wright." *Poesia* 149 (April 2001): 18–22.

_____. *In the Longfellow Line: Some Contemporary American Poets as Translators of Eugenio Mon-

tale: A Study in Theory and Practice. Ph.D. dissertation, Drew University, 1985.

———. "'The pale hems of the masters' gown': Mediterranean Voices and Shadows in the Poetry of Charles Wright." *America and the Mediterranean: AISNA, Associazione Italiana di Studi Nord-Americani, Proceedings of the Sixteenth Biennial International Conference, Genova, November 8–11, 2001.* Ed. Massimo Bacigalupo and Pierangelo Gastegneto. Torino: Otto Editore, 2003. 85–92.

———. "A Poet's Workshop: Charles Wright Translating Eugenio Montale." *L'Anello che non tiene: Journal of Modern Italian Literature* 4, nos. 1–2 (Spring-Fall 1992): 44–71.

———. "Trilogia triplice: riflessioni sulla poesia di Charles Wright." In Wright's *Crepuscolo americano e altre poesie (1980–2000)*, trans. Antonella Francini. Milan: Jaca Book, 2001. 261–81.

Franzek, Phyllis Jean. "Charles Wright's Half-Life: Elegiacally Inventive." *Pacific Coast Philology* 40 (2005): 138–57.

———. "Ibn 'Arabi to Charles Wright: Luminous Longings and Related Matters." Paper presented at the annual conference of the Pacific Ancient and Modern Language Association, 10–11 November 2006.

———. *Political Poetics: Revisionist Form in Adrienne Rich, John Ashbery, Charles Wright, and Jorie Graham.* Ph.D. dissertation, University of Southern California, 1996. See *Dissertation Abstracts International*, A (Humanities and Social Sciences). 57(1): 215. Dissertation Abstract Number DA9617098.

Gardner, Thomas. "Restructured and Restrung: Charles Wright's *Zone Journals* and Emily Dickinson." *Kenyon Review* 26, no. 2 (Spring 2004): 149–74. Rev. for inclusion in Gardner's *A Door Ajar: Contemporary Writers and Emily Dickinson*. New York: Oxford University Press, 2006.

Garrison, David. "'An Old Song Handles My Heart': Charles Wright and the Sweet Failure of Music." *Kentucky Philological Review* 6 (1991): 9–14.

———. "From Feeling to Form: Image as Translation in the Poetry of Charles Wright." *Midwest Quarterly* 4, no. 1 (Autumn 1999): 33–47.

Gewirtz, Ken. "The Age of Ozzy Osbourne." *Harvard Gazette*, 6 June 2002.

Gibson, Lydialyle. "'Not Dark, Not Dark, But Almost' Lurking in Shadows: Charles Wright's Poetry Wonders About History, Memory, and the Rest of Time." *Chicago Journal Poetry Center.* http://poetrycenter.org/involved/news/wrightjournal.html.

Gilchrist, David William. *Greening the Lyre: Environmental Poetics and Ethics (Poetry, Robert Frost, Wallace Stevens, Adrienne Rich, A.R. Ammons, Charles Wright).* Eugene: University of Oregon. Ph.D. dissertation, 1996.

Gitzen, Julian. "Charles Wright and Presences in Absence." *Mid-American Review* 14, no. 2 (1994): 110–21. Rpt. in Andrews, *The Point Where All Things Meet*, 172–83, and in Giannelli, *High Lonesome*, 192–202.

Guilford, Chuck. "Beyond the Great Wall of Language: Charles Wright's *The World of the Ten Thousand Things*." http://chuckguilford.com/uncollected/GRT_WALL_LNG.pdf.

Hahn, Robert. "The Mockingbird's Chops: Charles Wright in Italian." *Parnassus: Poetry in Review* 29, nos.1–2 (2006): 349–69.

———. "Versions of the Mediterranean in American Poetry." *America and the Mediterranean: AISNA, Associazione Italiana di Studi Nord-Americani, Proceedings of the Sixteenth Biennial International Conference, Genova, November 8–11, 2001.* Ed. Massimo Bacigalupo and Pierangelo Gastegneto. Torino: Otto Editore, 2003. 57–64. Revised version in *Poetry International* 6 (2002).

Hammer, Langdon. "The Latches of Paradise: Charles Wright's Meditations and Memories at Year's End." *American Scholar* 74, no. 4 (Autumn 2005): 73–4.

Harper, Margaret Mills. "Charles Wright (1935–)." *Contemporary Poets, Dramatists, Essayists, and Novelists of the South: A Bio-Bibliographical Sourcebook*, ed. Robert Bain and Joseph M. Flora. Westport, CT: Greenwood Press, 1994. pp. 553–61.

*Harris, Sally. "Emily Dickinson Challenges Modern Writers." *Virginia Tech Research* (Winter 2003). http://www.research.vt.edu/resmag/2003winter/emily.html.

*Harris, Sharon. "Dancing in the Distillery District: The 2007 Griffin Gala." *Torontoist.* 8 June 2007. http://www.torontoist.com/archives/2007/06/sometimes_write.php.

Hart, George Leslie. *The Poetics of Postmodernist and Neoromantic Nature Poetry.* Ph.D. dissertation, Stanford University, 1997.

Hart, Henry. "Charles Wright." *American Writers: A Collection of Literary Biographies, Supplement V: Russell Banks to Charles Wright.* Ed. Jay Parini. New York: Scribner's, 2000. 331–46.

———. "Charles Wright." *Oxford Encyclopedia of American Literature.* New York: Oxford University Press, 2004. 465–72.

———. "Charles Wright's *Via Mystica*." *Georgia Review* 58, no. 2 (Summer 2004): 409–32. Rpt. in Giannelli, *High Lonesome*, 325–44.

Hart, Kevin. "'La poesia è scala a dio': On Reading Charles Wright," *Heat* [Artarmon, NSW] 1, no. 6 (1997): 92–109. Rpt. in *Religion and the Arts* 8, no. 2 (June 2004): 174–99.

A SELECTED BIBLIOGRAPHY

———. "Poetry and Transcendence." 25 November 1997. http://home.vicnet.net.au/~ozlit/news9711.html.

Hawkins, Peter, and Rachel Jacoff. "Still Here: Dante after Modernism." *Yale Review* 89 (July 2001): 11–24.

Henry, Brian. "Exquisite Disjunctions, Exquisite Arrangements." *Antioch Review* 56 (Summer 1998): 281–93.

———. "New Scaffolding for New Arrangements: Charles Wright's Low Riders." *Virginia Quarterly Review* 80, no. 2 (Spring 2004): 98–112.

———. "Southern Cross: The Inheritance of Charles Wright." *Quarterly West* 46 (1998): 196–202.

Hirsch, Edward. "The Visionary Poetics of Philip Levine and Charles Wright." *The Columbia History of American Poetry*, ed. Jay Parini. New York: Columbia University Press, 1994. 777–805. Material on Wright rpt. in Andrews, *The Point Where All Things Meet*, 248–63.

Hix, H.L. "Charles Wright and a Case of Foreshortened Influence." *Notes on Contemporary Literature* 18, no. 1 (January 1988): 4–6.

*Hoagland, Sadie. "Poet Charles Wright Reinterprets Reality." *The Middlebury Campus*, 15 January 2004. http://www.middleburycampus.com/news/2003/10/10/Arts/Poet-Charles.Wright.Reinterprets.Reality-524165.shtml.

Holland, Diane. *Focusing the Dream: Image, Sequence and Pattern in Poems by Charles Wright.* M.F.A. thesis, Warren Wilson College, 2002.

Holland, Gill. "Charles Wright and the Presence of Chinese Poetry in Contemporary U.S. Poetry." *Crossing Borders: Interdisciplinary Intercultural Interaction*, ed. Bernhard Ketterman and Georg Marko. Tübingen: Gunter Narr Verlag, 1999. 313–23.

Ingalls, Zoe. "Charles Wright, Poet of Landscape, Melds Tradition and Innovation." *Chronicle of Higher Education* 45, no. 4 (18 September 1998): B10–11.

Irons-Georges, Tracy, and Philip K. Jason, eds. On *Homage to Paul Cézanne, Laguna Blues*, and *Reading Lao Tzu Again in the New Year*. *Masterplots II Poetry*. Pasadena, CA: Salem Press, 2002. vol. 4, pp. 1731, 2135; vol. 6, p. 3143.

Jarman, Mark. "The Pragmatic Imagination and the Secret of Poetry." *Gettysburg Review* 1, no. 4 (Autumn 1988): 647–77. Rpt. in Andrews, *The Point Where All Things Meet*, 105–9; and in Jarman's *The Secret of Poetry: Essays*. Ashland, OR: Story Line Press, 2001.

———. "The Trace of a Story Line." *Ohio Review* 37 (1986):129–47. Material on Wright rpt. in Andrews, *The Point Where All Things Meet*, 96–104.

*Johnson, Brian D. "The Griffin Groove." *Maclean's.ca*, 7 June 2007. http://forums.macleans.ca/advansis/?mod=for&act=dip&pid=55312&tid=55312&ref=rss&eid=44.

Johnson, Andrew. *Back To Splendour: Charles Wright's Poetry*. Ph. D. thesis, Monash University, 2005.

———. "'I Have Seen What I Have Seen': Charles Wright's 'Tattoos' and the Problem of Autobiography." *Colloquy: Text Theory Critique* 7 (May 2003). http://www.arts.monash.edu.au/others/colloquy/current/Issue%20Seven/Johnson.htm.

Johnston, Geranl Gordon. *The Poetry of Charles Wright*. Redlands, CA: University of Redlands. Honors thesis, 1981.

Kenzie, Mary. "Haunting." *American Poetry Review* 11, no. 5 (September-October 1982): 40–1.

King, Arthur H., Jr. *American Scholar* 75 (Winter 2006): 142. Letter to the editor.

Kirby, David. "Upward, Toward." *What Is a Book?* Athens: University of Georgia Press, 2002. 60–70.

*Kondracki, Elena. "Poets Sherod Santos and Charles Wright at the 'Y.'" *nycBigCityLit.com*, February 2001. http://www.nycbigcitylit.com/feb2001/contents/SeriesReviews.htmlSeries.

LaBlanc, Michael. *Poetry for Students. Volume 10: Presenting Analysis, Context and Criticism on Commonly Studied Poetry*. Detroit: Gale Research, 2001.

Lake, Paul. "Return to Metaphor: From Deep Imagist to New Formalist." *Southwest Review* 74, no. 4 (Autumn 1989): 515–29. Rpt. in *New Expansive Poetry: Theory, Criticism, History*, ed. R.S. Gwynn. Ashland, OR: Story Line, 1999.

Levine, Philip. "Citation: 1996 Lenore Marshall Poetry Prize." *American Poet*, Winter 1996–97: 25 Also at http://www.poets.org/poems/prose.cfm?45442B7C000C0702007A. Press release: http://www.poets.org/academy/news/pr961028.cfm.

Longenbach, James. "Disjunction in Poetry." *Raritan* 20, no. 4 (2001): 20–36. Incorporates "The Landscapes of Charles Wright," a paper presented at the meeting of the Association of Literary Scholars and Critics, 31 October 1999.

Lowinsky, Naomi. "Writing as Spiritual Practice in the Company of Tagore and Wright." Workshop at the C.J. Jung Institute, San Francisco, 8 May 2004.

McClatchy, J.D. "Reading." *White Paper on Contemporary American Poetry*. New York: Columbia University Press, 1989. 26–44. Material on Wright rpt. as "Under the Sign of the Cross" in Andrews, *The Point Where All Things Meet*, 72–85, and in Giannelli, *High Lonesome*, 142–53.

McCorkle, James. "Charles Wright." *Dictionary of*

A Selected Bibliography

Literary Biography: American Poets Since World War II, Fourth Series. Vol. 165, ed. Joseph Conte. Detroit: Gale, 1966. 267–82.

———. *Gaze, Memory, and Discourse: Self-reflexivity in Recent American Poetry (Bishop, Ashbery, Merwin, Wright).* Ph. D. dissertation, University of Iowa, 1984.

———. "Local Habitations." *American Poetry Review* 32, no. 5 (September-October 2003): 13.

———. "'Things That Lock Our Wrists to the Past': Self-Portraiture and Autobiography in Charles Wright's Poetry." *The Still Performance: Writing, Self, and Interconnections in Five Postmodernist American Poets.* Charlottesville: University Press of Virginia, 1989. 171–211. Rpt. in Andrews, *The Point Where All Things Meet*, 110–44, and in Giannelli, *High Lonesome*, 154–85.

McCurry, Sara Kathleen. *The Places of Contemporary American Poetry.* Ph.D. dissertation, University of Oregon, 2005. Chapter Two, "Transcending Place: Charles Wright and 'The Things That Must Fall Away.'"

McDonald, Jeanne. "Charles Wright and the Talking Eternity Blues." *Appalachian Life* 62 (December-January 2003): 26–8.

McFee, Michael. "Charles Wright's Pilgrimage." *Seneca Review* 14, no. 2 (1984): 85–97.

McGuiness, Daniel. "The Long Line in Contemporary American Poetry." *Antioch Review* 47, no. 3 (Summer 1989): 269–86. Rpt. as "The Long Line in Jorie Graham and Charles Wright," in *Holding Patterns: Temporary Poetics in Contemporary Poetry.* Albany: State University of New York Press, 2001. 139–54.

Merriman, Emily Taylor. *"Whatever": God as Absent Presence in the Poetry of Geoffrey Hill, Derek Walcott, and Charles Wright.* Ph.D. dissertation, Boston University, 2007.

*Messaros, Mike. "Pulitzer-winner Wright Reads at U. Massachusetts." *University Wire*, 9 April 1999.

Monacell, Peter. *Poetry of the American Suburbs (Louis Simpson, James Dickey, Donald Justice, Charles Wright).* M.A. thesis, University of Missouri, 2004.

Morris, John. "Making More Sense than Omaha." *Hudson Review* 27 (Spring 1974): 106–7.

———. "The Songs Protect Us in a Way." *Hudson Review* 27 (Autumn 1974): 453–5.

Mulvania, Andrew. "Confessions of St. Charles: Confession as Spiritual Autobiography in the Work of Charles Wright." *Valparaiso Poetry Review: Contemporary Poetry and Poetics* 4, no. 1 (Fall-Winter 2002-2003). http://www.valpo.edu/english/vpr/mulvaniaessaywright.html.

Muske, Carol. "Ourselves as History." *Parnassus: Poetry in Review* 4, no. 2 (Spring-Summer 1976): 116–21.

Ormsby, Eric. "Of Lapdogs and Loners: American Poetry Today." *New Criterion* 22, no. 8 (April 2004): 5–18.

Parini, Jay. "Charles Wright: The Remembered Earth." *Some Necessary Angels: Essays on Writing and Politics.* New York: Columbia University Press, 1997. 181–200.

Parisi, Joseph. "Charles Wright." *Poets in Person: A Listener's Guide.* 2nd ed. N.p.: Poetry Press, 1997. 168–83.

Perkins, David. *A History of Modern Poetry: Modernism and After.* Cambridge, MA: Harvard University Press, 1987. 561–2.

Perloff, Marjorie. "Charles Wright." *Contemporary Poets*, 4th ed. Ed. James Vinson and D.L. Patrick. New York: St. Martin's Press, 1985. 947–8.

Pittard, Shawn. "Charles Wright and 'The Minor Art of Self-Defense." *The Great American Pinup*, 5 May 2005. http://greatamericanpinup.blogspot.com/2005/05/charles-wright-and-minor-art-of-self.html.

*"Poet Wright Reflects on His Life." *Seattle Post-Intelligencer* (Seattle, WA), 26 March 2004.

Prampolini, Gaetano. "Charles Wright: Tre poesie e nota bio-bibliografica." *I poeti dell'antico fattore*, (1999): 40–5, 52–4.

———. "Nota" to a translation of *The Secret of Poetry*; *Is*; and *Nostalgia*. "Charles Wright: Il segreto della poesia." *La Luna*, Pensiero 12 [1999]. Poems with a graphic by Rossano Guerra laid in stiff paper wrapper.

———. "Nota del curatore." *Testo a fronte* 16 (March 1997): 136–7. Accompanies the translation of Wright's poem *The Southern Cross*.

———. "Poeti americani in Italia: Richard Hugo e Charles Wright." *Il Veltro: Rivista della Civilta Italiana* 38 (September-December 1994): 397–416.

———. "Postfazione." *L'altra riva del fiume*, trans. Gaetano Prampolini. Milano: ExCogita Editore, 2001. 135–45.

Prunty, Wyatt. "At Home and Abroad: Southern Poets with Passports and Memory." *Southern Review*, 30 (Fall 1994), 745–50.

Przybyszewski, Chris. "The Wright Words." *Memphis Flyer*, 29 March 2001. http://www.memphisflyer.com/MFSearch/full_results.asp?xt_from=1&aID=923.

Pugh, Christina Anne. *Revising the Pictorial: Ekphrasis and the Nature of Modern Lyric.* Ph.D. dissertation, Harvard University, 1998.

Rivara, Sara. *Forever Joined: Images of Landscape in the Poems of Charles Wright and Kay Stripling Byer.* M.F.A. thesis, Warren Wilson College, 2002.

Roman, Camile. *Postmodern Homemaking (Poetry).* Ph.D. dissertation, Brown University, 1990.

A Selected Bibliography

Rosenthal, M.L. "Sensibilities, Ltd." *Parnassus: Poetry in Review* 7, no. 2 (Spring-Summer 1979): 119.

Rowan, Tori. "A Wright-er's Landscape of the Impersonal." *The Declaration* November 1990.

Runciman, Lex. "Belief, Nonbelief, Invention: The Recent Poetry of Charles Wright." *Poet Lore* 78, no.1 (Spring 1983): 41.

Santos, Sherod. "A Solving Emptiness: C.K. Williams and Charles Wright." *A Poetry of Two Minds*. Athens: University of Georgia Press, 2000. 125–38.

St. John, David. "The Poetry of Charles Wright." *Wright: A Profile*. Iowa City: Grilled Flowers Press, 1979. 51–65. Part 1 of the essay first appeared in the *Seneca Review*.

*Shepherd, Lauren. "Poetry Earns Virginia Professor 1998 Pulitzer Prize." *University Wire*, 15 April 1998.

Smith, R.T. "The Appellations Yet Rising: A Birdseye View of Poetry from the Appalachians." *Poetry Daily* [Charlottesville, VA]. http://www.poems.com/essartsm.htm.

Spiegelman, Willard. "Landscape and Identity: Charles Wright's Backyard Metaphysics." *Southern Review* 40, no. 1 (Winter 2004): 172–96. A slightly different version of the essay rpt. in *"The Way Things Looks Each Day": How Poets See The World*. New York: Oxford University Press, 2005. 82–111. Rpt. in Giannelli, *High Lonesome*, 345–73.

———. "The Nineties Revisited." *Contemporary Literature* 42, no. 2 (Summer 2001): 206–37.

———. "The Vision of Charles Wright." Paper presented at the 1999 Association of Literary Scholars and Critics, 31 October 1999.

Stitt, Peter. "Resurrecting the Baroque." *Uncertainty and Plenitude*. Iowa City: University of Iowa Press, 1997. Rpt. in Giannelli, *High Lonesome*, 230–54.

*Sullivan, Sean Patrick. "Celebrated Canadian Poet Don McKay Wins $50,000 Poetry Prize." *Yahoo!TV*. 7 June 2007. http://tv.yahoo.com/show/31511/news/urn:newsml:cp.org:20070607:tv-35474024__ER:1. Also at *Canada.com*: http://www.canada.com/topics/entertainment/story.html?id=4f3a07a8-0085-42b6-8b56-3a0b752a9cb9&k=5819.

Swerdlow, David. "The Unknown Master of the Pure Poem Walks Nightly Among His Roses: Traveling Toward the Idea of God with Charles Wright." Paper presented at the annual meeting of the Associated Writing Programs on a panel "Charles Wright at 70: A Celebration and Retrospective," Vancouver, BC, 31 March 2005.

*Swift, Todd. "Commedia del Arte." *Eyewear* [London], 7 June 2007. http://toddswift.blogspot.com/2007/06/commedia-del-arte.html.

Theune, Michael. "The Dark Wood of Reading: The Diminished Pilgrimage of Charles Wright's Chickamauga." Paper presented at the 15th Annual Conference of the American Literature Association, 29 May 2004.

T[onge], J[ennifer]. "Wright, Charles." *Who's Who in Twentieth-Century World Poetry*, ed. Mark Willhardt and Alan Michael Parker. London: Routledge, 2000. 345.

Upton, Lee. "Charles Wright's Self-Portraiture: the Lyric Poet as Self-Traitor." *Poesis* 7, no. 5 (1987): 1–12.

———. "The Doubting Penitent: Charles Wright's Epiphanies of Abandonment." *The Muse of Abandonment: Origin, Identity, Mastery in Five American Poets*. 23–53. Lewisburg, PA: Bucknell University Press, 1998. Rpt. in Giannelli, *High Lonesome*, 255–84.

*"U.Va.'s Wright Wins Top Poetry Prize for 'Scar Tissue.'" *UVA Today*. 15 June 2007. http://www.virginia.edu/uvatoday/newsRelease.php?id=2255.

*"Va. Poet's Boat Makes a Sweet Landing." *Virginian Pilot*, 16 April 1998.

Vendler, Helen. "The Transcendent 'I.'" *New Yorker*, 29 October 1979, 160–74. Rpt. in *Part of Nature, Part of Us: Modern American Poets*. Cambridge, MA: Harvard University Press, 1988. 277–88; in Andrews, *The Point Where All Things Meet*, 1–12; and in Giannelli, *High Lonesome*, 115–25.

Walton, Anthony. "The Journey Within." *Oxford American* 37 (2001): 67–73.

West, Robert. "Everywhere but His Own Country: Three Essays on Charles Wright and the American South." *Asheville Poetry Review* 9, no. 1 (Spring-Summer 2002): 93–103.

———. "'Take Me as a Southern Writer, Please': Contextualizing Charles Wright in Southern Literature." Southern Writers Symposium, Fayetteville, North Carolina, September 2000.

"Wright, Charles." *Encyclopedia Britannica*. 2003.

Wright, Stuart. "Charles Wright: A Bibliographic Chronicle, 1963–1985." *Bulletin of Bibliography* 43, no. 1 (1986): 3–12.

Young, David. "Language: The Poet as Master and Servant." *Field* 14 (1976): 68–90. Rpt. in *A Field Guide to Contemporary Poetry and Poetics*, ed. Stuart Friebert and David Young. Oberlin, OH: Oberlin College, 1997. 179–97

———. "Looking for Landscapes." *Field* 58 (Spring 1998): 74–90. Rpt. in Giannelli, *High Lonesome*, 87–93.

Zawacki, Andrew. "Reading Wright in the Wrong Country." *Thumbscrew* 8 (Summer 1997).

Reviews

The titles of Wright's three major collections are marked with an asterisk.

POETRY

The Dream Animal (1968)
Poetry (February 1971): 322.

The Grave of the Right Hand (1970)
Agena, Kathleen. "The Mad Sense of Language." *Partisan Review* 43, no. 4 (1976): 625–30.
Kirkus Reviews (1 February 1970): 168.
Library Journal (15 March 1970): 1036.

The Venice Notebook (1971)
Library Journal (15 November 1972): 3717.

Hard Freight (1973)
Agena, Kathleen. "The Mad Sense of Language." *Partisan Review* 43, no. 4 (1976): 625–30.
Carpenter, John R. "The Big Machine." *Poetry* 125, no. 3 (1974): 166–73.
Choice 11 (April 1974): 264.
Gall, Sally M. "Seven from Wesleyan." *Shenandoah* 21, no. 1 (1974): 54–70.
Kennedy, X.J. "Lovers of Greece, Women, and Tennessee." *New York Times Book Review* (17 February 1974): 6.
Kessler, Edward. "The Shortest Distance between Two Poets." *Washington Post Book World* (5 May 1974): 3
Meinke, Peter. *New Republic* 169 (24 November 1973): 26–7.
Morris, John N. "Making More Sense than Omaha." *Hudson Review* 27, no. 1 (1974): 106–18.
National Observer (9 February 1974): 25.
Pinsky, Robert. "Description and the Virtuous Use of Words." *Parnassus* 3, no. 2 (1975): 134–46. Revised version rpt. in *The Situation of Poetry: Contemporary Poetry and Its Traditions*. Princeton, NJ: Princeton University Press, 1976. 111–18.
Ramsey, Paul. "American Poetry in 1973." *Sewanee Review* 82 (Spring 1974): 399.
Smith, Dave. *Library Journal* 99 (1 February 1974): 368.
Times Literary Supplement (29 March 1974): 339.

Bloodlines (1975)
Agena, Kathleen. "The Mad Sense of Language." *Partisan Review* 43, no. 4 (1976): 625–30. Partially rpt. in "Charles Wright," *Contemporary Literary Criticism*, Volume 13. Detroit, Michigan: Gale Research Company, 1984. 613.
Choice (September 1975): 848.
D'Aguiar, Fred. *Library Journal* (July 2001): 95.
Garrison, Joseph. *Library Journal* 100, no. 4 (15 February 1975): 398.
Kirkus Reviews (1 January 1975): 67.
McClatchy, J.D. "Recent Poetry: New Designs on Life." *Yale Review* 65, no. 1. (Autumn 1975): 103–5.
Morris, John N. 'The Songs Protect Us, in a Way." *Hudson Review* 28, no. 3 (1975): 446–58.
New York Times Book Review (7 September 1975): 6.
North American Review (Fall 1976): 91.
Sewanee Review (July 1976): 533.
Stitt, Peter. "The Inward Journey." *Ohio Review* 17 (1976): 91–2. Rpt. as part of "Five Reviews" in Andrews, *The Point Where All Things Meet*, 53–4.
Vendler, Helen. *New Yorker* 55 (29 October 1979): 160–9.

China Trace (1977)
America 138 (8 April 1978): 283.
Booklist (1 January 1978): 891.
Book World (11 December 1977): E6.
Bromwich, David. "I Showed Her My Darkness, She Gave Me a Stone." *Poetry* 133, no. 3 (1978): 169–76.
Choice (March 1978): 75.
Garrison, Joseph. *Library Journal* 102, no. 14 (1 August 1977): 1654.
Jackson, Richard. "Worlds Created, Worlds Perceived." *Michigan Quarterly Review* 17, no. 4 (Fall 1978): 555–6.
Kirkus Reviews (15 August 1977): 924.
Kliatt (Winter 1978): 19.
New Republic 177 (26 November 1977): 26.
New York Times Book Review (1 January 1978): 10.
North American Review (Fall 1979): 71.
Sadoff, Ira. *American Book Review* 1, no. 4 (October 1978): 8.
Sewanee Review (July 1978): 454.
Stitt, Peter. *Georgia Review* 32, no. 2 (1978): 474–80. Rpt. as part of "Five Reviews" in Andrews, *The Point Where All Things Meet*, 54–7.
Vendler, Helen. *New Yorker* 55 (29 October 1979): 160–9.

Wright: A Profile (1979)
Booklist (15 January 1980): 703.

Dead Color (1980)
American Book Collector (May 1983): 27.
Fine Print (January 1981): 20.

*Country Music (1982)
Atlas, James. "New Voices in American Poetry." *New York Times* 129 (3 February 1980): sec. 6, p. 16.
New York Times 132 (12 June 1983): 38.
New York Times Book Review 88 (12 December 1982): 14.

Parini, Jay. "From Scene to Fiery Scene." *Times Literary Supplement* (1 March 1985): 239.

St. John, David. "Charles Wright's *Country Music*." In *Country Music*, 2nd ed. Hanover, NH: Wesleyan / New England Press, 1991. xiii–xxi. Rpt. in Andrews, *The Point Where All Things Meet*, 86–93; in St. John's *Where the Angels Come Toward Us: Selected Essays, Reviews & Interviews*. Fredonia, NY: White Pine Press, 1995; and in Giannelli, *High Lonesome*, 3–9.

Stitt, Peter. "Words, Book Words, What Are You?" *Georgia Review* 37, no. 2 (Summer 1983): 428–38.

Tillinghast, Richard. "From Michigan and Tennessee." *New York Times Book Review* (12 December 1982): 14.

The Southern Cross (1981)

Axelrod, Steven Gould. *World Literature Today* 57 (Winter 1983): 111.

Bedient, Calvin. "Tracing Charles Wright." *Parnassus* 10 (Spring-Summer 1982): 55–74. Rpt. in Andrews, *The Point Where All Things Meet*, 21–38, and in Giannelli, *High Lonesome*, 126–41.

Brown, Gary. *Library Journal* 106, no. 20 (15 November 1981): 2240–1.

Buckley, Christopher. "From Here To There: A Review of Charles Wright's *The Southern Cross*." *Telescope* 4, no. 1 (1985): 81–94. Rpt. in Buckley's *Appreciations: Selected Reviews, Views & Interviews, 1975–2000*. Santa Barbara, CA: Millie Grazie Press, 2001. 39–51.

Conarroe, Joel. *Washington Post Book World* (27 June 1982): 10.

Kennedy, X.J. "A Tenth and Four-Fifths." *Poetry* 141, no. 6 (March 1983): 349–58.

Kirkus Reviews (15 September 1981): 1230.

Lodge, Sally. *Publishers Weekly* 220 (October 1981): 110.

Prado, Holly. "Respecting Poetry's Possibilities." *Los Angeles Times Book Review* (7 February 1982): 3.

St. John. "Raised Voices in the Choir: A Review of 1981 Poetry Selections." *Antioch Review* 40, no. 2 (Spring, 1982): 225–34. Rpt. in *Where the Angels Come toward Us: Selected Essays, Reviews, and Interviews*. Fredonia, NY: White Pine Press, 1995.

Stewart, Pamela. "In All Places at Once." *Ironwood*, No. 19 (1982): 162–6.

Stitt, Peter. "Problems of Youth ... and Age." *Georgia Review* 36, no. 1 (1982): 183–93. Rpt. as part of "Five Reviews" in Andrews, *The Point Where All Things Meet*, 57–60.

Walker, David. "*One for the Rose* and *The Southern Cross*." *Field* 26 (Spring 1982): 87–97. Rpt. in Andrews, *The Point Where All Things Meet*, 67–71, and in Giannelli, *High Lonesome*, 10–14.

Western American Literature (Fall 1982): 268.

The Other Side of the River (1984)

Bell, Madison. *New York Times Book Review* 89 (20 May 1984): 26.

Buckley, Christopher. "A Light in Our Eyes—*The Other Side of the River* by Charles Wright." *Bluefish* 2, nos. 3–4 (Spring 1984–85): 147–57. Rpt. in Buckley's *Appreciations: Selected Reviews, Views & Interviews, 1975–2000*. Santa Barbara, CA: Millie Grazie Press, 2001. 53–60.

Burris, Sidney. *Kenyon Review* 6 (Summer 1984): 127–34.

Eschelman, Clayton. "Life as a Poetic Puzzlement." *Los Angeles Times* 103 (19 August 1984): B7.

Frank, Elizabeth. "The Middle of the Journey." *The Nation* 238, no. 13 (7 April 1984): 421–3.

Hemstath, James B. *Library Journal* 109 (1 March 1984): 51.

Jarman, Mark. "The Trace of a Story Line." *Ohio Review* 37 (Fall 1986), 129–47. Rpt. in Andrews, *The Point Where All Things Meet*, 96–104, and in Giannelli, *High Lonesome*, 17–24. Also rpt. in Jarman's *Body and Soul: Essays on Poetry*. Ann Arbor: University of Michigan Press, 2000. 71–90.

Kalstone, David. "Lives in a Rearview Mirror." *New York Times Book Review* 89 (1 July 1984): 14. Material on Wright rpt. in Andrews, *The Point Where All Things Meet*, 94–5, and in Giannelli, *High Lonesome*, 15–16.

Koontz, Thomas. *Library Journal* 109, no. 4 (1 March 1984): 495.

Pettingell, Phoebe. *New Leader* 67 (20 August 1984): 17–18.

Publishers Weekly 225 (10 February 1984): 192.

Stitt, Peter. "The Circle of the Meditative Moment." *Georgia Review* 38, no. 2 (Summer 1984): 402–12. Rpt. as part of "Five Reviews" in Andrews, *The Point Where All Things Meet*, 60–3.

St. John, David. *Washington Post Book World* 107 (20 May 1984): 6.

Five Journals (1986)

Bringhurst, Robert. *Fine Print* 13, no. 2 (April 1987): 93–8.

Zone Journals (1988)

American Book Review 11 (March 1989): 6.

Clark, Kevin. "Stature." *Café Solo* 5, nos. 3–4 (1989): 63–8. Rpt. in Andrews, *The Point Where All Things Meet*, 163–6.

Corbett, William. *Harvard Book Review* 9–10 (Fall-Winter 1988): 11.

Enconomou, George. *World Literature Today* 62 (Autumn 1988): 660.

Galvin, B. *Choice* 25 (May 1988): 1407.

Gregerson, Linda. "Short Reviews." *Poetry* 155, no. 3 (December 1989): 229–31. Rpt. as "God's Concern for America" in *Negative Capability: Contemporary American Poetry*. Ann Arbor: University of Michigan Press, 2001. 120–2. Rpt. in *Contemporary Literary Criticism* 146 (2001).

Harris, Roger. "Place to Place." *Star Ledger* [Newark, NJ] 10 January 1988.

Jarman, Mark. "The Pragmatic Imagination and the Secret of Poetry." *Gettysburg Review* 1, no. 4 (Autumn 1988): 647–60. Material on Wright rpt. in Andrews, *The Point Where All Things Meet*, 105–9, and in Giannelli, *High Lonesome*, 25–8.

J.S. *Booklist* (15 December 1987).

Logan, William. "Season to Season, Day to Day." *New York Times Book Review* (4 September 1988): 9–10.

Pankey, Eric. "The Form of Concentration." *Iowa Review* 19, no. 2 (Spring-Summer 1989): 175–87.

Santos, Sherod. "Zone Journals." *New Virginia Review* 8 (Spring 1991): 369–72. Rpt. in Andrews, *The Point Where All Things Meet*, 155–9, and in Giannelli, *High Lonesome*, 36–9.

Shreve, Jack. *Library Journal* 112, no. 19 (15 November 1987): 84.

Smock, Frederick. "Tennessee: Burnished Edges." *American Book Review* 11, no. 1 (March-April 1989): 6.

Stitt, Peter. "To Enlighten, To Embody." *Georgia Review* 41, no. 4 (Winter 1987), 800–13. Rpt. as part of "Five Reviews" in Andrews, *The Point Where All Things Meet*, 64–6.

Stuttaford, Genevieve. *Publishers Weekly* 232 (27 November 1987): 76.

Thorpe, Peter. "Life's Answers Lie in Rhetorical Question." *Rocky Mountain News Sunday Magazine* (5 June 1988).

Van Winckel, Nance. "Charles Wright and the Landscape of the Lyric." *New England Review and Bread Loaf Quarterly* 12, no. 3 (Spring 1990): 308–12. Rpt. in Andrews, *The Point Where All Things Meet*, 167–71.

Vendler, Helen. "Travels in Time." *New Republic* 198, no. 3 (18 January 1988): 34–6. Revised version appears as "Charles Wright" in *The Music of What Happens: Poems, Poets, Critics*. Cambridge, MA: Harvard University Press, 1988. Rpt. in Andrews, *The Point Where All Things Meet*, 13–20; and in Giannelli, *High Lonesome*, 29–35.

Virginia Quarterly Review 64 (Spring 1988): 62.

A Journal of the Year of the Ox (1988)
Fine Print 15 (January 1989): 41.

Xionia (1990)
Buckley, Christopher. "Charles Wright's Hymn." *Poet Lore* 86, no. 3 (Fall 1991): 59–65. Rpt. in Andrews, *The Point Where All Things Meet*, 204–11; in Giannelli, *High Lonesome*, 61–7; and in Buckley's *Appreciations: Selected Reviews, Views & Interviews, 1975–2000*. Santa Barbara, CA: Millie Grazie Press, 2001. 121–7.

The World of the Ten Thousand Things (1990)

Andrews, Tom. "The Point Where All Things Meet: Improvisations on Charles Wright's *The World of the Ten Thousand Things*." *Iron Mountain Review* 8 (Spring 1992): 9–13. Rpt. as "Improvisations on Charles Wright's *The World of the Ten Thousand Things*" in Andrews, *The Point Where All Things Meet*, 212–21, and in Giannelli, *High Lonesome*, 52–60.

Bedient, Calvin. "Slide-Wheeling around the Curves." *Southern Review* 27 (1991): 221–34. Rpt. in Andrews, *The Point Where All Things Meet*, 39–52.

Blasing, Mutlu Konuk. "The American Sublime, c. 1992: What Clothes Does One Wear?" *Michigan Quarterly Review* 31 (Summer 1992): 425–41. Material on Wright (pp. 436–41) rpt. in Andrews, *The Point Where All Things Meet*, 198–203.

Collins, Floyd. "Metamorphosis within the Poetry of Charles Wright." *Gettysburg Review* 4, no. 3 (Summer 1991): 464–79.

Costello, Bonnie. "Voices from the Other Side." *Newsday* 23 December 1990: 19 ("Currents" section).

Garrison, David. *Choice* 28 (February 1991): 936.

Koeppel, Fredric. "Poems Register the Cosmic Touch." *Commercial Appeal* [Memphis] (23 December 1990): G3.

McClatchy, J.D. "Amid the Groves, Under the Shadowy Hill, the Generations Are Prepared." *Poetry* 158, no. 5 (August 1991): 280–95.

New York Times Book Review 96 (9 June 1996): 34.

Sampson, Dennis. "Poetry Chronicle." *Hudson Review* 44, no. 2 (Summer 1991), 333–42.

Stocking, Marion. *Beloit Poetry Journal* 41, no. 2 (Winter 1990–91): 38.

Tillinghast, Richard. "An Elegist's New England, a Buddhist's Dante." *New York Times Book Review* 96 (24 February 1991): 18–19. Rpt. in Andrews, *The Point Where All Things Meet*, 195–7, and in Giannelli, *High Lonesome*, 40–1.

Unsino, Stephen. *America* 166, no. 14 (25 April 1992): 361–2.

Virginia Quarterly Review 67, no. 2 (Spring 1991): 63.

Young, David. "The Blood Bees of Paradise." *Field*, No. 44 (Spring 1991): 77–90. Rpt. in Andrews,

The Point Where All Things Meet, 184–94, and in Giannelli, *High Lonesome*, 42–51.

Chickamauga (1995)

Alexander, Pamela. "A Measure of Measures." *Boston Book Review* (1 December 1995): 36. Also available at *Bookwire*: http://www.bookwire.com/bookwire/perlscript/review.pl?1944.

Andrews, Tom. "Via Negativa: A Symposium." *Ohio Review* 56 (1997): 123–37.

Bagby, George F. "Wright Sets Autumn of Life to Verse." *Richmond Times-Dispatch* (23 July 1995): F4.

Baker, David. "On Restraint." *Poetry* 168, no. 1 (April 1996): 33–47. Material on Wright rpt. in Baker's *Heresy and the Ideal: On Contemporary Poetry*. Fayetteville: University of Arkansas Press, 2000. 216–19, and in Giannelli, *High Lonesome*, 76–8.

Bastian, Kim. *The Alembic* [Providence College] (Spring 1996).

Bedient, Calvin. "Poetry and Silence at the End of the Century." *Salmagundi* 111 (Summer 1996): 195–207.

―――. "Facing the River." *Southern Review* 33 (Winter 1997): 136–49.

Brainard, Dulcy. *Publishers Weekly* 242, no. 9 (27 February 1995): 97–8.

―――. "Wanted More Complexity." *Southern Review* 33 (Winter 1997): 136–49.

Collins, Floyd. "A Fine Excess." *Gettysburg Review* 9, no. 2 (Spring 1996): 331–9.

Guillory, Daniel L. *Library Journal* 120, no. 6 (1 April 1995): 99.

Hart, Henry. *Verse* 14, no. 1 (1995): 114–18.

Hunter, Lynn Dean. "Three Collections Make Myth from American Memory." *Virginian-Pilot* (11 June 1995): J12.

Kitchen, Judith. "What Persists." *Georgia Review* 51, no. 2 (Summer 1997): 332–6.

Koeppel, Frederic. "Wright's Poems Search for Cosmic Touch in Daily Life." *Commercial Appeal* [Memphis] (30 April 1995).

LaFemina, Gerry. *Colorado Review* 22, no. 2 (Winter 1996–97): 214–23.

Longenbach, James. "Poetry in Review." *Yale Review* 83, no. 4 (October 1995): 148–51. Rpt. as "Earned Weight" in Giannelli, *High Lonesome*, 79–82.

Mason, David. "Poetry Chronicle." *Hudson Review* 49, no. 1 (Spring 1996): 166–7. Rpt. as "Charles Wright, Josephine Jacobsen and Ellen Bryant Voigt" in Mason's *The Poetry of Life and the Life of Poetry: Essays and Reviews*. Ashland, OR: Story Line Press, 2000. 146–51.

Pratt, William. *World Literature Today* 70, no. 4 (Fall 1996): 967.

Seaman, Donna. *Booklist* 91, no. 15 (1 April 1995): 1374.

Simpson, Megan. "Naked in the Workshop, or, Demystifying the Teaching and Writing of Poetry." *North Carolina Literary Review* 5 (1996): 226–35.

Sullivan, James. *Magill's Literary Annual 1996*. Pasadena, CA: Salem Press, 103–6.

Vendler, Helen. "The Nothing That Is." *New Republic* 213, no. 6 (7 August 1995): 42–5. Rpt. in Giannelli, *High Lonesome*, 68–75.

Virginia Quarterly Review 71, no. 4 (Autumn 1995): 137.

Walker, Kevin. "A Poetic Contradiction Gives a Clear View of the Mystical." *Detroit Free Press* (23 April 1995).

Ward, David C. "The Mask of Battle." *PN Review* 22, no. 6 (1996): 67–9.

Black Zodiac (1997)

Aaron, Jonathan. "Inner and Outer Landscapes: New Poems by Charles Wright and Les Murray." *Boston Globe* (17 August 1997): N13, N15.

Autry, Bruce. "*Black Zodiac* by Charles Wright." *Poetic Voices* (April 1998). http://www.poeticvoices.com/9804Wright.html.

Brainard, Dulcy. *Publisher's Weekly* 244, no. 8 (24 February 1997): 84.

Broaddus, Will. "All the Heart's Threads." *Boston Book Review* (September 1997): 32.

Byrne, Mairéad. *Sycamore Review* 9, no. 2 (1997): 146–50. Also found at http://www.sla.purdue.edu/academic/engl/sycamore/Vol9/v92-b1.html.

Collins, Floyd. "A Poetry of Transcendence." *Gettysburg Review* 10, no. 4 (Winter 1997): 683–701.

D'Angelo, Dennis. "Review of Charles Wright's *Black Zodiac*." Written for Professor Ira Sadoff, 5 March 1999. http://216.239.37.104/search?q=cache:GOkkDzyc9CIJ:www.colby.edu/~isadoff/apw/MODEL_Review-C.Wright.doc+%22Poem+Almost+Wholly+in+My+Own+Manner %22+%22charles+wright%22&hl=en&start=2&ie=UTF-8.

de la Fuente, Daniel. "Trae poetica de Wright." *El Norte* (México) (9 December 2002). Rev. of the Spanish translation.

Dilling, Jynne. "'*Zodiac*' Landscape Shines with Imagery." *Cavalier Daily* (31 March 1998).

Gussow, Mel. "A Good Ear for the Music of His Own Life." *New York Times* 147 (16 April 1998): B1.http://www.nytimes.com/library/books/041698 wright-poetry.html.

Harayda, Janice. "Why the Critics' Awards Usually Surprise." *Plain Dealer* [Cleveland] (29 March 1998).

Hecht, James. "Redactions." *American Book Review* 20, no. 2 (January-February 1999): 27.

Henry, Brian. "Charles Wright Puts Past To Good Use." *Richmond Times Dispatch* (21 September 1997): K4.

Hoffert, Barbara. *Library Journal* 122, no. 7 (15 April 1997): 85–6.

Hosmer, Robert Ellis, Jr. "Poetry Roundup." *America* 177 (20–27 December 1997): 24–6.

Koeppel, Fredric. "Mystical Poet Futilely Aspires to Wordlessness." *Commercial Appeal* [Memphis] (20 April 1997): G3.

Logan, William. "Hardscrabble Country." *New Criterion*. 15, no. 10 (June 1997): 68–76. Also at http://www.newcriterion.com/archive/15/jun97/logan.htm.

Longenbach, James. "Between Soil and Stars." *Nation* 264, no. 14 (14 April 1997): 27–30.

Maginnes, Al. "Poetry in Review." *Quail's Quill* [Raleigh, NC] (Summer 1997). Brief notice.

Marcus, Jacqueline. "The Imperishable Quiet at the Heart of Form." *Literary Review* 41, no. 4 (Summer 1998): 562–6.

Miller, Christopher R. "Poetic Standard Time: The Zones of Charles Wright." *Southern Review* 34, no. 3 (Summer 1998): 566–86. Rpt. in Giannelli, *High Lonesome*, 285–303.

Mobilio, Albert. "The Word's Worth." *Village Voice* (29 April 1997): 55.

Muske, Carol. "Guided by Black Stars." *New York Times Book Review* 102 (31 August 1997): 11–12. Rpt. in Giannelli, *High Lonesome*, 83–6.

New York Times Book Review 103 (31 May 1998): 50. Brief review.

Off the Wall [newsletter of Books & Co.] (February 1997).

Oser, Lee. *World Literature Today*. 71, no. 4 (Autumn 1997): 794–5.

Pankey, Eric. "The Woman Who Died in Her Sleep." *Partisan Review* 66, no. 2 (Spring 1999): 344–9.

Penn, David. "Wright Stuff: Poet Charles Wright's 'Black Zodiac' Is a Pulitzer Prize-Winning Tour de Force." *Tucson Weekly* (11 May 1998). http://weeklywire.com/ww/05-11-98/tw_book2.html.

Publisher's Weekly. 244, no. 8 (24 February 1997): 84.

Seaman, Donna. "Poetry on the Wing." *Booklist* 93, no. 16 (15 April 1997): 1377.

Silberg, Richard. *Poetry Flash* (September 1998).

Smith, Dave. *Oxford American* 17 (September 1997), 81–2.

Smith, Thomas R. *Star Tribune* [Minneapolis/St. Paul] (September 1997): F16.

Spiegelman, Willard. "Poetry in Review." *Yale Review* 85, no. 4 (October 1997): 166–75.

―――. "The Nineties Revisited." *Contemporary Literature* 42, no. 2 (Summer 2001): 206–37.

Sullivan, James. *Magill's Literary Annual 1998*. Pasadena, CA: Salem Press. 117–20.

Veale, Scott. *New York Times Book Review* 147 (31 May 1998): 50.

Virginia Quarterly Review 73, no. 4 (Autumn 1997): 136.

Walcott, Ellison Austen. *Ace* (5 November 1997): 26.

Wojahn, David. "Survivalist Selves." *Kenyon Review* 20, nos. 3–4 (Summer-Fall 1998): 180–9.

Appalachia (1998)

Beasley, Bruce. *Bellingham Review* 22, no. 1 (Summer 1999): 115–18.

Bagby, George F. "Spiritual Theme Marks Wright's New Verse." *Richmond Times-Dispatch* (27 June 1999): F4.

Branam, Harold. *Magill's Literary Annual 1999*. Pasadena, CA: Salem Press, 1999. 61–3.

Canady, John. *Poetry International* 4 (2000): 165–7.

Chasar, Mike. "'Appalachia' Is Homespun Meditation." *Dayton Daily News* (11 April 1999): 90.

―――. *Texas Review* 20, nos. 1–2 (1999): 116–18.

Cohea, David. *Florida Review* 24, no. 2 (1999): 106–16.

Daniels, Kate. "Old Masters." *Southern Review* 35, no. 3 (Summer 1999): 621–34.

Dilling, Jynne. "Wright's 'Appalachia' Springs with Beauty." *The Cavalier Daily: Online Edition*, 16 November 1998. http://www.cavalierdaily.com:2001/.Archives/1998/November/Book_Reviews/aef.asp.

Getty, Matt. "Straw Poetry." *Redland Review*, 1999. Also at http://mattgettynonfiction.blogspot.com/2005/03/straw-poetry.html.

Gioia, Dana, and James Wood. "Piddling Around by the Lemon Tree" and "Regularly Scheduled Passionate Intensity." *Slate* (13–14 January 1999). http://slate.msn.com/id/2000022/entry/1002201/ and http://slate.msn.com/id/2000022/entry/10022 03/.

Graber, Michael. "Dour Worldview Diminishes Power of Wright's New Effort in Poetics." *Commercial Appeal* [Memphis] (4 March 1999).

Hamill, Sam. *Seattle Weekly* (8 April 1999). Rpt. in issue of 4 March 1999.

Hass, Robert. "Poet's Choice." *Washington Post* (4 April 1999): X12.

Hoffert, Barbara. *Library Journal* 124 (1 April 1999): 96.

Hurley, Tom. "A Universe in the Back Yard: Collection Reflects 18 Dark and Light Months of Poet Charles Wright's Soul." *San Francisco Chronicle Book Review* (24 January 1999): 2. http://www.sfgate.com/cgi-bin/article.cgi?file=/chronicle/archive/1999/01/24/RV48236.DTL.

Kendrick, Leatha. "Poet Ends Trilogy by Examining Place and Its Effect." *Lexington Herald Leader* (19 April 1999).

Kirsch, Adam. "Between Heaven and Earth." *New York Times Book Review* 104 (28 February 1999): 21. Rpt. in Giannelli, *High Lonesome*, 98–100.

Logan, William. "Poetry." *Washington Post Book World* (10 January 1999): 11. Rpt. as a part of chapter 24 ("Three Magi") in Logan's *Desperate Measures*. Gainesville: University of Florida Press, 2002. 269–70.

Longenbach, James. *Boston Review* 23, no. 6 (December 1998-January 1999). Rpt. in Giannelli, *High Lonesome*, 94–7.

McClatchy, J.D. "*Ars Longa.*" *Poetry* 175, no. 1 (October-November 1999): 78–89. Rpt. in Giannelli, *High Lonesome*, 101–10.

Miller, Sarah. "Conclusion to Poetry Trilogy Set in Charlottesville." *Roanoke* [Virginia] *Times* (7 February 1999).

Muratori, Fred. *Library Journal* 123, no. 16 (1 October 1998): 94.

Oser, Lee. *World Literature Today* 73, no. 3 (Summer 1999): 535–6.

Pankey, Eric. "What Hast Thou, O My Soul, with Paradise: Charles Wright's *Appalachia.*" *Verse* 16, no. 2 (1999): 165–70.

Publishers Weekly 245 (28 September 1998): 95.

Rauschenbusch, Stephanie. "Serving a Darker Music." *American Book Review* 21, no. 1 (November-December 1999): 27.

Rector, Liam. *Harvard Review* (Spring 1999): 115–17.

Schuldt, Morgan. "*Appalachia* Springs Eternal." *The Angle* [University of Virginia Online Magazine] (27 October 1999). http://www.theangle.com/stgyle/1999_1027/appalachia.shtml.

Seaman, Donna. *Booklist* 95, no. 5 (1 November 1998): 466.

Smith, Thomas R. *Star Tribune* [Minneapolis] (28 March 1999).

Taylor, Henry. "Land of the Poets: Charles Wright and Eavan Boland Tell of the Landscapes of Fact and Poetry." *Boston Sunday Globe* (13 December 1998): M1, M4.

Virginia Quarterly Review 75, no. 3 (Summer 1999): 100–1.

Wall Street Journal 103 (2 April 1999): W6. Brief review.

Webster, Loren. "Charles Wright's *Appalachia.*" *In a Dark Time* (23 March 2003). http://lorenwebster.net/In_a_Dark_Time/archives/000395.html.

White, Edith R. "Award-winning Poets Offer New Volumes of Work." *Virginian-Pilot* (24 January 1999): J2.

Wood, James. See Gioia, above.

Negative Blue (2000)

Brown, Ashley. *World Literature Today* 74, no. 4 (Autumn 2000): 821–2.

Byrne, Edward. "Time and Again: Charles Wright's *Negative Blue: Selected Later Poems.*" *Valparaiso Poetry Review*. http://www.valpo.edu/english/vpr/byrnereviewwright.html.

Chelsea 70 (2001): 326.

Crippen, Jeri Lynn. "Delve into Genius Territory with These Creative Tomes." *Arizona Senior World* (April 2003). Brief notice.

Freeman, John. *City Pages: The Online News & Arts Weekly of the Tri-Cities* 21, no. 1019 (14 June 2002). http://www.citypages.com/databank/21/1019/article8744.asp.

Frimmer, Justin. Online review at http://btobsearch.barnesandnoble.com/booksearch/isbnInquiry.asp?sourceid=0039384190&btob=Y&isbn=0374220204&pwb=1.

High, Graham. "Charles Wright: *Negative Blue.*" *New Hope International Review On-line*, ed. Gerald England. http://www.nhi.clara.net/bs0289.htm.

Kirkus Reviews 68 (15 June 2000): 848.

Martinez, Dionisio D. "Ethereal Visions and the Everyday." *Herald of South Florida* (16 July 2000): 10M.

Oxley, William. "What? Again? More Kuppner? Or Just Wright? Right?" *Stride Magazine* http://www.stridemag.pwp.blueyonder.co.uk/2001/feb/what.htm.

Pankey, Eric. "Charles Wright's *Negative Blue.*" *VA Books* (Virginia Foundation for the Humanities) (January 2002). http://www.vabook.org/lit_links/columns/jan02-pankey.pdf.

Publishers Weekly 247 (24 April 2000): 81.

Pugh, Christina. *Harvard Review* 21 (Fall 2001): 177–8.

Redmond, John. "Backyard Poetics." *Thumbscrew* 18 (Spring 2001): 52–5.

Schuldt, M.L. "Search Light: Charles Wright Scans The Landscape Of Language." *Tucson Weekly* (16 November 2000): 34–5. http://www.tucsonweekly.com/tw/2000-11-16/book.html.

Seaman, Donna. "Spotlight on Poetry." *Booklist* 96, no. 14 (15 March 2000): 1317.

Smith, Ron. "Charles Wright Excels Once More in New Collection of Verse." *Richmond Times-Dispatch* (12 November 2000) F4. Rpt. as "An Enchanted, Diminished World" in Giannelli, *High Lonesome*, 111–12.

Suarez, Ernest. "The Year in Poetry." *Dictionary of Literary Biography Yearbook: 2000*, ed. Matthew J. Bruccoli. Detroit: Gale, 2001. 90–101.

Virginia Quarterly Review 76, no. 4 (Autumn 2000): 142.

Wadsworth, Lois. *Eugene Weekly* (13 April 2000).

Webster, Loren. "Charles Wright's *Negative Blue.*" *In a Dark Time* (10 March 2002). http://lorenwebster.net/In_a_Dark_Time/archives/000390.html.

Night Music (2001)

Beer, John. *Chicago Review* 47, no. 4/48, no. 1 (Winter 2001–Spring 2002): 263–70.

Caseley, Martin. "The Wheel, Turning." *Stride Magazine*. http://www.stridemag.pwp.blueyonder.co.uk/2001/nov/caseley.htm.

Higgins, Kevin. "Charles Wright: *Night Rider*." *New Hope International Review On-line*, ed. Gerald England. http://www.nhi.clara.net/bs0289.htm.

A Short History of the Shadow (2002)

Bere, Carol. *Boston Review* (December 2002-January 2003).

"Briefly Noted." *New Yorker* 78 (8 July 2002): 77.

Brier, Peter. *Magill's Literary Annual 2003*. Pasadena, CA: Salem Press, 2003. 741–5.

Brosi, George. *Appalachian Heritage* (Summer 2002): 120.

Buchanan, Oni. "Back Yard Blues: Charles Wright's Lawn-chair Poems." *Boston Phoenix* (19 July 2002).

Citino, David. *Columbus Dispatch* (16 June 2002): F7.

Crippen, Jeri Lynn. "Delve into Genius Territory with These Creative Tomes." *Arizona Senior World* (April 2003). Brief notice.

Daniels, Kate. "Don't Be Cruel: Appreciating the Year-round Joys of Poetry." *Book Page Online* (April 2002): 11. http://www.bookpage.com/0204bp/nonfiction/poetry_roundup.html.

Dargen, Kyle. *Meridian* 9 (Spring-Summer 2002): 180–1.

Doreski, William. *Harvard Review* 24 (Spring 2003): 178–80.

Flaherty, Dolores. "Poems to Read Aloud for All of Us." *Chicago Sun-Times* (13 April 2003). Brief notice.

Hammer, Langdon. "Ways of Seeing." *Los Angeles Times* (18 August 2002): R6.

Gonzalez, Garcia. *GOYA* 263 (March-April 1998): 127.

Johnson, Charles H. "Listen to the Rhythm of the Falling Verse." *New Jersey Home Tribune* (16 March 2003).

Kornbluth, Jesse. "Celebrating Poetry Month: Poetry Book Roundup." *Book Reporter.Com* http://www.bookreporter.com/features/020419-poetry.asp. Brief notice.

Lang, John. "Charles Wright's *A Short History of the Shadow*." *Appalachian Heritage* 30, no. 4 (Fall 2002): 79–84.

Lauzon, Lorraine. "In New Books, Authors Offer Poetry to Inspire, Ease the Spirit." *Catholic Observer* (25 July 2003): 21.

Logan, William. "Falls the Shadow." *New Criterion* 20, no. 10 (June 2002): 75–82.

Loydell, Rupert. "Lucky Dip: Thoughts on Recent American Poetry." *Slope* 17 (Winter-Spring 2003). Online journal at: http://www.slope.org/archive/issue17/criticism17loydell.html. Also at: http://www.stridemag.pwp.blueyonder.co.uk/2002/july/luckydip.htm.

McMaster, Arthur. *Tampa Tribune* (8 June 2003). Brief notice.

Muratori, Fred. *Library Journal* 127, no. 6 (1 April 2002): 112–3.

Oser, Lee. *World Literature Today* 77, no. 1 (April-June 2003): 105–6. Brief review.

Parini, Jay. "A 'Thirst for the Divine.'" *Nation* 274, no. 19 (20 May 2002): 31–2.

Podgurski, David. "'A Short History of the Shadow' is a Walk on the Dark Side." *Stamford Advocate & Greenwich Time* (7 April 2002): D5, D8.

Scharf, Michael. *Publishers Weekly* 249, no. 8 (25 February 2002): 56.

Simic, Charles. "You Can't Keep a Good Sonnet Down." *New York Review of Books* 49 (26 September 2002): 40–2.

Smith, Ron. "Wright Continues Lyrical Trips in Nature." *Richmond Times-Dispatch* (29 September 2002): F4.

Sparks, Amy. "Noted Poet Shares Fleeting Thoughts about Life." *Plain Dealer* [Cleveland] (26 May 2002).

Wilson, James Matthew. "Changing Shadows." *Notre Dame Review* 15 (Winter 2003).

Snake Eyes (2004)

Couth, John. *Shearsman* 62 online: www.shearsman.com/pages/magazine/back_issues/shearsman62/outh_cw.html.

Hardy, Alan. *New Hope International Reviews On-line*. http://www.nhi.clara.net/bs0289.htm.

Smith, Jules. "Method in Manners." *Times Literary Supplement* 5303 (19 November 2004): 34.

Buffalo Yoga (2004)

Freeman, John. "Paging Through: Poetry Books." *Milwaukee Journal Sentinel* (28 March 2004).

Garrett, George. "New Poems by Four Appalachian Masters." *Appalachian Heritage* 32, no. 3 (Summer 2004): 74–82.

Kennedy, Sarah. *Shenandoah* 54, no. 3 (Winter 2004): 184–6.

Lewis, Leon. *Magill's Literary Annual 2005*, ed. John D. Wilson and Steven G. Kellman. Pasadena, CA: Salem Press, 2005. 98–103.

Logan, William. "Stouthearted Men." *New Criterion* 22, no. 10 (June 2004): 60–7.

Lucas, Dave. *Meridian* 13 (Spring-Summer 2005): 150–2.

Publisher's Weekly 251, no. 17 (26 April 2004): 56.

Rand, Richard. *Harvard Review* 27 (2004): 203–5.

Seaman, Donna. *Booklist* 100, no. 14 (15 March 2004): 1259.

A Selected Bibliography

The Wrong End of the Rainbow (2005)
Zimmer, Paul. "The Alignments." *Georgia Review* 60 (Fall-Winter 2006): 791–802.

Scar Tissue (2006)
Bakken, Christopher. "Wisdom, Wisecrack." *American Book Review* 28, no. 4 (May-June 2007): 7–8.

Blakely, Diann. *The Nashville Scene* (7 December 2006). http://www.nashvillescene.com/Stories/Arts/Books/2006/12/07/Proud_Flesh/index.shtml.

Bowen, Kevin. *Harvard Review* 32 (2007): 206–8.

Brouwer, Joel. "A World in Permanent Flux." *New York Times Book Review* (17 September 2006).

Courtwright, Nick. *Front Porch* [Texas State University], issue 1.0. http://www.frontporchjournal.com/pdf/Issue10_Review_Wright.pdf.

Dings, Fred. *World Literature Today* 81, no. 2 (March-April 2007): 75.

Krajeski, Jenna. "A Poet's Metamorphosis." *San Francisco Chronicle* (6 August 2006): M2.

Muratori, Fred. *Library Journal* 131, no. 11 (15 June 2006): 74.

O'Conner, James. "Looking for Lethe." *PN Review* 33, no. 4 (March-April 2007): 80–1. Also appears in *The Brooklyn Rail* February 2007. http://www.brooklynrail.org/2007-02/books/looking-for-lethe#bio.

Open Books August 2006. http://www.openpoetrybooks.com/thegoods/archives/2006_08.html.

Phillips, Brian. *Poetry* 189 no. 3 (December 2006): 235.

Publishers Weekly 243, no. 18 (1 May 2006): 37.

Sattar, Sanyat. *Star Weekend Magazine* 5, no. 114 (26 September 2006). http://www.thedailystar.net/magazine/2006/09/05/books.htm.

Satterfield, Jane. *Antioch Review* 65, no. 1 (Winter 2007), 198, 201.

Seamon, *Booklist* 102, no. 21 (1 July 2006): 22.

Spaar, Lisa Russ. *Virginia Quarterly Review* 82, no. 2 (Spring 2007): 301.

Taylor, Ishan. "Paperback Row." *New York Times Book Review* (2 September 2007). Brief rev. of paperback ed.

Wilson, Melinda. "On Impending Twilight." *Coldfront* 12 (2006). http://reviews.coldfrontmag.com/2006/12/scar_tissue_by_.html.

Littlefoot: A Poem (2007)
Chitwood, Michael. "The Graceful Pilgrim Carries On." *Raleigh News and Observer* (2 September 2007). http://www.newsobserver.com/105/story/690134.html.

Cotter, John. "Two from FSG." *Open Letters: A Monthly Arts and Literature Review* (August 2007). http://openlettersmonthly.com/issue/two-from-fsg/.

Curwen, Thomas. "*Littlefoot: A Poem* by Charles Wright." *Los Angles Times* (24 June 2007). http://www.latimes.com/features/printedition/books/la-bk-curwen24jun24,1,1350181.story?coll=la-head-lines-bookreview&ctrack=1&cset=true.

D'Evelyn, Tom. "Poets Who Celebrate Nature." *Providence Journal* (29 July 2007). http://www.projo.com/books/content/BOOK-POETRY_07-29-07_1B62EOM.549625.html.

Garrison, David. "Meditating on Mortality." *America* 197 no. 8 (September 24 2007): 24–5.

Latta, John. "Metaphor, metaphor, metaphor ..." *Isola di Rifuti* (19 June 2007). http://isola-di-rifiuti.blogspot.com/2007/06/metaphor-metaphor-metaphor.html.

Logan, William. "The World Is Too Much with Us." *New Criterion* 26 (December 2007): 61–8.

MacDougall, Ian. "Littlefoot." *C-ville: Charlottesville's News Weekly* 19, no. 26 (26 June–2 July 2007). http://www.c-ville.com/index.php?cat=1990812060534937&ShowArticle_ID=11042506073456165.

Martinez, Dionisio. "Growing Old Gracefully, with No Regrets." *Miami Herald* (3 July 2007). http://www.miamiherald.com/215/v-print/story/157763.html.

Moffett, Joe. "'There is No End to Longing': Charles Wright's *Littlefoot*." *Review Revue* 4, no. 3 (December 2007): 16.

Mook, Lorne. "The Year of Turning Seventy." *Contemporary Poetry Review* (11 September 2007). http://www.cprw.com/littlefoot.htm.

Peterson, Katie. "Rhythms and Views: In Varied Voices, Authors Offer Moments Pastoral and Personal." *Books* (Chicago Tribune) (25 August, 2007): 9.

Vendler, Helen. "Snatched from the Air." *New York Review of Books* 55, no. 3 (6 March 2008): 36–8.

Translation

Campana, Orphic Songs
Vitti-Alexander, Maria R. *Modern Language Journal* 71 (1987): 11.

Essays

Quarter Notes (1995)
Simpson, Megan. "Naked in the Workshop, or, Demystifying the Teaching and Writing of Poetry." *North Carolina Literary Review* 5 (1996): 226–35. Also reviews books by Patrick Bizzaro and Fred Chappell.

Virginia Quarterly Review 72, no. 3 (Summer 1996): 98–9.

Index

ABC of Reading (Pound) 19
Acuff, Roy (1903–92) 12
Adam, Eve, and the Serpent (Pagels) 55
Adams, Andy (1859–1935) 27
Adventures in the Skin Trade (Thomas) 22
After Babel (Steiner) 34
After Rereading Robert Graves, I Go Outside to Get My Head Together (Wright) 1, 101
Aiken, Conrad (1889–1973) 143
The Alexandria Quartet (Durrell) 75
Allen, Woody (1935–) 81, 125
Altieri, Charles (1942–) 52
Álvarez Bravo, Manuel (1902–2002) 92
Amis, Kingsley (1922–95) 101
Ammons, A.M. (1926–2001) 143
Anderson, Jon (1940–2007) 25
Anecdote of the Jar (Stevens) 139
Antonioni, Michelangelo (1912–2007) 82, 135
Apologia Pro Vita Sua (Wright) 75, 93
Appalachia (book) (Wright) 8, 75, 76, 77–8, 83, 92, 99, 100, 102, 122, 123, 125, 138
The Appalachian Book of the Dead (Wright) 1, 99
Arbus, Diane (1923–71) 24
Arrowsmith, William (1924–92) 11
Ars Poetica (Wright) 1, 37–8, 39
As Good as It Gets (movie) 81
Ashbery, John (1927–) 26, 54, 87
Attila József (1905–37) 1, 12
Auden, W.H. (1907–73) 22, 23, 38, 57, 100, 144

Augustine, St. (354–430) 68
Austen, Jane (1775–1817) 21

Backwater (book) (Wright) 6
Bacon, Francis (painter) (1909–92) 16–17
A Bad Memory Makes You a Metaphysician, a Good One Makes You a Saint (Wright) 1, 90
Bar Giamaica 1959–60 (Wright) 1, 92
Barthelme, Donald (1931–89) 91
Baudelaire, Charles (1821–67) 1, 12
Beat poets 79–80
Beckett, Samuel (1906–89) 51, 94
Bedient, Calvin 58
Bernstein, Charles (1950–) 128
Berry, Wendell (1934–) 144
Berryman, John (1914–72) 130
Bible 26, 141
Bidart, Frank (1939–) 80
Black Mountain poets 79–80
Black Zodiac (book) (Wright) 1, 8, 76, 77–8, 83–4, 92, 93, 100, 122, 125, 126, 138
Black Zodiac (poem) (Wright) 1, 87
Blandula, Tenulla, Vagula (Pound) 40, 98, 119, 121, 130
Bloodlines (Wright) 6, 15, 16, 23, 49, 76, 83, 115, 122
Bly, Robert (1926–) 33
Book of Common Prayer 26
Bottoms, David (1949–) 72, 139
Bourgeois, Louis (interviewer) 143–8
Braque, Georges (1882–1963) 19

Bravo, Manuel Álvarez (1902–2002) 92
The Bridge (Crane) 90, 98–9
Brodsky, Joseph (1940–96) 147
Browning, Robert (1812–89) 98, 112
Buckdancer's Choice (Dickey) 75
La Bufera e alto (Montale) 29
Buffalo Yoga (book) (Wright) 9
Buffoni, Franco (1948–) 89
Bygones (Wright) 25

Called Back (Wright) 1, 14, 17
Campana, Dino (1885–1932) 1, 12, 30–1, 36, 88–9
Can I See Arcturus from Where I Stand? (Warren) 71–2
The Cantos (Pound) 40, 99, 128
Carter Family (musicians) 12
Caseley, Martin (interviewer) (1961–) 97–103
Catullus (84–54 B.C.E.) 21, 40, 119
Celan, Paul (1920–70) 1, 12, 112, 114, 127, 146–7
A Certain World (Auden) 57
Cézanne, Paul (1839–1906) 15, 18, 19, 39, 52, 55, 63, 86, 117
The Changing Light at Sandover (Merrill) 122
Chappell, Fred (1936–) 139
Charlottesville, Virginia 2
Chatwin, Bruce (1940–) 88
Chickamauga (book) (Wright) 8, 75, 76, 77–8, 83, 85, 92, 93–4, 100, 122, 138, 139
China Trace (book) (Wright) 6, 13, 15, 16, 17, 23, 25, 45, 70, 76, 83, 88, 122, 123, 145

INDEX

Ch'ing Yuan 130
Cioran, C.M. (1911–95) 146, 146–7
Clampitt, Amy (1920–94) 89
Clark, Mirian Martin (interviewer) 49–58
Clary, Killarney (1953–) 130
The Collected Poems (Stevens) 114
Colophons (book) (Wright) 6
Commedia (Dante) 23, 44, 69, 122
The Commitments (movie) 81
Confessions (St. Augustine) 1, 68
Corinth, Mississippi 5, 136
country music 58
Country Music (book) (Wright) 7, 55, 68, 99, 122, 12, 140
Crane, Hart (1899–1932) 1, 12, 20, 22, 66, 90, 98–9, 130
Creeley, Robert (1926–2005) 22
cummings, e.e. (1894–1962) 21
A Curtain of Green (Faulkner) 75

D'Annunzio, Gabriele (1863–1938) 30
Dante Alighieri (1265–1321) 1, 7, 12, 23, 30–1, 56, 64, 78, 99
Davidson College 5
Dead Color (book) (Wright) 7
Deconstructing Harry (movie) 81
Deep Image poets 79–80
Deliverance (Dickey) 75
Delta Traveller (Wright) 1, 27
Dickey, James (1923–97) 7, 74, 89, 143, 144
Dickinson, Emily (1830–86) 1, 12, 17, 19, 24, 26, 34, 44, 52, 61, 62, 66, 71, 71, 97, 140, 145
Didion, Joan (1934) 18
Disjecta Membra (Wright) 75, 93
Dog Creek Mainline (Wright) 1, 46–8, 69, 99, 137
La Dolce Vita (Fellini) 81
Donne, John (1572–1631) 17, 141
Donoghue, Denis (1928–) 20
The Dream Animal (book) (Wright) 6
Drowning with Others (Dickey) 75
Dryden, John (1631–1700) 33
Durrell, Lawrence (1912–90) 75
Dylan, Bob (1941–) 80

East Tennessee 26, 30, 41, 48, 59–60, 90, 113
Eastwood, Clint (1930–) 91
Edson, Russell (1935–) 130
The Egyptian Book of the Dead 99

Eliot, T.S. (1888–1965) 21, 56, 87, 98, 112, 130, 144, 146
Engle, Paul (1908–91) 120
Erigena, John Scotus (810–77) 98

Falling (Dickey) 75
Faulkner, William (1897–1962) 16, 21, 61, 75
Fellini, Federico (1920–93) 1, 81, 82, 135
Fitzgerald, F. Scott (1896–1940) 85
Flatt, Lester (1914–79) 12
Ford, Ford Madox (1873–1939) 98
Four Quartets (Eliot) 121–2
Frost, Robert (1874–1963) 21, 33, 40, 74, 98, 110, 144

Galassi, Jonathan (1949–) 32
Garda, Lake *see* Lake Garda
Gate City Breakdown (Wright) 139
Genoways, Ted (interviewer) (1972–) 119–26
Ginsberg, Allen (1926–97) 18, 45–6, 89
Glück, Louise (1943–) 80
The Gnostic Gospels (Pagels) 56
Godard, Jean-Luc (1930–) 135
Goethe, Johann Wolfgang von (1749–1832) 26
Gould, Glenn (1932–82) 58
Graham, Jorie (1950–) 80
The Grave of the Right Hand (Wright) 6, 17, 52, 70, 79, 120, 122, 145
Graves, Robert (1895–1985) 101
Grosseteste, Robert (1175–1253) 98
Gunn, Thom (1929–2004) 111

Halflife (Wright) 1, 7, 57, 62, 84, 100, 102
Hard Freight (Wright) 6, 15, 17, 17, 23, 52, 70, 76, 99, 115, 122
Hardy, Thomas (1840–1928) 74, 79, 114
Harmon, William (1938–) 144
Hass, Robert (1941–) 33
Heaney, Seamus (1939–) 148
Hecht, Anthony (1923–2004) 148
Helmets (Dickey) 75
Hemingway, Ernest (1899–1961) 75
Herbert, George (1593–1633) 141
Heyen, William (interviewer) (1940–) 37–48
High Plains Drifter (movie) 91

Hiwassee Dam, North Carolina 136, 137
Hobart, Peter 131
Hockney, David (1937–) 85, 86
Hoffman, Dustin (1937–) 81
Hollander, John (1929–) 89
Holy Thursday (Wright) 14, 18
Homage to Paul Cézanne (Wright) 1, 14, 15–16, 109
Homer 16
Hopkins, Gerard Manley (1844–89) 12, 15, 68–9, 121, 141
Howard, Richard (1929–) 67
Howl (Ginsberg) 25
Hudgins, Andrew (1951–) 144
Hummer, Terry (1950–) 73

The Idea of Order at Key West (Stevens) 139
If My Glasses Were Better, I Could See Where I'm Headed For (Wright) 102
If This Is Where God's At, Why Is That Fish Dead? (Wright) 102
Illuminations (Rimbaud) 147
In the Carolinas (Stevens) 139
Iowa writing program, University of 1, 6, 21, 40, 41, 79–80, 120
Italian Days (Wright) 116
It's Turtles All the Way Down (Wright) 102

January (Wright) 77
Jeffers, Robinson (1887–1962) 71
Johnson, Philip (1906–2005) 128
Johnson, Samuel (1709–84) 61
Jones, "Grandpa" Louis Marshall (1913–98) 58
Jones, James (1921–77) 18
Jones, Rodney (1950–) 73
A Journal of English Days (Wright) 36
A Journal of the Year of the Ox (Wright) 7, 53, 115
A Journal of True Confessions (Wright) 1, 36
Joyce, James (1882–1941) 21
Justice, Donald (1925–2004) 1, 12, 22, 57, 74, 80, 89, 99, 100, 111, 114–15, 120, 134, 143, 144, 148
Justine (Durrell) 75

Kaddish (Ginsberg) 25
Kafka, Franz (1883–1924) 127
Keats, John (1795–1821) 20, 34, 45, 101, 129, 146
Keeley, Edmund (1928–) 101

INDEX

Kenyon, Jane (1947–95) 89
Kingsport, Tennessee 5, 140
Kinnell, Galway (1927–) 34, 89, 91
Kitchen, Judith (interviewer) 37–48
Knoxville, Tennessee 5, 52, 135
Komunyakaa, Yusef (1947–) 73, 74, 134, 144

Laguna Beach, California 27
Lake Garda, Italy 1, 5, 61, 94
Lanier, Sidney (1842–81) 72
Larkin, Philip (1922–1985) 42, 100–1, 146
Laughlin, James (1914–97) 89
The Less Deceived (Larkin) 100–1
Levertov, Denise (1923–97) 89
Levine, Philip (1928–) 89, 90
Levis, Larry (1946–96) 80, 83
Littlefoot: A Poem (book) (Wright) 9
Lonesome Pine Special (Wright) 139
Lorca, Federico Garcia (1898–1936) 1, 12
Lost Bodies (Wright) 139
Lowell, Robert (1917–77) 33, 130, 141
Lytle, Andrew (1902–95) 136

Mandelstam, Osip (1891–1938) 1, 12, 14
Mantegna, Andrea (1431–1506) 15
Martin, Bill (1935–57) 145
Martin, Steve (1845–) 81
Matisse, Henri (1869–1954) 117
Matthews, William (1942–97) 89
Matthiessen, Peter (1927–) 12
May Day Sermon to the Women of Gilmer County (Dickey) 72
McClatchy, J.D. (1945–) (interviewer) 1, 59–64
McFee, Michael (interviewer) 49–58
Medea (Euripides) 112
Meditation on Form and Measure (Wright) 1, 76
Merrill, James (1926–95) 80, 89, 122
Merton, Thomas (1915–68) 141
Merwin, W.S. (1927–) 12, 80, 89, 91
Michaels, Leonard (1933–2003) 18
Milosz, Czeslaw (1911–2004) 2, 55
Milton, John (1608–74) 61
Mondrian, Piet (1872–1944) 117
Monet, Claude (1840–1926) 88
Monicelli, Mario (1915–) 82, 135

Montale, Eugenio (1896–1981) 1, 6, 7, 11–12, 29, 30, 31–2, 35, 36, 56, 57, 64, 66, 88–9, 147
Morandi, Giorgio (1890–1964) 117
Morgan, Robert (1944–) 55, 144
Moss, Howard (1922–87) 53
Motets (Montale) 6
Mt. Caribou at Night (Wright) 14
Mulas, Ugo (1928–73) 92

Negative Blue (book) (Wright) 1, 8, 99, 131, 140, 145
Neruda, Pablo (1904–74) 1, 12
Nerval, Gérard de (1808–55) 30
The New Poem (Wright) 22–3, 37, 38–9, 79
Night Journal (Wright) 36
Night Music (book) (Wright) 8
Night Rider (Wright) 1, 105–8, 109–10, 113, 114
North American Bear (book) (Wright) 8, 77

Oak Ridge, Tennessee 5
O'Connor, Flannery (1925–64) 140
Olson, Charles (1910–70) 80, 98, 99
Orphic Songs (Campana) 30
Ostinato and Drone (Wright) 102
The Other Side of the River (book) (Wright) 7, 55, 58, 88, 122, 137, 144

Pagels, Elaine (1943–) 2, 56
Pagliarani, Elio (1927—) 11
Palmer, Michael (1943–) 54, 128
Pascoli, Giovanni (1855–1912) 30
Pasolini, Pier Paolo (1922–75) 11, 29
Patchen, Kenneth (1911–72) 22
Pavese, Cesare (1908–50) 1, 11, 29
Pennies from Heaven (movie) 81
Perry, Anne 49–50, 86
Perry, Jim 49–50, 86
Pickwick Dam, Tennessee 5, 135
Piers Plowman 69
Pinsky, Robert (1940–) 52, 58
The Pisan Cantos (Pound) 111
Plath, Sylvia (1932–63) 26, 129
Poe, Edgar Allan (1808–49) 31
Polaroids (Wright) 133
Portrait of the Artist as a Young Dog (Thomas) 22
Portrait of the Poet in Abraham von Werdt's Dream (Wright) 1
Pound, Ezra (1885–1972) 1, 12, 17, 21, 22, 26, 29–30, 40, 57, 66, 71, 97–8, 99, 110, 111, 119–20, 121, 127, 128, 130, 137, 144, 146, 148
Prampolini, Gaetano 87
Private Madrigals (book) (Wright) 6

Quarter Notes (Wright) 1, 99
Quotations (Wright) 1, 102–3

Ransom, John Crowe (1888–1974) 74, 143, 144
Remnick, David (interviewer) (1958–) 21–7
Reply to Wang Wei (Wright) 1, 87
Residencias (Neruda) 1, 12
Rexroth, Kenneth (1905–82) 31
Rich, Adrienne (1929–) 91
Richard of St. Victor (d. 1173) 98
Ricks, Christopher (1933–) 80
Rilke, Rainer Maria (1875–1926) 1, 12, 19, 20, 69, 129
Rimbaud, Arthur (1854–91) 1, 12, 30, 67
Roethke, Theodore (1908–63) 40, 57, 64, 95–6
Rothko, Mark (1903–70) 109
Rubin, Stan Sanvel (interviewer) 37–48

St. John, David (interviewer) (1949–) 11–17, 80
St. John of the Cross (1542–91) 1, 12
Sampoli, Maria 6, 29
Sappho (d. ca 570 BCE) 98
Scalapino, Leslie (1947–) 54
Scar Tissue (book) (Wright) 9
Schimmel, Harold (1935–) 130–1
Schneeman, George (1934–) 131
Schuldt, Morgan Lucas (interviewer) 127–31
Schweiwiller, Vanni (1934–99) 120
Scruggs, Earl (1924–) 12
A Season in Hell (Rimbaud) 147
The Selected Poems (Pound) 21, 40, 119–20, 130
Self-Portrait (Wright) 1, 14, 16–17
Sentences (Wright) 77
Sexton, Anne (1928–74) 129, 130
Shelley, Percy Bysshe (1792–1822) 38
A Short History of the Shadow (book) (Wright) 9, 131
Sigodlin (Morgan) 55
Silliman, Ron (1946–) 128

— 173 —

INDEX

Simic, Charles (1938–) 12, 55, 80, 89, 102, 111
Sirmione, Italy 5, 40, 61, 119
The Situation of Poetry (Pinsky) 58
Skins (Wright) 1, 13, 23, 27, 60
Smith, Dave (1948–) 51, 72, 139, 144
Some Friends from Pascagoula (Stevens) 139
Song of Myself (Whitman) 71, 129, 145
The Southern Cross (book) (Wright) 7, 55, 115, 144
The Southern Cross (poem) (Wright) 139
Spiegelman, Willard (interviewer) 105–17
Sprung Narratives (Wright) 85, 139
Star Turn II (Wright) 124–5
Stein, Gertrude (1874–1946) 16
Steiner, George (1929–) 34
Stella, Frank (1936–) 43
Stevens, Wallace (1879–1955) 1, 22, 64, 65–6, 74, 98, 110, 112, 114, 139
Stoppard, Tom (1937–) 18
The Storm & Other Poems (Montale) 7, 11
The Story of a Cowboy (Adams) 27
Strand, Mark (1934–) 7, 11, 12, 40, 55, 80, 89, 111
Straw for the Fire (Roethke) 57
Suarez, Ernest (interviewer) 65–82
Sudek, Josef (1896–1976) 73, 134
Swarm (Graham) 112

T'ang poets 1, 12, 64, 68, 143
Tate, Allen (1899–1979) 18
Tate, James (1943–) 12, 80, 111, 125
Tattoos (Wright) 1, 13, 23, 24, 25, 27, 49
Taylor, Henry (1942–) 144
Teegarden, Troy (interviewer) 93–6
Tennessee Line (Wright) 137
Thomas, Dylan (1914–53) 22, 94
Thoreau, Henry David (1817–62) 91
The Tibetan Book of the Dead 78, 99
Tillinghast, Richard (1940–) 73
To a Friend Who Wished Always to Be Alone (Wright) 145
Trakl, Georg (1887–1914) 1, 12
Travis, Merle (1917–83) 58
Truffaut, François (1932–84) 135

Turner, Daniel Cross (interviewer) 133–41
Twain, Mark (1835–1910) 143
12 Lines at Midnight (Wright) 1, 16

Vallejo, César (1892–1938) 1, 12
Vendler, Helen (1933–) 52, 58
The Venice Notebook (book) (Wright) 6
Verner, Amy (interviewer) 65–82
Verona, Italy 1
Vietnam War 2, 38, 39, 79
Virginia Reel (Wright) 14
Virgo Descending (Wright) 1, 25
Voigt, Ellen (1943–) 73–4, 134, 144
The Voyage (book) (Wright) 6

Wag the Dog (movie) 81
Wales Visitation (Ginsberg) 45–6
Warren, Robert Penn (1905–89) 44, 71–2, 74, 75, 79, 136, 144
Welty, Eudora (1909–2001) 21
The White Goddess (Graves) 101
Whitman, Walt (1919–92) 1, 17, 52, 71, 97, 129, 140
The Whitsun Weddings (Larkin) 101
Wilbur, Richard (1921–) 40, 148
Williams, C.K. (1936–) 71, 80
Williams, William Carlos (1883–1963) 15, 22, 42–3, 98, 99, 100, 121
Wolfe, Thomas (1900–38) 21, 75
Wordsworth, William (1770–1850) 34, 45
The World of the Ten Thousand Things (Wright) 8, 55, 68, 70, 78, 99, 12, 140
Wright, Charles: on the absence of human beings in his poetry 73; on his army service 5, 11, 61; at Christ School 5, 49–50; on Christianity 24, 102, 140–1; church, experience with the 23–4; college years 40, 130; on contemplation of the divine 41, 62, 64; on creative writing classes 91–2; on dissatisfaction 116–17; on the dropped-down line 77, 108, 123; on the Episcopal Church 2, 23–4, 41, 50, 140–1; on film 81–2, 134–5; Fulbright Fellowship 6, 11, 29; as Fulbright lecturer 6; Guggenheim fellowship 6; on happiness 116; on history 137–8, 138; on iconostasis 110; on "inscape" 68–9; on his Italian experience 21, 61, 87–8, 94; on journal-keeping 17, 84, 95; on the journal poem 48 34, 40, 83–5, 95; on landscape 65, 68, 84, 139; on language 60–1, 90; on the Language Poets 53–4, 102, 128–9; on lineation 13, 14, 15, 70–1, 77, 99–100, 123, 140, 144–5; on melancholy 116; on memory 85–6, 140; on MFA programs 127, 146; at Monterey Language School 5, 29, 119, 119–20; on the music of poetry 41, 44; on the New Formalism 53–4, 124; orderliness of 41–2; on painting and poetry 15–16, 63, 135; on photography 92; on poetic content 41, 54; on poetic distance 26; on poetic form 54, 62–3; on poetic humor 124; poetic influences 12, 57, 65–6, 110–11, 143–4; on poetic measure 76; on poetic stanzas 15, 41–2, 114–15; on poetic story-telling 22, 40, 51, 61, 69, 124, 134, 137; on poetic voice 26, 44–5; on poetry and life 14; poetry awards 6–9; on Pound's influence 21, 22, 40–1, 57, 98, 110, 111; process of writing 45, 76–7; on the prose poem 88, 147; on prosody 43; on the Pulitzer Prize 93, 125–6; on reclusion 87; on the religious dimension of poetry 64, 68, 77, 113–14; as in the Romantic tradition 66; on the seasonal cycle 115–16; on sentimentality 26–7; at Sky Valley School 49–50, 141; on *sottonarrativa* (subnarrative) 51, 72, 124; on the South 59–6, 143; as a Southern poet 26, 51, 72, 74, 133–4, 143–4; spiritual awareness of 60, 78; on syllabics 43, 77, 120–1; on his synaptic sensibility 42, 61–2, 67, 117; on teaching 56; on the theme of the dead 63–4, 100; on title-ism 103; on translation 11–12, 29–36, 56–7, 88–9; on his trilogies 15, 68, 70, 76, 78, 83, 92–3, 99, 122–3, 138; at University of California, Irvine 6; visiting professor, Florence, Italy 8; on his visual

Index

sensibility 67; writing process of 25, 76, 86, 95, 110, 113, 115
Wright, Charles Penzel (father) (1904–72) 6, 74, 135–6
Wright, Holly (wife) 6, 58, 92
Wright, Jay (1934–) 80
Wright, Luke (son) (1970–) 6
Wright, Mary Winter (mother) (1910–64) 6, 21, 40, 61, 74, 75

The Wrong End of the Rainbow (book) (Wright) 9
Xionia (Wright) 8, 55, 84, 122

Yeats, William Butler (1865–1939) 100, 112, 114
You Can't Go Home Again (Wolfe) 75
Young, David (1936–) 80, 124

Zawacki, Andrew (interviewer) 83–92
Zen 130
Zeppa, Mary (interviewer) 29–36
Zone Journals (Wright) 7, 52, 55, 76, 84, 98, 122, 144–5

www.ingramcontent.com/pod-product-compliance
Lightning Source LLC
Chambersburg PA
CBHW081600300426
44116CB00015B/2945